The discovery of a new dish does more for the happiness of mankind than the discovery of a new star.

Anthelme Brillat-Savarin

Aloha Days *Hula Nights*

A third collection of recipes from
The Junior League of Honolulu, Inc.

The Junior League of Honolulu is an organization of women committed to promoting voluntarism, developing the potential of women, and improving communities through the effective action and leadership of trained volunteers. Its purpose is exclusively educational and charitable.

We are women of diverse backgrounds united to initiate significant change, build partnerships and inspire shared solutions that strengthen the community.

❧

This book is the third collection of recipes from the Junior League of Honolulu, and the recipes are not necessarily original.

Proceeds from the sale of *Aloha Days, Hula Nights* allow the League to continue to make a difference in the community. Thank you for your support.

Library of Congress Control Number: 2006932234
ISBN: 0-9612484-7-5

First printing August 2006 * 15,000 copies
The Junior League of Honolulu, Inc.
Commercial Products
1500 South Beretania Street, Suite 100
Honolulu, HI 96826
(808) 946-6466
info@juniorleagueofhonolulu.org

CREDITS:
Editor, Carole Berg and Tracy C. Jones
Photographer, John De Mello
Food Stylist, Nina Pfaffenbach
Graphic Designer, Lorry Kennedy
Printer, Everbest Printing Company, Ltd.
Mahalo nui loa.

Printed in China.

Aloha Days *Hula Nights*

A third collection of recipes from
The Junior League of Honolulu, Inc.

The thoughts of the day become the dreams of the night.

Chinese proverb

Table of Contents

Living Aloha Every Day...

Aloha Days, Hula Nights is the third collection of recipes from the Junior League of Honolulu. As with the previous collections, *A Taste of Aloha* and *Another Taste of Aloha*, this volume includes original artwork from island artists and a variety of flavors for a sampling of the many cultures that influence life in the Hawaiian Islands. Both local and imported ingredients blend together to create traditional and Pacific Rim culinary experiences. The recipes included within are as diverse as their contributors, and offer an opportunity for all to enjoy entertaining with island style.

About The League

The Junior League of Honolulu is an organization of women committed to promoting voluntarism, developing the potential of women, and improving communities through the effective action and leadership of trained volunteers. As women of diverse backgrounds, we are united in an effort to initiate significant change, build partnerships, and inspire shared solutions that will strengthen our island community.

Since 1923, the Junior League of Honolulu has been the impetus for creating positive social change in Honolulu. The Honolulu League's initial project was making layettes for Japanese earthquake victims. In addition, League members were involved with improving the health of Honolulu's immigrant children through nutrition education at the community's Free Kindergartens. This award-winning program continued until it was turned over to the Community Chest in 1938.

Through the decades, the aloha spirit of assisting the community by identifying needs, providing volunteers, and developing services has encompassed the Arts, Historic Preservation, Advocacy, the Elderly, the Young, Consumer Rights, Foster Care, and Developing the Potential of Women.

Our signature project, *My Story - a personal development course for adolescent girls*, is staffed with dedicated volunteers who help young women discover the power within and utilize this self-knowledge to deal with life's challenges. The proceeds from *Aloha Days, Hula Nights* support not only this project but also the broad range of initiatives of the Junior League of Honolulu, giving us the opportunity to improve our community through the collaborative efforts of our volunteers.

Mahalo for your support.

Morning

Breakfast
Breads

❧ *Breakfast Delight, by Susanne Ball*

Breakfast

Cereal

Breakfast Barley with Honey Walnuts	12
Rice Congee	12

Sides

Fried Green Tomato Stacks	13
Savory Kaffir Lime Flan	14
Leek and Mushroom Hash	15
Potato Cakes with Pear Sauce	16
Rosemary Bacon	18

Bakery

Bruschetta with Marmalade	18
Savory Bread Pudding	19
Lavender Coffee Cake	20
Berry Crumble Topped Breakfast Focaccia	22
Shrimp Quiche with Avocado	23
Roasted Tomato-Onion Tart	24
Vanilla Cinnamon Strata	25

Griddle

Poi Blini with Smoked Salmon	26
Banana Bread French Toast	29
Stuffed French Toast	30
Buttermilk Pancakes	31
Multi-Grain Pancakes	32
Cheddar Cheese Waffles	32
Lighter than Air Waffles	33

Eggs

Benedict Local Style	34
Eggs in Rice Nests	35
Eggs with Brandied Crab	36
Tarragon Egg Salad	37
Spinach Frittata	39
Avocado Manchego Omelet	40
Cinnamon Apple Omelet	41

Breakfast Barley with Honey Walnuts

INGREDIENTS

3 cups water
3/4 cup barley
1/4 teaspoon salt
1/2 cup chopped walnuts or pecans
2 tablespoons butter
2 tablespoons honey
1/4 teaspoon vanilla extract
    or 1 teaspoon brandy
1/4 cup packed golden brown sugar
1/8 teaspoon ground cinnamon
1/4 cup dried sweet cherries or
    chopped apricots

Bring 2 1/2 cups water to a boil in a medium saucepan over high heat. Stir in barley and salt. Bring back to a boil then reduce heat to low. Cover and cook until barley is tender, 45 to 50 minutes, adding more water as needed. Keep warm.

Place walnuts in a small skillet. Heat over medium, shaking occasionally, until walnuts are toasted, about 3 minutes. Add butter, heat to melt then stir to coat nuts. Mix together honey, vanilla, brown sugar, and cinnamon. Drizzle over buttered nuts. Heat, stirring, until nuts are well coated and any remaining sugar has melted. Remove from heat. Keep warm.

Divide barley among four serving bowls. Top with glazed nuts. Sprinkle with dried cherries and serve warm.

❧ Serves 4

Rice Congee

RICE

7 cups water
3 chicken bouillon cubes
1 cup long grain white rice
1/8-inch thick slice fresh ginger root
3x1-inch piece tangerine peel
1/2 teaspoon salt

GARNISH

3 fresh shiitake mushroom caps,
    thinly sliced
3 green onions, finely sliced
1 carrot, peeled and shredded
1 bunch fresh cilantro, chopped
Sliced preserved ginger

Combine 5 cups water, bouillon cubes, rice, ginger, and tangerine peel in a large pot. Bring to a boil over medium-high heat, stirring a few times to keep rice from sticking to bottom of pot. Reduce heat to low. Simmer about 1 hour, partially covered, stirring occasionally to prevent rice from sticking. Add remaining 2 cups water and continue cooking another 30 minutes until rice is very soft, falling apart, and mixture becomes a thick soup. Season with salt.

Ladle into serving dishes and garnish with mushrooms, green onion, carrot, cilantro, and ginger. Serve hot.

❧ Serves 4

Fried Green Tomato Stacks

INGREDIENTS

6 tomatillos, husks removed
   and rinsed well
8 ounces bacon
3 cloves garlic, divided
$1/2$ teaspoons salt
$1/2$ teaspoon black pepper
$1/2$ teaspoon paprika
1 bunch fresh basil
8 ounces cream cheese
4 ounces goat cheese
$1/3$ cup milk
1 teaspoon sugar
Peanut or olive oil
1 cup buttermilk
$1 1/2$ cups fine seasoned breadcrumbs
4 large green tomatoes,
   cut into 18 $1/4$-inch slices

Place tomatillos in a small saucepan. Add just enough water to cover. Bring to a boil over high heat. Reduce heat to medium-low and simmer 8 to 10 minutes until very tender.

Heat a small skillet over medium heat. Lay bacon in hot skillet and cook until crispy. Remove to paper towels to drain off fat. Save 2 tablespoons bacon drippings from pan.

Drain water from tomatillos. Place tomatillos and reserved bacon drippings in food processor. Put 2 cloves garlic through press and add to tomatillos with salt, pepper, and paprika. Puree until smooth. Pour into a bowl. Thinly slice enough basil to make $1/4$ cup and stir into tomatillo sauce. Cover and keep warm until ready to use.

Beat together cream cheese, goat cheese, and milk in a small bowl. Press remaining clove of garlic and beat into cheese mixture. Divide mixture in half and set aside.

Heat $1/2$-inch oil in a skillet over medium heat. Pour buttermilk in a shallow bowl. Place breadcrumbs in another shallow bowl. Dip tomato slices in buttermilk then coat with breadcrumbs. Carefully lay tomatoes in hot oil and fry about 2 minutes per side until golden. Drain on wire rack over paper towels.

Place 1 fried tomato piece on each of six salad plates. Spread each with an equal portion from half of cheese spread. Top each with another fried tomato. Spread with an equal portion from remaining cheese mixture. Top with last 6 fried tomato slices. Drizzle with tomatillo dressing, garnish with crumbled bacon and basil leaves, and serve.

❦ *Serves 6*

Savory Kaffir Lime Flan

INGREDIENTS
2 cups heavy cream
2 cups whole milk
12 to 16 kaffir lime leaves
3 cloves garlic, passed through press
8 eggs
Salt and black pepper
1/2 cup shaved Parmesan

Combine cream, milk, and kaffir lime leaves in a saucepan over medium heat. Bring to a boil, stirring to keep bottom from burning. Remove from heat. Cover. Let steep 30 minutes to develop flavor. Remove or strain out kaffir leaves.

Heat oven to 350°F. Butter and flour six 4-ounce ramekins. Divide pressed garlic among prepared dishes, set aside.

Using whisk, beat eggs in a medium bowl until smooth. Add cream mixture in a slow, steady stream, beating to mix well. Season with salt and pepper to taste. Ladle into prepared ramekins. Arrange in a shallow baking dish. Fill baking dish with 1 1/2 inches of water.

Place in center of oven. Bake 40 to 45 minutes until the custard shimmers in the middle when jiggled and is set around the edges. Test the flan by inserting a thin knife into the middle. Do not go all the way to the bottom. If just a film of custard clings to the knife, the flan is done. Remove from oven. Remove ramekins from water bath to wire rack, and let sit 5 minutes.

To unmold, run a thin, sharp knife around the edge of the flan. Shake ramekin gently to loosen. Place a flat serving plate on top. Holding the plate and ramekin together tightly, quickly flip them over. Shake a bit to loosen flan if it does not release easily. Garnish with shaved Parmesan and serve.

❋ *Serves 6*

Leek and Mushroom Hash

INGREDIENTS
$^1/2$ cup hazelnut or pecan pieces
1 tablespoon extra-virgin olive oil
2 leeks, trimmed, split, well rinsed,
   and cut into $^1/2$-inch pieces
1 bunch kale, finely sliced
3 cloves garlic, minced
$^1/4$ teaspoon black pepper
2 tablespoons butter
2 shallots, thinly sliced
8 ounces crimini mushrooms,
   cleaned and sliced
4 ounces shiitake mushroom caps,
   cleaned and sliced
1 cup shredded Mozzarella cheese
3 tablespoons chopped chives

Heat a large skillet over medium-high heat. Add nuts to dry skillet and toast 2 to 3 minutes until lightly browned. Remove from heat. Place nuts in a small bowl and set aside.

Reduce heat to medium. Return skillet to stove. Add oil and heat until hot. Add leeks, kale, and garlic. Season with pepper. Cook, stirring occasionally, about 10 minutes until tender. Remove greens from pan and set aside.

Add butter to skillet and return to heat. Let butter melt before adding shallots, crimini, and shiitake mushrooms. Cook, stirring occasionally, about 10 to 15 minutes until tender and liquid from mushrooms has evaporated. Return greens and stir to mix well. Heat through. Sprinkle with Mozzerella and stir lightly just to mix. Remove from heat and place sautéed vegetables on a warmed serving dish. Sprinkle with toasted nuts and chopped chives. Serve hot.

❧ *Serves 4 to 6*

Potato Cakes with Pear Sauce

PEAR SAUCE
2 tablespoons olive oil
1 large onion, finely diced
3 cups chicken broth
1 to 2 whole red chilies, minced
1 cinnamon stick
2 star anise
3 pears, peeled, halved, and cored
2 tablespoons butter
Salt and freshly ground black pepper

CAKES
2 cups cold mashed potatoes
1/4 cup panko, plus extra for coating
1/2 cup crumbled blue cheese
Salt and freshly ground black pepper
2 tablespoons olive oil
Crumbled blue cheese or
   dried sweetened cranberries

Heat oil in a large saucepan over medium-high heat. Add onion and cook until soft. Add broth, chilies, cinnamon, star anise, and pears. Cook 25 minutes to soften pears and reduce sauce. Remove cinnamon and star anise. Mash pears. Whisk in butter. Season with salt and pepper to taste. Keep warm. Sauce can be gently re-heated, but do not allow to boil or it will separate.

Combine potatoes and 1/4 cup panko in a medium bowl, stirring to mix well. Lightly stir in blue cheese, stirring just until blended. Season with salt and pepper to taste. Form into eight 2-inch cakes. Chill in the refrigerator at least 30 minutes.

Dredge the cakes lightly in remaining panko. Heat oil in a large skillet over medium-high heat. Cook the cakes until golden brown on both sides. Place on serving platter. Serve hot with warm Pear Sauce and garnish with blue cheese.

❧ *Serves 4 to 8*

Rosemary Bacon

INGREDIENTS
1 pound thickly sliced bacon
$1/4$ to $1/3$ cup brown sugar
2 tablespoons minced fresh rosemary

Heat oven to 375°F. Line a roasting or jellyroll pan with aluminum foil or parchment paper for easier clean up. Place wire rack on lining. Lay out strips of bacon on rack. Combine brown sugar and rosemary in small dish. Sprinkle over bacon.

Bake 20 to 25 minutes depending on desired crispness. Carefully transfer bacon to serving platter. Serve.

❈ *Serves 4*

Bruschetta with Marmalade

INGREDIENTS
12 $1/2$-inch thick slices
*   pain de campagne or rustic bread*
8 ounces Ricotta cheese
$3/4$ cup orange marmalade

Heat a grill pan or frying pan over medium-high heat. Add bread slices, in batches, and grill until golden brown, 3 to 4 minutes per side. Spread 1 to 2 tablespoons of Ricotta over each piece of toast. Spoon 1 tablespoon of marmalade over the Ricotta. Arrange on serving plate. Serve.

❈ *Serves 6 to 8*

Savory Bread Pudding

INGREDIENTS
4 red bell peppers
2 tablespoons olive oil
1 large Maui sweet onion, thinly sliced
8 ounces crimini or button mushrooms,
  thinly sliced
2 tablespoons minced fresh oregano or
  2 teaspoons dried oregano, crushed
8 ounces crusty Italian or French bread
2 tablespoons butter, softened
3 eggs
1 1/2 cups milk
Hot pepper sauce, such as Tabasco
Salt and freshly ground black pepper
1 cup shredded Fontina cheese
Tomato salsa

Heat broiler. Place peppers under heating element. Carefully turn with long handled tongs as skin blackens. Remove peppers from broiler, place in plastic bag or bowl with lid, and seal. Leave for 15 to 20 minutes to loosen skin.

Heat oil in a large skillet over medium heat. Add onion and sauté about 5 minutes until softened. Add mushrooms and continue to sauté until tender and most of liquid has evaporated, about 8 to 10 minutes. Stir in oregano and cook a few minutes to blend flavors. Remove from heat. Set aside.

Heat oven to 350°F. Grease a 1 1/2-quart soufflé or glass casserole dish. Remove peppers from plastic bag. Gently peel off charred skin. Cut each pepper in half and remove stem, seeds, and any pith. Dice peppers. Stir into onion mixture. Cut bread into 1-inch slices and spread with butter. Cut buttered slices into 1-inch cubes. Set aside.

Beat eggs with a fork in a large bowl until smooth. Beat in milk. Stir in vegetable mixture. Season with hot pepper sauce, salt, and pepper to taste. Add bread cubes and cheese, stirring to coat bread. Spoon into prepared dish. Bake uncovered for 40 minutes, until top is puffy, golden brown, and a knife inserted comes out clean. Let stand a few minutes to set slightly before serving. Serve with salsa as an accompaniment.

Serves 6 to 8

Lavender Coffee Cake

INGREDIENTS

^{1}/3 cup macadamia nut halves
^{3}/4 cup golden raisins
3 tablespoons sweet Marsala or sherry
2 ^{1}/4 cups all-purpose flour
1 ^{1}/2 teaspoons baking powder
^{1}/2 teaspoon baking soda
^{1}/4 teaspoon salt
1 tablespoon grated lemon zest
3 eggs
^{1}/2 cup olive oil
^{1}/2 cup honey, divided
^{3}/4 cup plain yogurt
^{1}/3 cup fresh lemon juice
1 tablespoon dried lavender flowers

Heat oven to 350°F. Butter and flour a 9-inch springform pan. Set aside. Spread nuts in a baking pan and place in center of oven. Heat 3 to 5 minutes, shaking frequently, until fragrant and the color deepens. Remove from pan. Set aside and let cool.

Put raisins in a small bowl, sprinkle with Marsala, and stir lightly. Let stand for 10 minutes. Stir together flour, baking powder, baking soda, salt, and lemon zest. Set aside.

In a large bowl, beat eggs with a whisk until well blended. Stir in oil, ^{1}/4 cup honey, and yogurt. Add soaked raisins with any liquid and dry ingredients. Stir with wooden spoon just until blended and almost smooth. Pour batter into prepared pan. Smooth top with spatula. Bake in center of oven 25 to 30 minutes, until a toothpick inserted in center comes out clean.

Combine remaining ^{1}/4 cup honey, lemon juice, and lavender in a small saucepan. Bring to a boil over medium heat, stirring occasionally. Remove from heat. Let cool.

When cake tests done, place pan on wire rack and poke the top all over with a wooden skewer or toothpick. Brush with half of the glaze. Let cool 10 minutes.

Remove sides of pan from coffee cake, invert cake onto rack, and remove bottom of pan. Poke bottom of cake with skewer. Brush with remaining glaze. Place inverted serving plate on bottom of cake. Turn cake upright. Sprinkle with toasted nuts. Cut into wedges and serve.

❧ *Serves 8 to 10*

Berry Crumble Topped Breakfast Focaccia

FOCACCIA
2 1/4 cups all-purpose flour
1/2 teaspoon salt
4 tablespoons granulated sugar
1 package rapid rise yeast
3 eggs, divided
1/2 teaspoon vanilla extract
2 teaspoons grated lemon zest
1/2 cup lukewarm milk
4 tablespoons unsalted butter, softened
1 tablespoon heavy cream
1 large Granny Smith apple,
    peeled and finely diced
1 2/3 cups blackberries, raspberries,
    or blueberries

TOPPING
1/2 cup oatmeal
3 tablespoons ground almonds
1/4 cup granulated sugar
1/4 teaspoon ground cinnamon
4 tablespoons unsalted butter, softened
2 tablespoons sliced almonds

Combine flour with salt, 2 tablespoons sugar, and yeast in a large bowl. In another bowl, beat 2 eggs until frothy. Beat in vanilla and half the lemon zest. Add milk. Stir the liquid ingredients into the dry ingredients to make a soft dough, adding more flour if too sticky. Work in butter. Knead by hand about 10 minutes until dough is smooth and springy. Clean and lightly oil mixing bowl. Return dough, cover with a clean kitchen towel, and place in warm place to rise until doubled in size, about 1 to 1 1/2 hours. Punch down dough. Roll out onto a 13 x 9-inch jelly roll pan, or baking sheet with low sides. Stretch to fit. Set aside for 15 to 20 minutes.

Heat oven to 400°F. Beat together remaining egg and heavy cream in a small cup. Brush over dough. Combine apple, berries, remaining 2 tablespoons sugar, and remaining lemon zest. Sprinkle over dough.

Stir together oatmeal, ground almonds, sugar, and cinnamon, using fork. Dice and blend in butter. Sprinkle oatmeal mixture over fruit, then sprinkle on sliced almonds.

Bake for 15 minutes. Turn heat down to 350°F and cook for 20 minutes or until dough has risen, is golden at the edges, and the crumble is set; however, it will remain soft.

Remove from the oven and place on cutting board. Cut into squares or diamonds. Place on serving platter and serve.

❋ Serves 8

Shrimp Quiche with Avocado

QUICHE

9-inch flaky pie crust, baked
1 tablespoon olive oil
1 tablespoon butter
1 large onion, finely diced
4 ripe tomatoes, seeded and diced
4 cloves garlic, minced
1 pound raw shrimp, peeled,
    deveined, and chopped
$1/2$ teaspoon salt
$1/4$ teaspoon black pepper
1 $1/2$ cups shredded Cheddar cheese
1 firm ripe avocado, halved,
    seeded and peeled
3 eggs
1 cup whole milk or half-and-half
Salsa, lime wedges and sour cream

FLAKY PASTRY

1 $1/3$ cups all-purpose flour
$1/4$ teaspoon salt
5 tablespoons cold butter,
    cut into small pieces
3 tablespoons cold vegetable shortening
4 to 6 tablespoons ice water

Heat oven to 350°F. Heat oil and butter in a skillet over medium heat. Add onion and sauté 8 to 10 minutes until golden. Stir in tomatoes and garlic. Continue to sauté to soften tomatoes and evaporate some of the liquid. Add shrimp and cook, stirring frequently, until opaque. Remove from heat. Season with salt and pepper. Spread cheese on bottom of baked 9-inch pie crust. Top with shrimp mixture.

Slice each avocado half into a fan shape starting at wide end and cut $1/4$-inch thick slices to within $1/2$-inch of stem end. Gently separate slices from each other but keep attached at top, to form fan shape. Place on shrimp mixture with stem end facing center. Continue, forming a circle of slices out of both halves of avocado.

Beat eggs with milk in a small bowl until blended. Pour over quiche filling. Bake in center of oven about 45 minutes until eggs are set. Serve in wedges with salsa, lime wedges, and sour cream.

Flaky pastry: Stir together flour and salt in a large bowl. Cut in butter and shortening using a fork or a pastry blender until the texture of coarse sand. Drizzle in ice water 1 tablespoon at a time, stirring after each addition, until dough is evenly moist and comes together but does not quite form a ball. Transfer to work surface and shape dough into a disk. Wrap in plastic and chill for at least 1 hour.

Remove from refrigerator. Heat oven to 400°F. Dust work surface and rolling pin with flour. Unwrap dough. Working quickly, start from the center and roll out dough in all directions. Lift, turn dough, sprinkling with more flour as needed to keep from sticking. Form a 12-inch circle about $1/8$-inch thick. Carefully fold dough in half and place in 9-inch pie pan. Unfold dough, adjusting to center it. Press gently but firmly against bottom and sides. Roll in overlapping edge, trimming off excess if more than an inch. Crimp using fork or flute with fingers to make an attractive edge along rim of pan. Line with foil, fill with baking weights or dried beans, bake 15 minutes. Remove weights and foil. Reduce heat to 350°F. Bake about 10 minutes until golden. Remove from oven. Let cool.

❋ *Serves 4 to 6*

Roasted Tomato-Onion Tart

BASIC CRUST
2 cups all-purpose flour
1 teaspoon salt
$1/2$ cup butter, cut into small pieces
6 tablespoons ice water

FILLING
6 to 8 Roma or plum tomatoes,
   cut into $1/4$-inch slices
$1/2$ cup grated Parmesan, divided
4 tablespoons olive oil, divided
3 medium Maui onions, thinly sliced
3 cloves garlic, passed through press
2 teaspoons minced fresh thyme, or
   1 teaspoon dried, crumbled
1 teaspoon minced fresh rosemary or
   $1/2$ teaspoon dried, crumbled
Salt and freshly ground black pepper
1 to 2 tablespoons red wine or
   balsamic vinegar

Sift flour and salt into a medium bowl. With fork or pastry blender, cut in butter until the texture of coarse sand. Stir in ice water 1 tablespoon at a time until dough gathers into a ball. May not need to use all of the water. Wrap in plastic. Chill 15 minutes.

Heat oven to 400°F. Lay tomato slices in single layer on two jellyroll or roasting pans. Bake 15 to 20 minutes until tomatoes are nicely wilted and most of the liquid has evaporated. Check occasionally during baking and pour off any liquid that accumulates. Remove from oven. Set aside.

Keep oven at 400°F. On lightly floured surface, roll dough out to $1/8$-inch thick circle. Gently wrap dough over rolling pin. Place in a 10-inch round quiche or tart pan. Press gently into place. Line the inside of unbaked crust with aluminum foil and then add pie weights, beans or rice on top of the foil and bake crust for about 10 minutes, then remove the weights and finish baking until the crust is golden. Or bake 7 to 8 minutes, remove from oven, press crust down gently with wooden spoon, and bake another 4 minutes. Remove crust from oven and place on cooling rack. Sprinkle with 2 tablespoons Parmesan. Set aside.

Reduce oven to 350°F. In a large skillet, heat 2 tablespoons oil over medium heat. Add onions and cook, stirring occasionally, 12 to 15 minutes until golden. Add garlic, thyme, rosemary, and season with salt and pepper. Cook, stirring frequently, 10 more minutes until onions are a deeper golden color. Add vinegar and cook until liquid is evaporated. Remove from heat.

Spread half of onions over crust. Top with layer of tomato slices. Sprinkle with half of remaining cheese. Spread in rest of onions, layer with remaining tomatoes, and sprinkle with last of cheese. Drizzle with remaining 2 tablespoons olive oil. Bake 30 minutes. Serve warm or at room temperature.

❀ *Makes one 10-inch tart*

Vanilla Cinnamon Strata

STRATA

2 tablespoons butter
4 eggs
1 1/2 cups vanilla yogurt, divided
1 cup milk
1 teaspoon vanilla extract
1/4 teaspoon ground cinnamon
1/4 teaspoon ground nutmeg
Pinch of salt
8 thick slices cinnamon raisin bread

RUM RAISIN SAUCE

1/2 cup raisins
2 tablespoons dark rum
3 tablespoons butter
1/4 cup packed brown sugar
1/8 teaspoon ground cinnamon
1/4 cup chopped macadamia nuts

Heat oven to 350°F. Generously butter a baking dish with butter. Beat eggs in a large bowl until light and frothy. Beat in 1 cup yogurt, milk, vanilla, cinnamon, nutmeg, and salt until smooth. Dip bread slices into egg mixture. Arrange in prepared dish overlapping as necessary. Pour in any remaining egg mixture. Bake 25 to 30 minutes until lightly browned and eggs are set.

Top with dollops of remaining 1/2 cup yogurt. Drizzle with Rum Raisin Sauce, and serve.

Rum Raisin Sauce: Put raisins in small bowl and sprinkle with rum. Cover and let stand 15 minutes to plump. In small saucepan, melt butter over medium heat. Stir in raisins with liquid, brown sugar, and cinnamon. Cook a few minutes to melt sugar, creating syrup. Stir in macadamia nuts. Remove from heat and cover until ready to use.

❧ Serves 4

Poi Blini with Smoked Salmon

CREAM

1 1/2 cups sour cream
6 tablespoons lemon juice
1/2 cup chopped shallots
1/3 cup chopped fresh dill or
    1 1/2 tablespoons dried
1/2 teaspoon salt
1/2 teaspoon black pepper

BLINI

1 1/4 cups all-purpose flour
1 teaspoon baking powder
1/4 teaspoon salt
2 teaspoons chopped fresh chives
2 teaspoons chopped fresh parsley
1 teaspoon chopped fresh thyme
3/4 cup buttermilk
1/4 cup milk
1 egg, lightly beaten
2 tablespoons butter, melted
3/4 cup poi

TOPPING

4 ounces thinly sliced smoked salmon
4 tablespoons ikura (small salmon roe)
1/4 cup radish or alfalfa sprouts
1 1/2 cups tiny mixed salad greens

In a non-reactive bowl, stir together sour cream, lemon juice, shallots, dill, salt, and pepper. Cover with plastic wrap. Chill in the refrigerator at least 2 hours.

In a bowl, stir together flour, baking powder, salt, chives, parsley, and thyme. In another bowl, stir together buttermilk, milk, and egg. Blend in the melted butter and poi. Add wet ingredients to dry, folding gently. Cover bowl with plastic wrap. Let batter rest in the refrigerator for 1 hour.

Heat griddle or skillet over medium heat. Scoop the batter onto the griddle 2 tablespoons at a time to form 3-inch pancakes. A small ice cream scoop or coffee measuring scoop can be used to make it easier to portion out batter. Cook until golden, about 2 minutes per side, flipping over when bubbles appear on the top. There should be 20 to 24 blini.

Put 3 to 4 blini on each serving plate. Spread centers with herbed cream. Drape with smoked salmon, and garnish with ikura and sprouts. Place a few greens on the side and serve.

Serves 5 to 6

Banana Bread French Toast

FRENCH TOAST
2 tablespoons butter, divided
3 eggs
2 heaping tablespoons plain
    or vanilla yogurt
Pinch ground nutmeg
8 thick slices Banana Bread*

BRANDY ORANGE BUTTER
4 tablespoons butter, softened
3 tablespoons confectioners' sugar
1 tablespoon brandy
1 teaspoon grated orange zest

*Recipe on page 45

In a large frying pan or griddle, melt 1 tablespoon butter over medium heat. In a small bowl, beat eggs with yogurt until smooth. Add nutmeg, stirring to blend well. Pour into shallow dish.

One at a time, dip four bread slices in beaten egg, coating well. Place in hot skillet and cook until golden brown, about 3 minutes, turn, and cook other side. Place on serving platter and keep warm. Add remaining butter to skillet, dip rest of bread in beaten egg, and cook until golden. Place on platter, serve warm with Brandy Orange Butter.

Brandy Orange Butter: In a small bowl, cream together butter and confectioners' sugar until smooth. Beat in brandy and orange zest until well incorporated. Set aside.

Blend again before serving if brandy starts to separate. This can be made ahead and refrigerated, but allow to return to room temperature before serving.

❧ *Serves 4*

Stuffed French Toast

SAUCE

10 to 12 ounces frozen red raspberries,
    thawed and drained; reserving juice
1/2 cup sugar
2 tablespoons raspberry jam

FILLING

3/4 cup Ricotta cheese
3 ounces cream cheese, softened
1 teaspoon almond extract
2 tablespoons granulated sugar

FRENCH TOAST

1 loaf French or Italian bread
    cut into 1 1/2-inch slices
6 eggs
1/3 cup half-and-half
1 tablespoon butter

In a medium saucepan, combine reserved raspberry juice and sugar. Stir in raspberry jam. Bring mixture to a boil, then lower heat and simmer 7 to 8 minutes, allowing mixture to thicken slightly.

Meanwhile, in a medium bowl, combine Ricotta, softened cream cheese, almond extract, and sugar, stirring until well blended. Make a pocket in each slice of bread by cutting through center of top crust down into bread to within 3/4-inch from side and bottom edges, being careful not to cut through. Fill each pocket with 1 to 2 tablespoons of filling and set aside.

Remove thickened raspberry sauce from heat and stir in raspberries. Cover and set aside.

In a medium bowl, whisk together eggs and half-and-half until well blended. Melt butter in a large skillet over medium-high heat. Dip each side of filled bread pockets into egg mixture until well coated. Place bread into hot skillet and fry both sides until golden brown and filling is warm, about 6 to 8 minutes. Place on warmed individual serving plates, top with raspberry sauce, and serve.

❋ *Serves 4*

Buttermilk Pancakes

INGREDIENTS
2 eggs
2 tablespoons butter, melted
2 cups buttermilk
$1/2$ cup whole milk
2 cups all-purpose flour
1 teaspoon baking soda
1 $1/2$ teaspoons baking powder
1 teaspoon salt
2 to 3 tablespoons granulated sugar

Heat a large pan over medium heat. Lightly beat eggs in a large bowl. Stir in melted butter, buttermilk, and milk. In another bowl, stir together flour, baking soda, baking powder, salt, and sugar. Add dry ingredients to wet ingredients in three parts, folding gently without over mixing.

Scoop out batter making 3 or 4-inch pancakes on hot griddle. When bubbles appear evenly in pancakes and edges are slightly dry, turn to cook other side a few minutes. Total cooking time should be about 4 to 5 minutes. Remove to plate and keep warm while cook remaining batter. Serve with butter and syrup.

Serves 4

Multi-Grain Pancakes

INGREDIENTS
$1/3$ cup all-purpose flour
$2/3$ cup whole wheat flour
$1/3$ cup cornmeal
$1/2$ cup wheat germ
$1/4$ cup flax seed meal
1 $1/2$ teaspoon baking powder
$3/4$ teaspoon baking soda
2 eggs
1 cup buttermilk
$1/2$ to $3/4$ cup milk
2 tablespoons canola oil
Maple or fruit syrup
Vanilla yogurt
Diced fresh fruit

Heat griddle over medium heat. In a large bowl, mix together all-purpose flour, whole wheat flour, cornmeal, wheat germ, flax seed meal, baking powder, and baking soda. In a separate bowl, beat eggs until smooth. Beat in buttermilk, $1/2$ cup milk, and oil. Add wet ingredients to dry ingredients mixing just until blended. Adjust batter thickness with additional milk as desired.

Pour $1/4$ cup batter on hot griddle. When bubbles appear and edges begin to dry out, flip pancakes to cook other side. Serve with syrup or yogurt, and fruit.

Note: Whole flax seed can be ground in food processor or clean coffee mill to make meal. Due to the nature of the grains, these pancakes are not light and fluffy unless the eggs are separated and the whites beaten to a soft peak stage.

❋ *Serves 4 to 6*

Cheddar Cheese Waffles

INGREDIENTS
1 $1/2$ cups all-purpose flour
$2/3$ cup grated Cheddar cheese
1 tablespoon baking powder
$1/4$ teaspoon salt
2 eggs
1 $1/2$ cup milk
4 tablespoons butter, melted
8 crisply cooked bacon slices, crumbled
Maple syrup

Preheat waffle iron. Stir together flour, cheese, baking powder, and salt in small bowl. Set aside.

In a medium bowl, beat eggs. Beat in milk and melted butter. Stir in dry ingredients just until blended.

Set waffle iron to medium heat. Spoon batter in center of hot waffle iron until batter covers half the grid. Close top and cook until golden. Remove to serving plate and keep warm while cooking the rest of the waffles. Serve sprinkled with bacon and drizzled with maple syrup.

❋ *Serves 2 to 3*

Lighter than Air Waffles

INGREDIENTS
¹/2 teaspoon baking soda
¹/2 teaspoon baking powder
2 cups buttermilk
2 cups all-purpose flour
Pinch of salt
2 eggs, separated
1 ¹/2 tablespoons canola oil
Butter

Stir baking soda and baking powder into buttermilk and set aside.

Mix flour with salt in a large mixing bowl. Make a well in middle. Separate eggs, putting whites in one bowl and yolks in another. Beat the egg whites with whisk until stiff and set aside.

Beat egg yolks with fork until smooth. Stir in buttermilk and oil. Pour liquid into flour well and stir to blend. Gently fold in egg whites just to blend, leaving some lumps of egg white. Cover with a clean cloth and let batter rest for 10 minutes before cooking, allowing the batter to rise which will give the waffles their lovely light texture.

Set waffle iron to medium heat. Spoon batter into the center of hot waffle iron until it covers half the grid. Close top and cook until golden. Remove to serving plate and keep warm while cooking the rest of the waffles. Serve hot with butter.

Leftover waffles can be put in a plastic bag, frozen, and toasted for a quick breakfast or snack.

Note: For lighter than air pancakes, do not separate eggs, simply add them whole to the flour well with the other ingredients and let the batter rest covered for 10 minutes.

❋ *Serves 3 to 4*

Benedict Local Style

CAKES
1 cup sushi rice
1 1/4 cups water
1/4 teaspoon salt

HOLLANDAISE SAUCE
2 egg yolks
4 tablespoons cream
2 tablespoons butter
Juice of 1/2 lemon
Pinch salt
Pinch sugar
Chicken broth
1 tablespoon white vinegar

TOPPING
3 tablespoons unsalted butter, divided
8 slices Canadian bacon
4 eggs
1/8 teaspoon salt
1/8 teaspoon black pepper
1 scallion, trimmed and thinly sliced

Rinse rice in a large fine-mesh sieve under cold running water. Drain well. Combine rice, water, and salt in a 2-quart heavy saucepan and bring to a boil over high heat. Reduce heat to low and cook, covered, 15 minutes. Remove from heat and let stand, covered, 10 minutes.

Stir rice from bottom to top. Lightly grease a metal 1-cup measure. Firmly pack enough rice in measure using rubber spatula to fill halfway. If spatula becomes sticky, dip in water. Invert onto a buttered plate, tapping to unmold rice. Repeat with remaining rice, greasing mold each time, to make four cakes. Chill, uncovered, at least 15 minutes.

Combine egg yolks, cream, butter, lemon juice, salt, and sugar in the top of a double boiler, over boiling water. Stir until thick, approximately 3 minutes. Set aside, leaving pot over hot water. Thin, if needed, with a little chicken broth. Stir in the vinegar. Do not reheat or cover the pot.

Melt 1 tablespoon butter in a large nonstick skillet over medium-low heat. Add rice cakes and cook, until pale golden, about 8 to 10 minutes. Turn cakes, add 1/2 tablespoon butter and cook until other side is golden, about 5 minutes. Transfer to plates.

Increase heat to medium-high and melt 1/2 tablespoon butter in skillet. Add Canadian bacon and cook, turning once, about 1 minute per side until browned. Place 2 slices bacon on each rice cake.

Melt remaining tablespoon butter. Crack eggs one by one into skillet. Sprinkle with salt and pepper and fry until whites are cooked and yolks begin to set, 2 to 4 minutes. Turn and cook other side. Place 1 egg on each stack and top with some Hollandaise sauce. Sprinkle with scallion and serve.

Note: Sushi rice cooks up slightly moist and sticky, forming a cake easily. Chilling the cakes before browning helps to hold their shape. Rice cakes can be shaped one day ahead. Allow to cool 15 minutes before covering and refrigerating. Allow 2 to 5 minutes longer to heat.

Serves 2 to 4

Eggs in Rice Nests

INGREDIENTS

1 1/2 cups water
3/4 cup brown rice
1 teaspoon instant vegetable or
  chicken bouillon
1/2 cup finely chopped
  green onions with tops
4 ounces canned,
  chopped green chilies, drained
4 eggs
1/2 cup shredded sharp Cheddar cheese
Tomato salsa
Finely diced ripe avocado

In a medium saucepan, bring water and rice to a boil over high heat. Stir in bouillon. Reduce heat to low. Cover and cook 15 to 20 minutes until tender. Remove from heat. Stir in onions and chilies. Set aside.

Heat oven to 350°F. Lightly grease four 10-ounce ovenproof bowls, custard cups, or ramekins. Spoon 1/2 cup of the rice mixture into each of the prepared cups. With back of spoon, gently push mixture up side of each cup making an indentation in center to create a nest. Break 1 egg into each rice cup. Sprinkle each with 2 tablespoons cheese. Bake 12 to 18 minutes until egg whites are completely set and yolks begin to thicken but are not hard. Remove from oven. Garnish with salsa and avocado, and serve hot.

❧ Serves 4

Eggs with Brandied Crab

CHEESE SAUCE
2 tablespoons butter
$^1/_2$ cup thinly sliced green onions
$^1/_2$ teaspoon salt
$^1/_4$ teaspoon black pepper
Ground nutmeg
2 tablespoons all-purpose flour
2 cups milk
1 cup shredded Gruyere cheese
2 tablespoons brandy

EGGS
4 tablespoons butter, divided
$^1/_2$ cup thinly sliced green onions
8 ounces spinach, washed, stemmed,
   and chopped
8 ounces crabmeat, picked through
   for cartilage and shell
1 tablespoon fresh lemon juice
$^1/_4$ to $^1/_2$ teaspoon hot pepper sauce,
   such as Tabasco
Salt and freshly ground black pepper
4 whole English muffins, split
8 eggs
$^1/_2$ cup milk
Paprika

In a medium saucepan, melt butter over medium heat. Add green onions and season with salt, pepper, and dash of nutmeg. Sauté 2 minutes, stirring occasionally. Using whisk, stir in flour and cook about 2 minutes. Whisk in milk and continue stirring until comes to a gentle boil. Reduce heat and simmer, stirring frequently, until thickened. Stir in Gruyere and brandy and continue to heat until cheese is melted. Remove from heat. Cover and keep warm.

In a large heavy skillet, melt 2 tablespoons butter over medium low heat. Add green onions and spinach and sauté about 3 minutes until soft. Add crabmeat and heat through. Stir in lemon juice, season with hot pepper sauce and salt and pepper to taste.

In a large bowl, beat eggs until light. Beat in milk. Pour egg mixture over crab in skillet. Let cook 3 minutes before stirring gently. Cook until eggs are firm but not dry.

Toast English muffins and butter with equal portions of remaining 2 tablespoons butter. Place 2 muffin halves on each plate. Arrange egg mixture on top. Cover with brandied sauce. Sprinkle with paprika and serve.

❧ *Serves 4 to 6*

Tarragon Egg Salad

INGREDIENTS
8 eggs
1/4 cup olive oil
2 tablespoons white wine vinegar
2 teaspoons Dijon mustard
1 tablespoon finely minced onion
1 clove garlic, finely minced
1 teaspoon minced fresh tarragon
1/4 teaspoon sugar
1/2 cup finely diced celery
3 to 5 tablespoons mayonnaise
1/2 head red cabbage
Fresh parsley

Place eggs in a saucepan. Cover with water, place over medium-high heat and bring to a boil. Turn off the heat, cover, and let stand 15 minutes. Drain off warm water, place in bowl, and cover with cold water. Let stand 5 minutes to cool.

In a small bowl or jar with lid, combine oil, vinegar, mustard, onion, garlic, tarragon, and sugar with a whisk until well blended. Set dressing aside to let flavors blend.

Peel eggs. Chop into pea-sized pieces. Place in a bowl. Mix in celery and 2 tablespoons of salad dressing. Stir in enough mayonnaise to coat. Shred cabbage, lay on bottom of shallow serving dish. Top with egg salad. Drizzle with remaining dressing. Garnish with fresh parsley. Serve.

Note: Try to use fresh tarragon. Often the flavor of tarragon gets lost in the drying process requiring almost twice as much of the dried type to be used to achieve full flavor.

If the eggs are cooked too quickly they will become tough and chewy. Immediately cooling the eggs will make the shells easier to remove.

Serves 4

Spinach Frittata

INGREDIENTS
3 tablespoons olive oil, divided
1 large potato, scrubbed,
  quartered, and thinly sliced
1 medium onion,
  quartered and thinly sliced
8 ounces fresh spinach, washed,
  stemmed, and finely chopped
4 eggs
1 teaspoon fresh dill or
  1/2 teaspoon dried
Salt and black pepper
1/2 cup crumbled Feta or
  grated Swiss cheese

Heat 2 tablespoons oil in a large skillet over medium heat. Add potato and onion and sauté 5 to 8 minutes until soft. Add spinach. Cover and reduce heat to medium-low. Cook, stirring occasionally, until spinach is wilted. Remove from pan and set aside.

Clean pan and return to heat. Add remaining tablespoon oil. Beat eggs. Add to hot pan. Cook 5 minutes to set. Season with dill, salt, and pepper. Sprinkle with sautéed vegetables and cheese. Continue to cook until thoroughly set and eggs are cooked through. Gently run spatula under frittata to release from pan. Slide onto serving plate. Serve immediately.

Serves 2

Avocado Manchego Omelet

INGREDIENTS

Olive oil

1/2 each yellow, red, and green
   bell pepper, finely diced

1 jalapeno pepper,
   seeded and finely diced

1 small onion, finely diced

Salt and freshly ground black pepper

1 tablespoon minced fresh cilantro

2 teaspoons minced fresh parsley

8 eggs

1/4 cup milk

1 1/2 cups shredded Manchego cheese,
   divided

1 large ripe avocado, peeled,
   seeded, and thinly sliced

Sprigs of fresh cilantro

Heat a small amount of oil in a small skillet over medium heat. Add peppers and onion and sauté until tender. Remove from heat and season with salt and pepper to taste. Sprinkle with cilantro and parsley. Remove from skillet and divide into four portions. Set aside. In a large bowl, beat eggs until light in color. Beat in milk and set aside.

Set aside 1/4 cup shredded cheese for topping. Heat a skillet over medium heat. Pour in one-fourth of beaten eggs. Stir in one-fourth of sautéed vegetables, cook until set. Flip omelet and cook other side just until done. Add one-fourth of sliced avocado and top with one-fourth of remaining cheese. Fold omelet and turn out onto warm serving plate. Top with 1 tablespoon reserved cheese and garnish with cilantro sprigs. Repeat process to create four servings.

Note: Manchego, a Spanish cheese, is available in the cheese section of many grocery and specialty food stores.

Serves 4

Cinnamon Apple Omelet

FILLING
2 tablespoons butter
4 large apples such as Fuji, Braeburn,
  or Granny Smith,
   peeled and thinly sliced
1 tablespoon grated fresh ginger root
1/4 cup granulated sugar
1/2 teaspoon ground cinnamon

OMELET
8 eggs, separated
1 teaspoon grated fresh ginger root
1/2 teaspoon salt
1/8 teaspoon freshly ground black pepper
2 tablespoons butter
Confectioners' sugar

Heat oven to 400°F. Melt butter in a large skillet over medium heat. Add apples and sauté until soft, about 5 minutes. Add ginger, sugar, and cinnamon, stirring to mix well. Cook a few minutes to melt sugar and blend flavors. Set aside.

In large bowl, combine egg yolks, ginger, salt, and pepper. Beat 2 to 3 minutes until thick and light in color. In another large bowl, beat egg whites with electric mixer at high speed until stiff peaks form. Add 1/3 of whites to egg yolk mixture, folding gently to combine. Fold in remaining whites.

Melt butter in a large oven-proof skillet over medium heat. Add egg mixture and cook, without stirring, 2 minutes. Remove from stove and place in oven. Bake about 5 minutes until set and top is lightly browned. Run spatula under eggs to release from pan. Remove to warmed serving plate, spread with apple mixture, and fold over slightly allowing filling to be exposed. Sprinkle with confectioners' sugar and serve.

Serves 4

Breads

Avocado Bread

INGREDIENTS
1 egg
$^1/2$ cup avocado puree,
   about 1 medium avocado
$^1/2$ cup plain yogurt
$^1/4$ cup chopped pecans
1 teaspoon lime zest
2 cups all-purpose flour
$^3/4$ cup granulated sugar
1 teaspoon baking powder
$^1/2$ teaspoon baking soda
$^1/2$ teaspoon salt

GLAZE
$^1/4$ cup granulated sugar
$^1/4$ cup fresh lime juice

Heat oven to 350°F. Grease a 9 x 5-inch loaf pan and set aside.

Beat egg in a large bowl using fork. Blend in avocado and yogurt. Stir in nuts and lime zest, mixing well. Sift in flour, sugar, baking powder, baking soda, and salt. Stir just until smooth and moistened. Batter will be thick but do not over mix. Pour into prepared pan.

Bake in center of oven about 50 to 55 minutes, or until a cake tester inserted into the center of the loaf comes out clean. Remove to wire rack.

Heat sugar and lime juice in a small saucepan over medium heat until sugar dissolves and glaze is hot. Remove from heat. Pierce warm bread evenly with skewer 10 to 12 times. Drizzle with glaze. Let cool for 30 minutes in pan, then turn out onto rack and cool completely. Wrap tightly in plastic wrap or put in an airtight container and let stand at room temperature overnight before serving.

✳ *Makes one loaf*

Banana Oat Bread

INGREDIENTS

$^2/3$ cup whole wheat flour,
   plus $^1/3$ cup wheat germ; or
   1 cup whole wheat flour
1 cup all-purpose flour
$^1/3$ cup instant nonfat powdered milk
1 $^1/4$ teaspoons baking powder
1 $^1/2$ teaspoons baking soda
$^3/4$ teaspoon salt
$^1/2$ cup unsalted butter, softened
$^3/4$ cup packed brown sugar
$^1/2$ cup honey
3 eggs
3 medium bananas, mashed
1 teaspoon vanilla extract
$^2/3$ cup rolled oats
$^1/2$ cup chopped pecans or walnuts

Heat oven to 375°F. Grease a 9 x 5-inch loaf pan. Set aside.

Combine whole wheat flour, wheat germ, all-purpose flour, powdered milk, baking powder, baking soda, and salt in a bowl. Set aside.

In a large bowl, cream together butter and sugar until light and fluffy. Beat in honey. Add eggs, one at a time, beating well after each addition. Beat in bananas and vanilla. Stir in dry ingredients. Add oats and nuts stirring just until blended. Pour into prepared pan. Bake 45 to 55 minutes or until a cake tester inserted in the center of the loaf comes out clean. Cool on wire rack.

Note: Spray measuring cup with vegetable oil spray before measuring honey. It will help honey slide out. This bread is great for French Toast.

❋ *Makes one loaf*

Lemon Blueberry Cornbread

INGREDIENTS
1 egg
1 tablespoon grated lemon zest
1 tablespoon lemon juice
4 tablespoons butter, melted
2 tablespoons canola oil
1 cup buttermilk
1 cup all-purpose flour
1 cup yellow cornmeal
1 1/2 teaspoons baking powder
1/2 teaspoon baking soda
1/4 cup granulated sugar
1/2 teaspoon salt
1 cup fresh blueberries

Heat oven to 400°F. Grease a 9 x 9-inch baking pan or 9 x 5-inch loaf pan and set aside.

Whisk together egg, lemon zest, lemon juice, melted butter, and oil in a large bowl. Whisk in buttermilk. Mix together flour, cornmeal, baking powder, baking soda, sugar, and salt in another bowl. Add the flour mixture to the buttermilk mixture. Stir gently with a few swift strokes just until combined. Fold in blueberries. Do not over mix. Scrape batter into prepared pan.

Bake 20 to 25 minutes for 9 x 9-inch pan, 40 to 50 minutes for loaf or until edges start to pull away from the sides of pan. Remove from oven and place on wire rack until cool. Cut into squares or slices and serve.

❋ *Makes one pan*

Cornbread with Basil and Roasted Peppers

INGREDIENTS

8 tablespoons unsalted butter, divided
1 large onion, diced
1 jalapeno pepper, seeded and minced
1 3/4 cups yellow cornmeal
1 1/4 cups all-purpose flour
1/4 cup granulated sugar
1 tablespoon baking powder
1 1/2 teaspoons salt
1/2 teaspoon baking soda
1 1/2 cups buttermilk
3 eggs
1 1/2 cups grated Monterey Jack cheese
1 1/3 cups canned corn kernels, drained
1/2 cup chopped roasted red peppers
1/2 cup chopped fresh basil

Heat oven to 400°F. Grease a 9 x 9 x 2-inch baking pan. Set aside.

Melt 1 tablespoon butter in a medium skillet over medium-low heat. Add onion and jalapeno. Sauté until tender about 10 minutes, set aside.

Mix cornmeal, flour, sugar, baking powder, salt, and baking soda in a large bowl. Cut remaining butter into 1/2-inch pieces. Mix butter into dry ingredients until mixture resembles coarse meal. In a medium bowl, whisk together buttermilk and eggs until blended. Add to dry ingredients and stir just until blended. Stir in cheese, corn, red peppers, basil, and onion mixture. Pour into prepared pan.

Bake about 45 minutes until golden and a cake tester inserted into the center of the pan comes out clean. Let cool for 5 minutes in pan on rack before cutting. Serve warm or at room temperature.

Note: Can be made up to eight hours ahead; cool completely, cover loosely with foil, and keep at room temperature. Reheat at 350°F about 10 minutes to serve warm.

❋ *Makes one pan*

Not Quite Malasadas

INGREDIENTS
1 egg
1 1/4 cups granulated sugar
1/4 cup sour cream
3 tablespoons butter, melted
1/2 teaspoon vanilla extract
5 cups all-purpose flour
1 1/2 teaspoons baking soda
1/2 teaspoon salt
1/4 teaspoon ground nutmeg
1 1/4 cups buttermilk
Vegetable oil for deep frying
Confectioners' sugar

In a large bowl, beat egg until smooth. Add sugar, sour cream, melted butter, and vanilla, stirring until blended. Combine flour, baking soda, salt, and nutmeg. Add to egg mixture alternately with buttermilk, stirring after each addition. Turn onto lightly floured surface. Roll to 1/4-inch thickness, and cut with a 2 1/2-inch doughnut cutter. Let rest 5 to 10 minutes.

Heat 2 to 3 inches of oil to 375°F in a deep fryer or skillet. Fry a few pieces at a time turning once with a slotted spoon, until golden, about 2 minutes per side. Drain on paper towel. Dust with confectioners' sugar. Serve.

Note: Malasadas, a local treat, were brought to the Hawaiian Islands by the Portuguese. This recipe is more of a doughnut.

❀ *Makes 2 1/2 dozen*

Green Tea Bread with Candied Ginger

INGREDIENTS

2 cups all-purpose flour
2 teaspoons ground ginger
1 teaspoon baking powder
1 teaspoon salt
1/4 teaspoon baking soda
*1/4 cup loose green tea leaves,
    finely ground*
1/4 cup finely chopped candied ginger
Grated zest of 1 lemon
4 eggs
1 cup granulated sugar
3/4 cup mild olive oil
2 tablespoons fresh lemon juice
2 teaspoons vanilla extract

Position a baking rack in the lower third of the oven. Heat oven to 350°F. Lightly oil a 9 x 5-inch loaf pan and line with parchment or waxed paper.

In a medium bowl, sift together flour, ginger, baking powder, salt, and baking soda. Stir in green tea, candied ginger, and lemon zest. Set aside.

Break eggs into a large bowl. Beat 2 minutes until light in color and frothy. Slowly add the sugar in three stages, beating 30 seconds between each addition. Combine oil, lemon juice, and vanilla in measuring cup. Drizzle into egg mixture while beating. Stir in dry ingredients all at once mixing just until blended. Scrape batter into prepared pan.

Bake 50 to 55 minutes until a knife inserted in the center of the loaf comes out clean. Remove from oven and let bread cool at least 30 minutes on cooling rack. Remove from pan and cool completely. Store wrapped tightly in plastic wrap.

❋ *Makes one loaf*

Ginger Peach Bread

INGREDIENTS
1 cup finely diced peaches
3 tablespoons bourbon
1/2 cup butter, softened
1/3 cup packed brown sugar
1/2 cup molasses
1/2 cup hot water or buttermilk
2 eggs
2 1/2 cups all-purpose flour
1 teaspoon baking soda
1 teaspoon baking powder
1 teaspoon ground ginger
1 teaspoon ground cinnamon
3/4 teaspoon salt
3/4 cup chopped pecans

Heat oven to 350°F. Grease and flour a 9 x 9 x 2-inch pan, set aside. Place peaches in small bowl, sprinkle with bourbon, and set aside.

In a large bowl, combine butter, brown sugar, molasses, and hot water or buttermilk. Beat until smooth. Add eggs and beat until light and fluffy. In another bowl, stir together flour, baking soda, baking powder, ginger, cinnamon, and salt. Add half the dry ingredients to butter mixture, beating lightly to mix. Beat in remaining dry ingredients. Fold in peaches with bourbon and pecans. Scrape into prepared pan. Bake 45 to 50 minutes until a cake tester inserted in center of the loaf comes out clean. Let sit at least 5 minutes before cutting.

Note: Mangoes can be substituted for peaches when in season.

❋ *Makes one pan*

Pineapple Macadamia Nut Bread

INGREDIENTS

2 cups all-purpose flour
1 1/2 tablespoons baking powder
1/2 teaspoon salt
1/2 teaspoon ground ginger
1/4 teaspoon ground nutmeg
1/4 cup butter, softened
3/4 cup granulated sugar
2 eggs
1 teaspoon almond extract
2/3 cup milk
3/4 cup crushed pineapple, drained
3/4 cup diced macadamia nuts

Heat oven to 350°F. Grease and flour a 9 x 5-inch loaf pan. Set aside.

In a medium bowl, sift together flour, baking powder, salt, ginger, and nutmeg. In a large bowl, cream together butter and sugar. Beat in eggs one at a time, until well blended. Combine almond extract and milk. Add the dry ingredients to the butter mixture, alternately with the milk, beating to combine. Fold in pineapple and nuts. Scrape into prepared pan and lightly smooth the top.

Bake for 45 to 55 minutes or until a cake tester inserted in the center of the loaf comes out clean. Let bread cool in pan on rack for 10 minutes, then remove from pan and continue to cool.

❋ *Makes one loaf*

Cider Pumpkin Bread

INGREDIENTS
1 cup butter, softened
1 1/2 cups packed brown sugar
2 teaspoons ground cinnamon
1 teaspoon grated fresh ginger root
3 eggs, beaten
2 cups pumpkin puree
1 cup apple cider
1 cup shredded fresh pumpkin or apple
1 cup raisins
1 cup chopped walnuts
3 cups all-purpose flour
1 1/2 cups whole wheat flour
2 1/2 teaspoons baking soda
1/2 teaspoon baking powder
1/2 teaspoon salt

Heat oven to 350°F. Grease two 9 x 5-inch loaf pans. Set aside.

Beat butter until creamy in a large bowl. Stir in brown sugar, cinnamon, and ginger, mixing well. Beat in eggs. Stir in pumpkin puree and cider. Add shredded pumpkin, raisins, and walnuts. Mix thoroughly. In another bowl, stir together all-purpose flour, whole wheat flour, baking soda, baking powder, and salt. Add dry ingredients to pumpkin mixture and mix just until moistened. Divide batter between prepared pans.

Place in oven and bake for 50 to 60 minutes, or until a cake tester inserted near the center of the loaves comes out clean. Cool in pans on rack until room temperature. Store in airtight container.

Note: Great with a slightly sweetened cream cheese spread.

❋ *Makes two loaves*

Sage Tea Bread

INGREDIENTS
1/2 cup whole milk
2 tablespoons minced fresh sage
1/2 cup butter, softened
1/2 cup granulated sugar
2 eggs
2 cups all-purpose flour
1 teaspoon baking powder
1 teaspoon salt

Heat oven to 350°F. Grease a 9 x 5-inch loaf baking pan. Set aside.

In small saucepan, heat milk and sage just until warm, being careful not to boil. Set aside to cool.

Cream together butter and sugar in a bowl. Add eggs one at a time, beating well after each addition. Combine flour, baking powder, and salt. Add to butter mixture alternately with cooled milk. Stir just to blend. Scrape into prepared loaf pan.

Bake for 40 to 50 minutes or until a cake tester inserted near the center of the loaf comes out clean. Cool 10 minutes on a wire rack before removing bread from the pan, then cool completely. Store in airtight container.

❋ *Makes one loaf*

Spring Tea Loaf

INGREDIENTS
1 cup butter, softened
1 cup super fine sugar
4 eggs, beaten
2 cups all-purpose flour
1 teaspoon baking powder
Grated zest of 1 orange
Grated zest of 1 lemon
2 tablespoons dried calendula petals
Granulated sugar

Heat oven to 350°F. Grease and line or flour a 8 x 4-inch loaf pan. Set aside.

Cream together butter and sugar until smooth. Add the beaten eggs a little at a time, beating well after each addition. Sift together flour and baking powder and fold into the creamed mixture. Add the orange zest, lemon zest, and calendula petals. Stir to blend. Spoon into prepared pan.

Bake 55 to 60 minutes or until a cake tester inserted near the center of the loaf comes out clean. Sprinkle with granulated sugar about halfway through baking. Cool for 5 minutes then remove from pan. Serve when just cool. This keeps well and can be frozen.

Note: Calendula is easy to grow. It's also known as 'pot marigold', so be careful not to confuse it with the regular marigold. Calendula petals can be added to soups, stews, and salads and give beautiful color to puddings, rice dishes, and fish recipes. The young leaves are edible as well. Petals are available at nature food stores. With home grown plants be sure they are chemical-free.

❋ *Makes one loaf*

Sweet Potato Bread

INGREDIENTS

2/3 cup butter, softened
2 1/3 cups granulated sugar
4 eggs
2 cups mashed sweet potatoes
2/3 cup water
3 1/2 cups all-purpose flour
2 teaspoons baking soda
1 1/2 teaspoons salt
1 teaspoon ground cinnamon
1/2 teaspoon ground cardamom
1/2 teaspoon baking powder
1 cup coarsely chopped pecans
1 1/2 cups raisins

Heat oven to 350°F. Generously grease two 9 x 5-inch loaf pans. Set aside.

In a large bowl, cream together butter and sugar. Beat in eggs one at a time, until well blended. Stir in sweet potatoes and water, mixing thoroughly. Sift in flour, baking soda, salt, cinnamon, cardamom, and baking powder. Stir, mixing just until combined. Fold in pecans and raisins with just a few strokes. Do not over mix. Divide batter between prepared pans.

Bake for 50 to 60 minutes or until a cake tester inserted near the center of the loaves comes out clean. Cool in pan 30 minutes. Remove from pan and cool to room temperature.

❋ *Makes two loaves*

Tomato Spice Bread

INGREDIENTS

2 eggs
1/3 cup canola or safflower oil
1/2 cup granulated sugar
1/2 cup packed light brown sugar
1 1/4 cups puree from seeded,
*   fresh ripe red tomatoes; or*
*   1 1/4 cups canned unseasoned*
*   diced tomatoes, drained*
1 1/2 cups all-purpose flour
1 teaspoon ground cinnamon
1/2 teaspoon ground allspice
1/2 teaspoon ground nutmeg
1/2 teaspoon ground cloves
1 teaspoon baking soda
1/2 teaspoon baking powder
Pinch salt
1/4 cup sliced almonds

Heat oven to 350°F. Grease a 6-cup ring mold, bundt pan, or 8 1/2 x 4 1/2-inch loaf pan, set aside.

Beat eggs in a large bowl until creamy. Add oil, granulated and brown sugars. Beat 3 minutes until doubled in volume and light in color. Stir in tomato puree mixing well. Sift in flour, cinammon, allspice, nutmeg, cloves, baking soda, baking powder, and salt. Beat 2 minutes until smooth. Batter will be thin. Pour into prepared pan and sprinkle with almonds.

Bake for 45 to 50 minutes in ring or bundt pan, 60 to 65 minutes in loaf pan, or until bread springs back when touched and a cake tester inserted into the center of the bread comes out clean. Let cool in pan about 5 minutes, then turn out onto rack to cool completely before slicing. Store wrapped in plastic.

Note: A moist sweet and spicy tea bread, a great way to use a bumper crop of ripe tomatoes.

❋ *Makes one loaf*

Orange Zucchini Bread

INGREDIENTS
2 eggs
$1/2$ cup canola oil
1 $1/2$ cups grated fresh zucchini
1 $1/2$ cups all-purpose flour
$3/4$ cup granulated sugar
2 teaspoons baking powder
$1/2$ teaspoon baking soda
$1/4$ teaspoon salt
$1/4$ teaspoon ground ginger
Pinch ground cloves
1 $1/2$ teaspoons orange zest
$1/2$ cup chopped pecans or walnuts

Heat oven to 375°F. Grease a 9 x 5-inch loaf pan. Set aside.

In a large bowl, beat eggs until light and frothy. Stir in oil and zucchini. Sift in flour, sugar, baking powder, baking soda, salt, ginger, and cloves. Add orange zest and pecans. Stir to mix. Pour batter into prepared pan.

Bake 50 minutes or until a cake tester inserted near the center of the loaf comes out with crumbs adhering. Let cool in the pan 5 minutes, then turn out onto a rack to cool completely.

Note: This bread can be frozen and the recipe doubles easily.

❋ *Makes one loaf*

Pineapple Zucchini Loaf

INGREDIENTS

3 eggs
2 cups granulated sugar
1 cup vegetable oil
3 tablespoons vanilla
2 cups grated fresh zucchini, with or
 without peel, well drained
3 cups all-purpose flour
1 teaspoon baking powder
1 teaspoon baking soda
1 teaspoon salt
1 teaspoon ground cardamom
8 ounces crushed pineapple, drained
1 cup chopped pecans, walnuts
 or macadamia nuts
1/2 cup raisins

Heat oven to 350°F. Grease and flour two 9 x 5-inch loaf pans. Set aside. In a large bowl, beat eggs until light and fluffy. Add sugar, oil, and vanilla. Blend well. Stir in zucchini, mixing thoroughly. Sift in flour, baking powder, baking soda, salt, and cardamom. Stir to blend. Add pineapple, nuts, and raisins. Mix well. Pour into prepared pans.

Bake for 60 minutes or until a cake tester inserted in the center of the loaves comes out clean. Cool on wire rack about 10 minutes before removing from pans. Cool completely. Store wrapped tightly in plastic wrap.

Note: This bread gets better the next day as the flavors have time to develop overnight.

❀ *Makes two loaves*

Whole Wheat Biscuits

INGREDIENTS

1 1/4 cups whole wheat flour
1 cup all-purpose flour
1 tablespoon baking powder
1/2 teaspoon salt
1/2 teaspoon baking soda
1/2 cup butter or shortening,
 cut into small pieces
1/2 to 2/3 cup milk

Preheat oven to 400°F. Lightly grease baking sheet. Set aside.

In a large bowl, stir together whole wheat flour, all-purpose flour, baking powder, salt, and baking soda until thoroughly blended. Add butter. Work into flour using fork, blending until mixture is the texture of coarse sand. Stir in milk until evenly moistened. Turn dough out onto a floured board and shape into a ball. Knead dough lightly 5 or 6 times, then roll out until 1-inch thick using lightly floured rolling pin. Cut into 2-inch circles with biscuit cutter or juice glass. Place on prepared baking sheet.

Bake 20 minutes until lightly browned, and serve hot.

❀ *Makes 10 to 12 biscuits*

Goat Cheese and Green Onion Scones

INGREDIENTS
2 cups all-purpose flour
1 tablespoon baking powder
1 teaspoon salt
$^1/_4$ to $^1/_2$ teaspoon cayenne pepper
4 ounces goat cheese
3 green onions, thinly sliced
1 egg
$^3/_4$ cup half-and-half

Heat oven to 375°F. Stir together flour, baking powder, salt, and cayenne in a large bowl. Using pastry blender or fork, blend in cheese until mixture resembles coarse sand. Stir in green onions.

In small bowl, beat egg until blended. Stir in half-and-half, mixing well. Stir into flour mixture mixing gently just until soft dough forms. Divide dough in half. On lightly floured surface, shape each piece of dough into a ball. Flatten to $^3/_4$-inch thick round. Place on baking sheet. Cut each round into six wedges. Separate wedges about $^1/_4$-inch or so, enough to allow to rise but remain somewhat as one round.

Bake about 25 minutes until gently browned. Do not let bottoms burn. Cool 10 minutes and serve warm.

Note: Delicious with butter or split, spread with mustard, and filled with thinly sliced ham and tomatoes.

✺ *Makes one dozen*

Orange Cranberry Scones

INGREDIENTS
3 cups all-purpose flour
1 tablespoon baking powder
$1/2$ teaspoon baking soda
$1/2$ teaspoon salt
$1/4$ cup granulated sugar
1 tablespoon orange zest
$3/4$ cold butter, cut into small pieces
$1/2$ cup sweetened dried cranberries
1 egg
1 cup cream
$1/2$ teaspoon vanilla extract

Heat oven to 425°F. Lightly flour baking sheet, set aside.

In a large bowl, sift together flour, baking powder, baking soda, and salt. Stir in sugar and orange zest, add butter. Using a pastry blender or fork, work in butter until mixture resembles coarse sand. Stir in cranberries. Make a well in the center. In a small bowl, beat together egg, cream, and vanilla. Pour into the well in the flour. Stir just until dough begins to combine. Do not over mix.

Form dough into a ball and place on a lightly floured surface. Knead 6 to 8 times. Pat dough down to 1-inch thick. Cut out twelve 2 to $2 \, 1/2$-inch rounds with floured cutter or rim of glass, or six 3-inch rounds if using for sandwiches. Press the scraps together and continue to cut out rounds until all the dough is used. Place on baking sheet about 1-inch apart.

Bake 10 to 12 minutes until scones have risen, are golden, and bottoms are lightly browned. Remove to wire rack to cool slightly. Serve warm.

Note: Dough can be wrapped in plastic and chilled in refrigerator overnight before baking, resulting in a flakier scone but may require an extra minute or two of baking time.

Makes 6 to 12 scones

Kahala Challah

INGREDIENTS
2 packages active dry yeast
1 cup warm water (105°-115°F)
1/2 cup granulated sugar, divided
4 eggs
5 cups all-purpose flour
2 teaspoons salt
1/2 cup butter, softened
1 tablespoon poppy seeds

In a large bowl, dissolve yeast in warm water with a few tablespoons of sugar and let stand until foamy, about 5 to 10 minutes. With wooden spoon, stir in remaining sugar and 3 eggs, blending well. Add 4 1/2 cups flour, salt, and butter, stirring until mixture comes together to form a sticky dough. Knead dough by hand or electric stand mixer about 8 minutes, adding very little flour, until smooth and elastic. Be careful not to add too much flour. The dough should stay soft and will become less sticky with kneading. Form into a ball. Place in a lightly oiled bowl, turning to coat. Cover with a clean, damp cloth and let rise in a warm, draft free place until double in bulk, about 2 hours.

Oil baking sheet or line with parchment paper. Set aside. Punch dough down. Scrape out onto floured work surface. Divide dough in half. Cut each half into three equal pieces. Gently roll each piece by starting in center of dough and working outward to form a 12-inch rope. Line up the three pieces vertically. Starting at the top, braid ropes by crossing the strand on the right over the middle strand, then the left strand over the new middle piece. Repeat until all of the ropes have been incorporated into the braid. Pinch the ends together and tuck under. Tidy up the top by crossing any loose ends under each other, pinching together, and tucking under the loaf.

Place braided loaves on prepared baking sheet, cover with a dry cloth, and let rise in a warm place until double in size and spongy to touch, about 1 hour.

Position rack in lower third of oven and heat to 350°F. Beat remaining egg and brush over the top of the bread. Sprinkle with poppy seeds. Bake for 30 to 35 minutes until nicely browned and loaves sound hollow when tapped on bottom. Transfer to wire rack to cool.

This recipe can be cut in half for just one loaf. Break eggs into a cup, beat until smooth, and reserve 1 to 2 tablespoons for egg wash.

Note: Yeast is a living organism that needs food, warmth, and moisture to thrive. Proofing or activating the yeast before adding it is one step to take in assuring the success of the bread. High heat can kill it and not enough heat will slow it down.

❁ *Makes two loaves*

Maui Onion Focaccia

INGREDIENTS

1 package dry yeast
1/2 teaspoon granulated sugar
1 cup warm water (105° - 115°F),
   divided
3 cups all-purpose flour
1 teaspoon salt
4 tablespoons olive oil, divided
2 Maui or Ewa Sweet onions,
   diced or thinly sliced
8 cloves garlic, minced
1 tablespoon fresh chopped rosemary
   or basil
Parmesan or chopped walnuts

In a large bowl, dissolve yeast and sugar in $1/4$ cup warm water. Let sit 5 to 10 minutes until foamy. Add remaining $3/4$ cup of water, flour, salt, and 1 tablespoon of oil, stirring to make a soft dough. Turn out onto floured surface. Knead dough for 8 to 10 minutes. Let rest for 2 or 3 minutes. Knead another 5 minutes until dough is very smooth and elastic. Place in a lightly oiled bowl, turning to coat lightly. Cover and let rise in a warm place until double in bulk, about 1 $1/2$ hours. Punch dough down. Lightly oil a 12 x 16-inch pan with slight rim. Place dough on pan and press evenly to reach edges. Set aside.

Heat remaining oil in a medium skillet over medium-high heat. Add onion, garlic, and herbs. Sauté until golden, 8 to 10 minutes. Dimple dough by poking with finger. Spread with sautéed onions. Let rise uncovered in a warm place for 30 minutes. Heat oven to 400°F. Sprinkle focaccia with cheese or walnuts. Bake in the middle of the oven about 25 minutes until golden and bottom is lightly browned. Remove to wire rack and let sit a few minutes before cutting into squares or on diagonal for diamonds. Serve warm.

Note: This can be frozen. Thaw at room temperature and bake at 350°F just until heated through, about 10 minutes.

Onion varieties include yellow, white, Spanish, red, or Bermuda; and sweet onions, such as Vidalia, Maui, and Walla Walla - named after the locations in which they're grown. The true Maui onion grows in the deep red, volcanic earth on the upper slopes of Haleakala, on the island of Maui, and is considered one of the best and most flavorful onions in the world.

✻ Makes one loaf

Onion Sage Rolls

INGREDIENTS

2 tablespoons olive oil
2 cups finely chopped onions
2 packages active dry yeast
1/4 cup honey
1/2 cup warm water (105° - 115°F)
2 cups warm milk (105° - 115°F)
1/4 cup vegetable shortening
2 teaspoons salt
5 to 6 cups all-purpose flour
2 tablespoons rubbed fresh sage or
   2 teaspoons dried sage
1 1/2 cups whole wheat flour
Olive oil

Heat oil in a medium skillet over medium heat. Add onions and sauté until soft but not brown. Set aside and let cool.

In a large bowl, stir yeast and honey into water to proof about 5 minutes. Add milk, shortening, salt, 2 cups all-purpose flour, and cooled onions. Beat vigorously for 2 minutes. Whisk together sage and whole wheat flour. Add to yeast mixture, stirring to incorporate. Gradually add some of the remaining all-purpose flour, 1/4 cup at a time, just until dough begins to pull away from the sides of the bowl. Knead dough by hand or electric stand mixer, adding more flour as necessary, until smooth and elastic. Place in a lightly oiled bowl, turning to coat. Cover with a clean towel and let rise in a warm, draft free place until double in bulk, about 1 hour.

Line baking sheets with parchment paper or lightly oil 36 muffin cups. Turn the dough out onto a lightly oiled work surface (do not punch down) and divide into 36 equal pieces. Shape each piece into an 8-inch strand and tie it into a single knot. Place about 3 inches apart on prepared baking sheets or in muffin cups. Cover with a towel and let rise until almost doubled, about 45 minutes. Heat oven to 400°F. For a shiny, soft crust, brush the tops of the rolls with olive oil. Bake for 15 to 20 minutes, until light golden brown. Immediately remove the rolls from baking sheets or muffin tins to wire rack. Serve hot.

Note: Great for a festive dinner and turkey sandwiches. The rolls can be made ahead and kept in the freezer. This recipe can be cut in half.

❋ *Makes 3 dozen rolls*

Pineapple-Coconut Bread

INGREDIENTS
1/2 cup warm water (105° - 115°F)
1/4 cup warm milk (105° - 115°F)
2 tablespoons honey
1 package yeast
2 tablespoons butter, softened
1/4 teaspoon ground ginger
1/4 teaspoon ground nutmeg
1/2 teaspoon salt
1/2 cup whole wheat flour
2 cups all-purpose flour
1/4 cup finely diced dried pineapple
1/4 cup shredded coconut
1/4 cup diced macadamia nuts

Mix water, milk, and honey in a large bowl. Sprinkle in yeast and let stand to proof about 5 minutes. Add butter, ginger, nutmeg, salt, and whole wheat flour, stirring to blend. Add all-purpose flour a 1/2 cup at a time, mixing well after each addition, until dough pulls away from side of bowl. Knead dough by hand or electric stand mixer, adding more flour as necessary, until smooth and elastic. Place in a lightly oiled bowl, turning to coat lightly. Cover with a clean cloth and let rise in warm, draft free place for 1 hour.

Punch dough down. Add pineapple, coconut, and macadamia nuts. Knead 5 minutes to incorporate well. Grease and flour an 8-inch loaf pan. Shape dough into loaf and fit into pan. Cover and let rise for 45 minutes. Heat oven to 400°F. Place bread in center of oven and bake 35 to 40 minutes until top is crusty, bottom is browned and sounds hollow when tapped. Let bread rest in pan for 5 minutes on wire rack before removing from pan to wire rack to cool completely. Store wrapped tightly in plastic wrap.

Makes one loaf

Midday

Salads
Sandwiches
Soups

Growing from the Inside Out, by Patrice Federspiel

Salads

Ahi Poke

INGREDIENTS

12 ounces good quality fresh ahi,
  diced into $1/2$-inch cubes
2 teaspoons sesame oil
1 $1/2$ teaspoons soy sauce
1 medium Maui onion, diced
2 green onions, thinly sliced
$1/8$ to $1/4$ teaspoon crushed
  red pepper flakes

Place ahi in shallow dish in single layer. Lightly cover with oil and soy sauce. Sprinkle with onion, green onion, and red pepper flakes. Toss to mix. Cover and chill for at least 2 hours. Serve.

Note: Just play with the amounts of everything to taste. Great paired with the Watercress and Daikon Salad.

Serves 4

Ahi Poke with Chayote Slaw

INGREDIENTS

12 ounces fresh ahi, thinly sliced
3 tablespoons chopped fresh Thai basil
2 tablespoons soy sauce
1 teaspoon wasabi paste
1 green onion, thinly sliced
$1/4$ cup shredded coconut
1 teaspoon sesame seeds
1 cup julienned chayote squash
1 cup julienned Crenshaw or
  Honeydew melon
2 tablespoons orange juice concentrate
1 teaspoon rice vinegar
Few drops sesame oil
1 green onion, thinly sliced
Salt

Place ahi in shallow dish. Combine basil, soy sauce, wasabi, and green onion in small bowl. Pour over ahi and gently mix. Cover and chill at least 1 hour.

Place chayote and melon in mixing bowl. In small bowl, stir together orange juice concentrate, vinegar, oil, and green onion. Pour over squash-melon mixture and toss lightly to coat. Season with salt to taste. Cover and chill slaw at least 1 hour.

Heat broiler. Lay coconut and sesame seeds in small baking pan. Place at least 6 inches from heating element. Toast until golden. Be careful as coconut burns easily. Remove from oven and set aside.

Place equal portions of slaw on four salad plates. Top with slices of ahi. Sprinkle with toasted sesame seeds and coconut. Serve.

Serves 4

Asian Pear and Green Beans

SALAD

2 teaspoons white sesame seeds

$^1/_2$ cup water

1 pound Chinese long beans,
 trimmed and cut into 2-inch pieces
 on diagonal or 4 ounces snow peas,
 trimmed and julienned

2 Asian pears, or 4 red-skinned pears,
 cored and diced

$^1/_2$ cup unsalted macadamia nut halves

5 cups mixed salad greens, washed
 and dried (avoid radicchio)

DRESSING

$^1/_4$ cup macadamia nut or
 extra-virgin olive oil

Juice of 1 lime

1 to 2 red chilies, finely sliced

$^1/_2$ teaspoon salt

$^1/_8$ teaspoon black pepper

$^1/_2$ to 1 teaspoon granulated sugar

Heat a skillet over medium heat. Add sesame seeds and toast in dry skillet for several minutes, stirring frequently, until lightly golden. Remove from skillet and set aside.

Fill a large bowl with cold water and ice. In a medium saucepan, bring $^1/_2$ cup water to a boil over high heat. Add green beans. Blanch by cooking about 1 minute until bright green, drain, and immediately plunge into ice water to stop cooking process. Let sit a few minutes to cool. Drain beans well and pat dry. Place in bowl with pears and half of macadamia nuts. Arrange greens on serving platter. Top greens with pear-bean mixture. Sprinkle with remaining nuts and sesame seeds.

Mix oil, lime juice, and chilies in a small bowl with whisk or jar with lid. Blend in salt and pepper. Adjust seasonings adding sugar if desired. Drizzle dressing over pear-bean mixture and toss lightly to coat well. Serve.

☗ *Serves 4*

Asian Pear Julienne

SALAD
2 ribs celery, trimmed, julienned into
   3-inch lengths and $1/4$-inch thick
2 firm Asian pears,
   julienned $1/4$-inch thick
1 ripe but firm mango,
   julienned $1/4$-inch thick

DRESSING
3 tablespoons fresh lime juice
2 tablespoons rice vinegar
1 teaspoon peeled, finely grated
   fresh ginger root
$1/2$ to 1 small fresh hot red chili,
   finely minced
2 scallions or green onions,
   thinly sliced on the diagonal
$1/4$ cup fresh cilantro leaves
Salt and freshly ground black pepper

Place celery, Asian pear, and mango in a bowl.

Whisk together lime juice, vinegar, ginger, and chili in small bowl. Pour over celery-pear mixture and toss lightly to coat. Sprinkle in scallion and cilantro. Season with salt and pepper to taste. Cover and let stand at room temperature 15 minutes. Arrange in shallow serving dish and serve.

Note: To julienne means to cut into narrow, fine sticks that can measure from 2 to 3 inches long and $1/8$-inch wide. A finer julienne measures $1/16$ of an inch wide.

꙳ *Serves 4 to 6*

Asparagus and Snow Peas

SALAD
1 pound fresh asparagus,
   trimmed and cut in half
4 ounces snow peas, stems removed
1 pint cherry tomatoes, quartered

DRESSING
2 tablespoons lemon juice
2 tablespoons peanut butter
2 tablespoons soy sauce
1 tablespoon honey
2 to 3 teaspoons sesame oil
Sliced green onions

Steam asparagus 2 to 3 minutes until bright green but still crisp. Drain. Rinse with cold water to cool quickly. Pat dry and place in serving dish. Set aside.

Steam snow peas for 1 minute until bright green but still crisp. Drain. Rinse with cold water. Pat dry and add to asparagus. Mix tomatoes with asparagus and snow peas.

Whisk together lemon juice, peanut butter, soy sauce, honey, and oil in small bowl until smooth. Drizzle over the vegetables. Garnish with green onions and serve.

꙳ *Serves 4 to 6*

Beet with Walnuts

INGREDIENTS

1/4 cup walnut pieces
1 1/2 pounds assorted colored beets,
  with tops
1 1/2 tablespoons sherry vinegar
3 tablespoons extra-virgin olive oil
1 tablespoon finely chopped fresh
  flat-leafed parsley
Salt and freshly ground black pepper
2 bunches arugula, trimmed and washed

Heat a small frying pan over medium heat. Add walnuts and toast, shaking occasionally, until golden and fragrant, 5 to 8 minutes. Remove from pan and set aside.

If beets still have tops attached, trim stems to 1/2-inch in length. Save leaves for another recipe. Peel beets. Carefully quarter, giving each piece a little of leaf stems. In a large saucepan, cover beets with water. Bring to a boil over medium-high heat. Reduce heat and simmer until just tender, about 30 minutes. If beets are large they may take longer to cook. Drain. Place in a bowl. Toss warm beets with vinegar. Beets and nuts may be prepared two days ahead and kept separately, covered in refrigerator.

Just before serving, toss beets with nuts, oil, and parsley. Season with salt and pepper to taste. Arrange arugula on individual plates or serving platter. Top with beets. Serve.

✾ *Serves 6 to 8*

Broccoli with Lime Vinaigrette

INGREDIENTS
1 pound broccoli, cut into small florets
Juice of 1 lime
1 shallot, minced
2 teaspoons Dijon mustard
1/4 cup extra-virgin olive oil
Salt and black pepper
1/4 cup shaved Parmesan Reggiano

Place broccoli in a saucepan with 1-inch of water. Bring to a boil and cook 2 minutes, stirring frequently, just until broccoli turns bright green. Drain, rinse with cold water, and drain again. Place in serving bowl.

Whisk together lime juice, shallot, and mustard in a small bowl. Slowly pour in oil while continuing to whisk. Season with salt and pepper to taste. Drizzle over broccoli and toss to coat. Sprinkle with Parmesan and serve.

Serves 4

Couscous with Black Beans

INGREDIENTS
3 1/2 cups water
1 cup couscous
1/2 cup olive oil
1/4 cup balsamic vinegar
1 large clove garlic, crushed and minced
1 cup finely diced celery
2 cups cooked black beans, drained
Salt and black pepper
*1 small head iceberg lettuce,
  washed and thinly sliced*
1 large tomato, diced
2 cups crumbled Feta

In a medium saucepan, bring water to a boil over high heat. Stir in couscous. Cover and remove from heat and let sit 10 minutes to absorb the water.

Whisk together oil and vinegar in a small bowl. Stir in garlic, celery, beans, and couscous. Toss all together until couscous is slightly purpley-black in color. Season with salt and pepper to taste. Spread lettuce on serving platter. Top with couscous. Garnish with tomato and Feta. Serve.

Serves 4 to 6

Cucumber-Peanut Salad

INGREDIENTS
3 large cucumbers, peeled
Juice of 1 lime
1 tablespoon peanut oil
1 tablespoon granulated sugar
4 to 6 tablespoons chopped fresh mint
1 small red chili, minced
3/4 cup coarsely chopped roasted
    salted peanuts

Cut cucumbers in half lengthwise and remove seeds. Slice into pieces 2 inches long and 1/4-inch thick. Place in a medium glass bowl.

In a small bowl, combine lime juice, oil, sugar, mint, and chili, stirring to combine. Pour over cucumber. Cover and set aside for at least 30 minutes to blend flavors.

Sprinkle with peanuts. Serve.

Note: A refreshing summer salad that can be served at room temperature or chilled. But, consider peanut allergies.

☀ *Serves 4*

Cucumber with Adzuki Beans

SALAD
1/2 cup dried adzuki beans
8 cups water, divided
3 quarter-sized slices fresh ginger root,
   bruised
3 large cloves garlic, peeled and smashed
6 scallions, washed and trimmed, divided
1 cup peeled, seeded, and diced
   Japanese cucumber

DRESSING
1 teaspoon sesame oil
2 teaspoons tamari or soy sauce
2 teaspoons rice vinegar
1 teaspoon granulated sugar
1/4 teaspoon prepared wasabi

Pick through beans and remove debris. Rinse well, cover with 4 cups water, and soak overnight.

Drain and rinse beans. Put into a medium saucepan. Add remaining 4 cups water, ginger, and garlic. Cut 3 scallions into 1-inch pieces and add to beans. Bring to a boil over high heat. Reduce heat and simmer, partially covered, for 45 minutes, until tender but not mushy. Drain well. Remove ginger, garlic, and scallion pieces. Cool the beans to room temperature. If making ahead, refrigerate. The beans can be kept chilled up to 3 days. Place beans and cucumber in serving bowl.

Combine oil, tamari, vinegar, sugar, and wasabi in a small bowl or jar with lid. Whisk or shake to blend well. Thinly slice remaining scallions and toss over bean mixture. Blend dressing again, and pour over vegetables. Toss to coat, and serve.

Note: Bruising ginger means to give it a good whack with something flat, which releases the flavor.

Serves 4

Warm Goat Cheese Salad

SALAD

1 pound plain goat cheese
1/2 cup crushed roasted pistachios
1 to 2 tablespoons olive oil
3/4 to 1 pound mixed greens
Freshly ground black pepper
Edible flowers, olive slices,
*   radish rosettes or grape tomatoes*

MUSTARD VINAIGRETTE

5 tablespoons good quality olive oil
2 to 3 tablespoons balsamic vinegar
1 heaping teaspoon Dijon mustard
1 teaspoon granulated sugar
1 large clove garlic, smashed
Freshly ground black pepper

Shape 2 tablespoons of goat cheese into a circle about 2 inches in diameter and 1/2-inch thick. Place on sheet of plastic wrap. Make 12 to 16 patties, depending on number of servings desired. Place the crushed pistachios on a small shallow plate. Add cheese patties a few at a time. Press firmly to coat both sides thoroughly with nuts. Set aside.

Brush a heavy skillet lightly with oil. Heat over medium heat. Add coated patties, in batches, to hot skillet and sauté about 2 minutes per side until golden brown. Remove, set aside, and continue to cook all the patties. Arrange salad greens on individual salad plates. Drizzle with a little vinaigrette. Place 2 sautéed cheese patties in the center of each. Sprinkle with freshly ground pepper. Garnish as desired. Serve immediately.

Vinaigrette: In a small bowl, whisk together oil, vinegar, and mustard in small bowl until well blended. Stir in sugar and garlic. Season with pepper to taste. Mix well. If the vinaigrette is made in advance, whisk again just before serving to blend ingredients.

Serves 6 to 8

Green Lentils with Feta and Sun-Dried Tomato

Dressing
1/4 cup extra-virgin olive oil
3 tablespoons white wine vinegar
1 teaspoon dried thyme
Salt and black pepper
1 cup oil packed sun-dried tomatoes, drained and cut into slivers

Salad
2 cups French green lentils, picked over and rinsed
4 cups water
1 cup crumbled Feta
2 tablespoons chopped fresh parsley
1 tablespoon chopped pine nuts, optional

Whisk together oil, vinegar, and thyme in large bowl. Season with salt and pepper to taste. Stir in tomatoes. Adjust seasonings and set aside.

Put lentils and water in a large saucepan. Bring to a boil over high heat. Reduce heat to low and simmer just until tender, about 20 minutes. Drain in sieve, gently rinse, and drain again.

Remix dressing. Add lentils and stir lightly to coat. Sprinkle in Feta and toss lightly. Garnish with parsley and pine nuts. Serve.

Serves 6 to 8

Green Mango Salad

INGREDIENTS
2 large green mangoes, just starting to ripen
1 tablespoon vegetable oil
$^1/_2$ teaspoon mustard seeds
1 small fresh red chili, finely minced with seeds
15 ounces canned black beans, drained
3 tablespoons shredded coconut
2 teaspoons soy sauce
1 small head of Manoa or red leaf lettuce, washed and patted dry
1 large ripe avocado, peeled and diced

Peel mangoes. Grate into a mixing bowl and set aside.
Discard seed. Heat oil in saucepan over medium heat. Add
mustard seeds and chili. When mustard seeds start to pop,
add mango, beans, coconut, and soy sauce. Sauté, stirring
frequently, about 5 minutes until heated through.

Slice lettuce into thin strips and spread in shallow bowl. Mound
mango mixture in center. Sprinkle with avocado. Serve.

Note: The texture of this dish is softer than a green papaya
salad and the green mango has a tangier flavor.

Serves 4

Hearts of Palm and Crab

Dressing

1 medium firm ripe avocado, peeled, seeded, and cubed
2/3 cup buttermilk
1/4 cup sour cream
3 tablespoons minced sweet onion
2 1/2 tablespoons fresh lime juice
2 tablespoons olive oil
1 teaspoon minced garlic
1 teaspoon minced fresh dill or 1/2 teaspoon dried
1/2 teaspoon salt
1/8 teaspoon cayenne pepper

Salad

1 head Butter or Manoa lettuce, separated, washed and patted dry
2 large vine-ripened tomatoes, thinly sliced
3/4 pound fresh hearts of palm, trimmed and poached until tender, or 14 ounces jarred or canned; drained and cut into 1/4-inch slices
1 pound fresh or canned crab, picked through to remove cartilage or shell

Place avocado in a mixing bowl and mash well. Beat in buttermilk and sour cream. Stir in onion, lime juice, oil, garlic, dill, salt, and cayenne. Cover and refrigerate until ready to use. This can be done up to 4 hours in advance. Dressing can be made in a blender for a smoother texture.

Lay lettuce leaves overlapping on each of six large plates. Fan out equal amounts of tomato slices on the lettuce. Scatter with hearts of palm slices. Mound crabmeat in the center. Drizzle dressing over all and serve.

Serves 6

Hearts of Palm with Prosciutto

VINAIGRETTE
2 teaspoons granulated sugar
1 teaspoon grated lemon zest
1 teaspoon chopped fresh chives
$1/2$ teaspoon salt
$1/2$ cup macadamia nut or
   extra-virgin olive oil
$1/4$ cup sherry vinegar
1 tablespoon fresh lemon juice
$1/4$ teaspoon black pepper

SALAD
6 cups mixed baby greens
1 pound fresh hearts of palm,
   poached until tender or
   14 ounces jarred or canned;
   cut into $1/4$-inch slices
4 ounces Prosciutto or
   Westphalian Ham, cut into slivers
6 julienned strips of lemon peel,
   tied into a knot

In a bowl, combine sugar, lemon zest, chives, and salt with whisk. Add oil, vinegar, lemon juice, and pepper. Whisk ingredients until blended. Adjust seasonings, set aside.

Toss the mixed greens in a salad bowl. Scatter in hearts of palm slices and Prosciutto. Drizzle with vinaigrette. Garnish with lemon peel. Serve.

♛ Serves 4 to 6

Island Salad Nicoise

AHI
12 ounces good quality fresh ahi fillet
1 teaspoon soy sauce
1 tablespoon olive oil
1 tablespoon fresh thyme
1/4 teaspoon black pepper

VINAIGRETTE
3/4 cup olive oil
1/3 cup balsamic vinegar
1/4 cup minced Maui onion
3 tablespoons Dijon mustard
1 tablespoon chopped fresh parsley
1 tablespoon chopped fresh thyme
1 teaspoon dried Maui lavender flowers
1/2 teaspoon salt
1/4 teaspoon black pepper

SALAD
1 pound red potatoes, quartered
3/4 pound green beans, trimmed
4 ripe Kula tomatoes, diced
1/3 cup sliced black olives
1/4 cup finely chopped green onion
1/4 cup chopped fresh basil
4 cups Kula salad greens or Manoa
    lettuce, washed and patted dry
4 hard cooked eggs, peeled and quartered
4 large anchovy fillets, minced
1 tablespoon capers
1 lemon, thinly sliced
Several sprigs of fresh basil

Brush ahi with soy sauce and oil. Sprinkle with thyme and pepper. Cover and chill for 30 minutes.

Whisk together oil and vinegar in a small bowl until blended. Whisk in onion, mustard, parsley, thyme, lavender, salt, and pepper. Pour into bottle or jar with lid and set aside.

In a large saucepan, cover potatoes with water and bring to a boil over high heat. Reduce heat to medium and cook until tender, about 15 minutes. Drain and place in a large bowl. Steam green beans about 2 minutes until bright green but still crisp. Drain, and add to potatoes with tomatoes, olives, green onion, and basil. Shake dressing well, pour half the vinaigrette over the vegetables. Toss gently to coat.

Heat grill or heavy skillet over medium-high heat. Brush with olive oil. Add ahi and sear both sides about 3 minutes each side. Remove and let stand a few minutes before slicing thinly. Ahi will be rare. Place greens on serving platter. Top with vegetable mixture. Layer ahi slices on top. Arrange quartered eggs around platter. Sprinkle with anchovies and capers. Drizzle with remaining vinaigrette. Garnish with fresh lemon slices and basil. Serve.

Note: To hard cook eggs, place eggs in saucepan, cover with water, place over medium-high heat and bring to a boil. Turn off the heat, cover, and let stand 15 minutes. Drain off warm water, place in bowl, cover with cold water. Let stand 5 minutes to cool.

Edible dried lavender flowers can be obtained from natural food stores.

Serves 4 to 6

Mango Jicama Slaw

INGREDIENTS

1 firm ripe mango, peeled and julienned
2 carrots, peeled and julienned
1 small jicama, peeled and julienned
1 red bell pepper, seeded and julienned
$^{1}/_{4}$ cup chopped fresh cilantro
$^{1}/_{4}$ cup fresh lime juice
1 teaspoon granulated sugar
1 to 2 teaspoons soy sauce
Freshly ground black pepper

Place mango, carrots, jicama, and bell pepper into a serving bowl. Sprinkle with cilantro, lime juice, sugar, and soy sauce. Season with freshly ground pepper. Stir gently. Cover with plastic wrap and refrigerate at least 1 hour, stirring occasionally. Serve.

Note: Jicama is also known as Asian yam.

♛ *Serves 4*

Melon with Paprika Dressing

PAPRIKA DRESSING
2 tablespoons fresh lime juice
$1/2$ teaspoon sweet or hot paprika
$1/4$ teaspoon salt
$1/8$ teaspoon black pepper
5 $1/2$ tablespoons extra-virgin olive oil

SALAD
2 cups 1-inch pieces cantaloupe melon
2 cups 1-inch pieces honeydew melon
2 large bunches arugula or mixed greens,
 trimmed, washed, and patted dry
4 ounces Prosciutto, cut into slivers

In a small bowl, whisk together lime juice, paprika, salt, and pepper. Add oil in a slow stream, whisking until well blended. Adjust seasonings. Set aside.

Place cantaloupe and honeydew in a medium bowl. Drizzle with half the dressing. Stir gently to coat. Arrange arugula decoratively on a platter. Top with melon. Drizzle with remaining dressing. Garnish with Prosciutto. Serve.

✾ *Serves 4 to 6*

Sautéed Mushrooms with 'Nalo Greens

DRESSING

3 tablespoons extra-virgin olive oil
2 tablespoons raspberry vinegar
1 teaspoon Dijon style mustard
Salt and black pepper
1 medium shallot, minced

SALAD

1 tablespoon olive oil
1 small onion, finely diced
8 ounces mushrooms, scrubbed
 and thinly sliced
2 tablespoons raspberry or
 red wine vinegar
Salt and black pepper
4 cups mixed Waimanalo greens
Fresh thyme or tarragon leaves
Crispy won ton strips

In a small bowl, whisk together oil, vinegar, and mustard. Season with salt and pepper to taste. Stir in shallot. Set aside.

Heat oil in a large skillet over medium heat. Add onion and sauté 3 minutes until soft. Stir in mushrooms and cook 8 to 10 minutes until tender and most of liquid has evaporated. Stir in vinegar and cook 1 minute. Season with salt and pepper to taste. Remove from heat.

Place 1 cup greens on each of four salad plates. Top with sautéed mushrooms. Blend dressing and drizzle over all. Garnish with fresh herbs and won ton strips. Serve.

Note: Try using the dressing over hot boiled potatoes with additional chopped shallots for a country-style potato salad.

♛ *Serves 4*

New Potato Green Bean Salad

DRESSING
1/4 cup olive oil
2 tablespoons whole grain mustard
3 tablespoons balsamic vinegar
4 cloves garlic, crushed
Salt and freshly ground black pepper

SALAD
1 pound whole small new potatoes or
  red skinned potatoes, quartered
1/2 cup water
1/2 pound green beans,
  trimmed and cut into 2-inch pieces
1/2 cup thinly sliced green onions
1/2 cup chopped black olives
1/4 cup slivered oil packed
  sun-dried tomatoes
4 ounces Parmesan, diced

In a small bowl, whisk together oil, mustard, vinegar, and garlic. Season to taste with salt and pepper, until well blended. Set aside.

Place potatoes in pan and cover three-quarters with water. Bring to a boil over high heat, reduce heat to medium and cook just until tender, 12 to 15 minutes. Drain and set aside.

In pan, bring 1/2 cup of water to a boil. Add green beans and cook 30 seconds. Drain and plunge into ice water. Let chill a few minutes. Place in colander and drain.

In a large salad bowl, mix warm potatoes, green onions, olives, and sun-dried tomatoes. Whisk dressing again and pour over vegetables. Toss lightly to mix, then let stand a few minutes. Sprinkle with green beans and cheese. Serve.

♛ *Serves 6*

Papaya Avocado Salad

SALAD
5 to 6 cups mixed greens,
  washed and patted dry
1 large ripe firm papaya, peeled,
  seeded, and diced
1 large ripe firm avocado, peeled,
  seeded, and diced
2 tablespoons chopped fresh cilantro
$^1/_2$ small Maui onion, minced

DRESSING
$^1/_3$ cup rice vinegar
2 tablespoons packed brown sugar
2 tablespoons macadamia nut or
  olive oil
$^1/_4$ teaspoon salt
$^1/_4$ teaspoon paprika
$^1/_4$ cup toasted macadamia nuts

Place greens in serving bowl. Scatter papaya and avocado over greens. Sprinkle with cilantro and onion.

In a small bowl, whisk together vinegar, sugar, oil, salt, and paprika until well blended.

Drizzle over salad. Sprinkle with macadamia nuts. Serve.

Serves 4

Snap Peas with Bacon Mint Dressing

INGREDIENTS
$^1/_2$ cup water
1 pound fresh snap pea pods
  or 8 ounces snow peas, trimmed
2 teaspoons granulated sugar
2 tablespoons light olive oil
$^1/_4$ cup rice vinegar
3 tablespoons minced fresh mint
4 ounces bacon, cooked and crumbled

Fill a bowl with iced water. Bring $^1/_2$ cup water to a boil over high heat in a medium saucepan. Add snap peas and cook about 30 seconds, just until tender and bright green. Drain, then plunge into cold water. Place in colander and set aside to drain.

In a small bowl, whisk together sugar, oil, and vinegar until well blended. Whisk in mint. Put snap peas in serving dish. Drizzle with dressing and sprinkle with crumbled bacon. Serve.

Serves 4 to 6

Spinach-Radicchio Salad

INGREDIENTS
4 cups fresh spinach leaves, rinsed and patted dry
1 large head radicchio, rinsed and patted dry
2 ruby red grapefruit, peeled and cut into bite-sized pieces
$1/4$ cup extra-virgin olive oil
2 tablespoons balsamic vinegar
Salt and black pepper
$1/2$ cup chopped pitted dates
2 green onions with tops, thinly sliced
$1/4$ chopped pecans

Combine spinach and radicchio in a large salad bowl. Scatter grapefruit over leaves.

Whisk together oil and vinegar. Season with salt and pepper. Stir in dates and green onions. Drizzle dressing over salad and toss. Sprinkle with pecans. Serve.

Serves 4

Spinach Salad with Warm Cranberry Dressing

DRESSING
1 cup cranberry relish
2 tablespoons granulated sugar
1 teaspoon salt
1 teaspoon black pepper
1 tablespoon grated fresh ginger root
Dash or two ground nutmeg
2 cups walnut or olive oil

SALAD
2 pounds fresh spinach leaves,
  washed and stemmed
$1/2$ to $3/4$ cup walnut halves
15 ounces canned Mandarin
  orange sections, drained well
$1/2$ cup crumbled Feta

CRANBERRY RELISH
12-ounce bag fresh cranberries
1 orange, quartered with peel
3 tablespoons sugar

Place cranberry relish in blender or food processor. Add sugar, salt, pepper, ginger, and nutmeg. Pulse to combine. With machine running, slowly add oil until well blended. Scrape into saucepan. Heat over low heat until warmed through.

In a salad bowl, toss spinach with half the warm dressing. Add walnuts, orange sections, and Feta. Serve with additional dressing and remaining relish on the side.

Cranberry Relish: Place cranberries, orange, and sugar in blender or food processor. Pulse until finely chopped, about 30 seconds. Scrape into container, cover, and chill until ready to use.

Note: You may use canned whole berry cranberry relish when fresh berries are out of season.

Serves 4

Star Fruit and Artichoke Hearts

INGREDIENTS

1 small head red leaf lettuce,
  washed and patted dry
14-ounce jar marinated artichoke
  hearts, quartered, reserve marinade
3 star fruit, washed and thinly sliced
1 sweet red pepper, diced
1 tablespoon fresh lime juice
1 tablespoon fresh lemon juice
1 to 2 teaspoons honey
$1/8$ teaspoon salt
Fresh parsley

Tear lettuce into bite-sized pieces and arrange on a serving platter. Arrange artichoke hearts in center of lettuce. Arrange star fruit in circle around artichoke hearts. Scatter red pepper over all.

In a small bowl, whisk together $3/4$ cup artichoke marinade, lime juice, lemon juice, honey, and salt until well blended. Drizzle over salad. Garnish with parsley and serve.

✿ *Serves 6 to 8*

Star Fruit with Sesame Vinaigrette

VINAIGRETTE

2 tablespoons olive oil
Juice of 1 large lime
2 teaspoons granulated sugar
2 teaspoons sesame oil
1 clove garlic, very finely minced
1 teaspoon grated fresh ginger root
$1^1/2$ tablespoons soy sauce
Black pepper

SALAD

6 cups mixed salad greens,
  washed and patted dry
3 star fruit, washed and thinly sliced
2 large mangoes, peeled, seeded,
  and diced
Oil for frying
2 to 4 ounces rice noodles

In small bowl or jar with lid, combine olive oil, lime juice, sugar, sesame oil, garlic, ginger, and soy sauce. Whisk or shake until well blended. Season with pepper and set aside. Place greens in serving bowl. Arrange star fruit on greens and top with mango.

Heat $3/4$-inch of oil in small frying pan until hot but not smoking. Break noodles into 3 to 4-inch lengths. Carefully add a few pieces to hot oil to test readiness. When oil is hot enough, the noodles will instantly puff up and turn opaque. Carefully place a layer of noodles in hot oil. When noodles puff up, turn to cook other side. Remove from oil and drain on paper towels. Repeat with remaining noodles. Place puffed noodles on salad and drizzle with sesame vinaigrette. Serve.

Note: To cut mango, slice it in half slightly off center to remove the flesh while avoiding the seed. Remove flesh from other side in the same manner. Cut away any remaining flesh from edges of seed.

✿ *Serves 4 to 6*

Sweet Potato and Green Beans

DRESSING
1/4 cup mashed cooked pumpkin
2 tablespoons olive oil
2 tablespoons lemon juice
1 tablespoon rice or apple cider vinegar
1 1/2 teaspoons light miso
1 1/2 teaspoons Dijon style mustard
2 cloves garlic, passed through press
2 tablespoons minced parsley
2 tablespoons minced cilantro
Salt and black pepper

SALAD
1 pound sweet potatoes, quartered
1/2 cup water
1/2 pound Chinese or green beans,
    cut in 2-inch pieces
1 small red onion, finely diced
1 sweet red pepper, seeded and
    finely diced
Manoa lettuce, washed and patted dry

In a small bowl, whisk together pumpkin, oil, lemon juice, vinegar, miso, and mustard. Stir in garlic, parsley, and cilantro. Season with salt and pepper to taste. Chill until ready to use.

Cook sweet potatoes in boiling water over medium heat until tender. Drain and set aside until cool enough to handle. Cut into 1-inch cubes, with or without peels. Place in a bowl.

Bring 1/2 cup water to boiling in a medium saucepan over high heat. Add green beans and cook about 30 seconds until bright green. Drain, rinse under cold water a few seconds, then drain again. Add to bowl of potatoes. Add onion and sweet pepper.

Drizzle with dressing and gently stir all together. Arrange lettuce on a shallow serving platter, top with potato-bean mixture, and serve.

♛ *Serves 4 to 6*

Watercress and Daikon Salad

INGREDIENTS
1/4 pound daikon radish,
    peeled and grated
1/4 cup olive oil
1 1/2 tablespoons white wine vinegar
1 teaspoon sugar
1/2 teapoon hondashi
Few drops sesame oil
Salt and freshly ground black pepper
1 bunch watercress, washed, patted dry,
    and cut into 2-inch pieces
1 red bell pepper, seeded and julienned

Squeeze excess moisture from daikon. Place in a serving bowl. Whisk together with olive oil, vinegar, sugar, hondashi, and sesame oil. Season with salt and pepper to taste. Pour over daikon and stir to mix well. Add watercress and bell pepper. Toss lightly. Serve.

Note: Hondashi is a Japanese dried fish soup base that is made from bonito flakes.

♛ *Serves 4*

Autumn Fruit Salad

INGREDIENTS

1 large pomegranate
$^1/4$ cup pine nuts
1 head Manoa or other soft leaf lettuce,
    washed and patted dry
2 ruby red grapefruit
2 Asian pears, cut in chunks
4 firm-ripe Fuyu persimmons,
    cut in chunks
6 tablespoons lime juice
6 tablespoons rice vinegar
$^1/4$ cup honey
Salt

Peel pomegranate, separate seeds, and set aside. Heat a small frying pan over medium heat. Add pine nuts and toast until golden, about 2 to 3 minutes, shaking pan frequently. Remove from pan. Set aside.

Arrange lettuce leaves on a serving platter with slight rim. Peel grapefruit. Cut into bite-sized pieces using serrated knife over a bowl to collect juice. Scatter grapefruit over lettuce with Asian pear and persimmon. Sprinkle with pomegranate seeds and pine nuts.

In jar with lid, mix 6 tablespoons of collected grapefruit juice, lime juice, vinegar, and honey. Drizzle over salad. Sprinkle lightly with salt and serve.

Note: Gloves may be worn to protect hands from pomegranate juice stains.

Serves 6 to 8

Fresh Figs with Basil

INGREDIENTS
3 tablespoons olive oil
1/4 cup balsamic vinegar
24 ripe fresh black or green figs,
*   washed and cut into eighths*
1/4 cup chopped fresh basil
Salt and black pepper

In a small bowl, whisk together oil and vinegar. Arrange figs on a shallow serving platter. Drizzle with dressing. Sprinkle with basil. Season with salt and pepper to taste. Serve chilled or at room temperature.

Note: Nice accompaniment to grilled chicken and pork. Can also be served as a dessert with a plate of assorted cheese.

❦ *Serves 8*

Peaches with Mint-Almond Pesto

SALAD
4 firm ripe peaches
8 cups baby salad greens

DRESSING
1 cup fresh mint leaves
$1/4$ cup granulated sugar
2 tablespoons balsamic vinegar
Dash or two black pepper
2 tablespoon chopped almonds, toasted

Fill a large bowl with ice and water, set aside. Bring a large saucepan of water to a boil. Score skin but not flesh of peaches by carefully cutting an "x" on the bottom. Immerse peaches for 20 seconds in boiling water, remove with slotted spoon, and plunge in ice water. Remove skin with a paring knife. Cut peaches in half and remove pits. Place in a large bowl.

Finely chop mint leaves. Place in a small bowl with sugar, vinegar, pepper, and almonds, stirring well. Pour over peaches. Cover and chill at least 4 hours.

Wash and pat dry greens. Arrange equal amounts on plates. Top each with one or two peach halves. Drizzle with pesto marinade. Serve.

Note: Salad can be served with a wedge of cheese and a thick slice of French bread.

Serves 4 to 8

Pears with Raspberry Vinaigrette

VINAIGRETTE
1 cup fresh or frozen raspberries, thawed
1/3 cup white or apple cider vinegar
1/2 cup extra-virgin olive oil
2 teaspoons granulated sugar
1/2 teaspoon salt
1/4 teaspoon black pepper

SALAD
2 heads radicchio, leaves separated,
    washed, and dried
4 fresh Bosc pears, peeled, halved,
    cored, and diced
1/2 cup crumbled Gorgonzola
3/4 cup chopped walnuts
1/4 cup chopped Italian parsley

Combine raspberries, vinegar, oil, sugar, salt, and pepper in a jar with lid and shake to combine. Set aside.

Make an attractive bed of radicchio leaves on serving platter. Scatter pears over radicchio. Sprinkle with cheese, walnuts, and parsley. Shake dressing to blend again, drizzle over salad, and serve.

Note: Radicchio varies in size from the equivalent of a baseball to a softball. You can substitute fresh spinach leaves when radicchio is not in season.

♨ *Serves 6 to 8*

Pineapple and Jicama with Basil

INGREDIENTS

1 medium pineapple, peeled,
    cored, and diced
1 small jicama, peeled and diced
1 to 2 tablespoons extra-virgin olive oil
1 teaspoon granulated sugar
1 teaspoon fresh lemon juice
1 teaspoon grated orange zest
$^1/_2$ teaspoon ground paprika
2 tablespoons chopped fresh basil
Fresh basil leaves

Place pineapple and jicama in a large bowl. Drizzle with olive oil. Sprinkle with sugar, lemon juice, orange zest, paprika, and chopped basil. Toss lightly to mix. Cover and refrigerate at least 1 hour. When ready to serve, garnish with basil leaves.

Note: To prepare a pineapple, twist off leafy top. Using a serrated or sharp knife, trim off both ends. Stand pineapple up, and starting at top edge, cut toward bottom in a sawing motion to remove peel, being careful to not remove too much of the flesh. Turn pineapple and repeat peeling motion to remove next section. Continue to turn and peel until finished. Cut pineapple in half lengthwise, then in quarters. Stand up each quarter and carefully run knife between pineapple flesh and center core.

☸ *Serves 8*

Holiday Waldorf Salad

INGREDIENTS

4 firm tart apples (such as Granny
    Smith) peeled, seeded, and diced
1 tablespoon fresh lemon juice
1 cup dried sweetened cranberries
1 cup halved green seedless grapes
1 cup diced celery
$^1/_4$ cup chopped dried apricots
$^1/_4$ cup raisins
1 cup plain yogurt
$^1/_4$ cup mayonnaise

Place apples in a large salad bowl. Sprinkle with lemon juice and toss lightly. Add cranberries, grapes, celery, apricots, and raisins. Blend together yogurt and mayonnaise. Pour over fruit and stir gently to coat all. Cover and chill at least 30 minutes. Serve.

Note: Try using fresh chopped cranberries instead of dried. Add a little sugar to dressing to mellow the tartness of berries.

☸ *Serves 8*

Thai Watermelon with Strawberry Dressing

INGREDIENTS
2 pounds chilled Thai watermelon,
  peeled and cubed
1 small jicama, peeled and julienned
1 pound fresh strawberries, washed,
  hulled, and halved
Juice of 2 limes
1/8 teaspoon cayenne pepper
1 bunch fresh cilantro, chopped
Sea salt

Combine watermelon and jicama in a large serving bowl. Place strawberries, lime juice, and cayenne in blender or food processor and pulse until a coarse puree. Drizzle over melon-jicama mixture. Sprinkle with chopped cilantro and sea salt. Serve or cover and chill up to 2 hours.

Note: The hull is the dry outer covering of a fruit, seed, or nut; a husk. Also, the enlarged calyx of a fruit, such as a strawberry, that is usually green and easily detached, hence a hulled berry is one that has had the calyx removed.

☙ *Serves 6*

Watermelon with Lime Ice

INGREDIENTS
1 3/4 cups granulated sugar
2 1/4 cups water
4 whole cloves
1 tablespoon grated lime zest
1 3/4 cups fresh lime juice
  (10 to 12 limes)
1/2 chilled watermelon, cut into slices
  or wedges

In a medium saucepan, bring sugar, water, cloves, and lime zest to a boil, stirring until sugar is dissolved. Remove from heat. Remove cloves and discard. Set syrup aside to cool.

Place a 9 x 9 x 2-inch glass dish in freezer. When syrup has cooled, stir in lime juice. Pour into chilled glass dish. Return to freezer. Stir every 45 to 60 minutes with a fork, until liquid is frozen and granular, about 4 to 6 hours.

Make a small indentation in watermelon slices. Fill with small scoop of lime ice. Serve.

Note: Lime ice may be made 2 days ahead, covered, and kept frozen.

☙ *Serves 8*

Sandwiches

BEEF

Barbequed Beef Brisket	104
London Broil and Portobello Mushroom	105
Roast Beef with Wasabi Mustard	105

PORK

Hoisin Pork with Pineapple Relish	106

POULTRY

Chicken Cordon Bleu Burgers	107
Grilled Chicken on a Scone	108
Turkey Burgers with Ginger Mayonnaise	109
Turkey Salad on Blueberry Cornbread	110

SEAFOOD

Smoked Salmon Salad in Toast Cups	111
Warm Scallop BLT	112
Ahi Wraps	114
Tuna with Tapenade	115
Seared Tuna with Fruit Salsa	117

Barbecued Beef Brisket

INGREDIENTS

$^3/4$ cup tomato sauce
$^1/2$ cup packed brown sugar
2 tablespoons tomato paste
1 tablespoon soy sauce
1 tablespoon prepared mustard
$^2/3$ cup apple cider vinegar
2 tablespoons Worcestershire sauce
1 teaspoon hot pepper sauce,
  such as Tabasco
2 medium onions, diced
4 pounds beef brisket
1 teaspoon liquid hickory smoke
Garlic powder
Salt and black pepper
Multi grain buns

In a bowl, stir together tomato sauce, sugar, tomato paste, soy sauce, mustard, vinegar, Worcestershire, and hot sauce. Add onion and blend well. Cover and refrigerate.

Heat broiler. Trim excess fat from brisket. Pat brisket dry with paper towels and place in a large roasting pan. Place under broiler and sear both sides. Remove from oven. Set oven to bake at 300°F.

Spread liquid smoke over meat and season with garlic powder, salt, and pepper. Add 2 inches of water to pan and cover tightly with lid or heavy-duty aluminum foil. Place in oven and braise 2 $^1/2$ hours, checking every 30 to 40 minutes, adding water as needed.

Spread barbeque sauce over beef brisket and cook 1 to 1 $^1/2$ hours more until liquid reduces to a thick sauce. Do not let liquid evaporate. Test for doneness by piercing thickest part of the brisket with fork. If it pierces easily, it is done. If not, cook longer, adding water to sauce a little at a time if necessary. Remove meat from pan and let cool. The meat can be wrapped and refrigerated for use the next day and the sauce can be put in container, covered and refrigerated; or, slice meat across the grain or shred apart with two forks. Toast buns, place meat on bun, top with sauce, and serve.

Note: Braising is a wet-heat cooking method where food is first seared in hot fat, then slowly simmered in liquid in a pan with a tight lid.

✿ *Serves a crowd*

London Broil and Portobello Mushroom

INGREDIENTS

1 ^{1}/2 pounds London broil
5 tablespoons olive oil, divided
Salt and black pepper
2 portobello mushrooms, rinsed,
   patted dry, and sliced ^{1}/4-inch thick
1 Maui or other sweet onion,
   cut crosswise into ^{1}/8-inch thick slices
^{1}/4 cup balsamic vinegar
4 tablespoons butter, softened
2 teaspoons prepared horseradish
^{1}/4 cup chopped fresh parsley
1 teaspoon Worcestershire sauce
2 cloves garlic, passed through press
4 multi-grained bread rolls, split
1 cup arugula leaves, washed
   and patted dry

Heat broiler or grill. Brush London broil with 2 tablespoons olive oil and season with salt and pepper. Place on a broiler pan and broil on upper rack, about 5 minutes per side. Line a baking sheet with parchment paper or aluminum foil. Lay mushroom slices in a single layer on prepared baking sheet. Separate onion into rings and arrange over mushrooms. Drizzle with remaining oil and vinegar. Place in oven on middle or lower rack to roast while meat cooks on upper rack, about 10 minutes. Remove steak from oven, place on cutting board, and let rest for 5 minutes. Remove mushrooms and onions from oven. Set aside.

In a small bowl, combine butter, horseradish, parsley, Worcestershire, and garlic. Spread flavored butter on bottom pieces of the split rolls. Slice meat against the grain ^{1}/4-inch thick. Lay slices of steak on buttered bread and top with a bit of mushrooms and onions. Garnish with arugula. Serve.

❀ *Serves 4*

Roast Beef with Wasabi Mustard

INGREDIENTS

^{3}/4 cup coarse-grained mustard
3 tablespoons honey
2 teaspoons wasabi paste
Sprigs of watercress, alfalfa sprouts,
   or radish sprouts
6 pita bread rounds
1 to 1 ^{1}/2 pounds thinly sliced roast beef

In a small bowl, stir together mustard, honey, and wasabi. Wash and pat dry watercress. Cut pita bread in half. Divide roast beef equally among bread, tucking slices in each. Add watercress. Drizzle in mustard sauce. Serve.

❀ *Serves 6 to 8*

Hoisin Pork with Pineapple Relish

PINEAPPLE RELISH

2 cups fresh or canned pineapple tidbits,
  well drained
1 jalapeno pepper, minced
1 tablespoon lime juice
1 tablespoon honey
1 tablespoon olive oil
3 green onions, thinly sliced
2 tablespoons chopped cilantro
Salt and black pepper

SANDWICH

$^1/2$ cup hoisin sauce
1 tablespoon apple cider vinegar
1 tablespoon soy sauce
2 cloves garlic, crushed
1 teaspoon sesame oil
8 thin boneless pork chops
4 pita pocket breads, cut in half

Stir together pineapple, jalapeno, lime juice, honey, olive oil, green onion, and cilantro in a non-reactive bowl. Season with salt and pepper to taste. Cover and set aside.

In a small bowl combine hoisin, vinegar, soy sauce, garlic, and sesame oil. Place pork chops in self-sealing bag. Pour hoisin mixture over pork, seal bag, and toss gently to coat well. Set aside for 30 minutes.

Prepare medium-high fire in grill. Remove chops from bag and discard any remaining marinade. Grill pork directly over fire for about 2 minutes per side, until nicely browned. Lightly toast pita bread. Gently open pita pocket and insert grilled chop. Drain any excess liquid from pineapple relish and place spoonfuls over chop. Serve.

Note: Aluminum, unlined copper, and cast iron by themselves react poorly with acidic ingredients such as tomatoes, citrus juice, wine, and vinegar by imparting a metallic taste and an off color. It is extremely important to use non-reactive substances such as stainless steel and glass when cooking or preparing acidic foods.

✿ Serves 4

Chicken Cordon Bleu Burgers

Ingredients

1/4 cup sour cream
1 heaping tablespoon Dijon mustard
1 tablespoon fresh chopped tarragon
    or 2 tablespoons dried tarragon
1 pound ground chicken
1 teaspoon paprika
1 teaspoon grill seasoning blend, such as
    Montreal Steak Seasoning
1 shallot, finely diced
Olive oil
4 slices Canadian bacon
4 slices Jarslberg cheese
4 sour dough English muffins or
    sandwich rolls, split
1 vine ripe tomato, sliced
4 leaves Manoa or Boston lettuce,
    washed and patted dry

Stir together sour cream, mustard, and tarragon in a small bowl. Cover and refrigerate. In a large bowl, combine chicken, paprika, grill seasoning, and shallot. Divide meat into four equal portions and shape into patties about 1-inch thick. Rub patties with oil and set aside.

Heat grill pan or skillet over medium heat. Add bacon and cook 2 to 3 minutes on each side until crisp at edges. Remove from pan and set aside. Place chicken patties in hot pan. Cook 5 minutes on each side, until chicken is cooked through and lightly browned. Top with Canadian bacon and cheese. Cover loosely with lid or aluminum foil, reduce heat to low and let cheese melt, about 2 minutes.

Toast English muffins. Slather muffin tops with tarragon sauce. Place burgers on bottom halves. Top with tomato and lettuce. Put muffin tops in place. Serve.

❈ *Serves 6*

Grilled Chicken on a Scone

INGREDIENTS

2 tablespoons oil, divided
1 large onion, thinly sliced
1/4 cup slivered almonds
*6 Orange Cranberry scones**
2 cups fresh mesclun or
*   other small leaf salad greens,*
*   washed and patted dry*
3 boneless, skinless chicken
*   breast halves*
2 teaspoons paprika
1 teaspoon garlic powder
1 teaspoon salt
1/2 teaspoon black pepper
1 tablespoon butter
Splash of dry white wine
1 cup Cranberry Relish
1 fresh orange, cut into 6 slices

CRANBERRY RELISH

3 cups fresh or frozen cranberries,
*   rinsed and sorted*
1/2 cup granulated sugar
1 tablespoon cider vinegar
1/2 teaspoon mixed whole pickling spice

* Recipe on page 62

Heat 1 tablespoon oil in a medium frying pan and sauté onion 8 to 10 minutes, stirring occasionally, until slightly golden. Add almonds and cook about 3 more minutes. Remove from pan and set aside. Split scones in half, and place on individual serving plates. Arrange 1/3 cup of greens on bottom of each scone and set aside.

Cut each piece of chicken in half to make 6 pieces. Place chicken breasts between two sheets of plastic wrap. Pound to flatten with the flat side of a meat pounder until 3/8 to 1/2-inch thick. Mix paprika, garlic powder, salt, and pepper. Rub on one side of each breast. Heat remaining tablespoon of oil with butter in frying pan over medium high. Add chicken, spiced side down, and sauté 3 to 4 minutes until golden. Turn, add a splash of wine, and sauté the other side until wine evaporates and chicken is golden. Remove chicken from pan and set on greens. Top with some of the onions with almonds, and a spoonful or two of cranberry relish. Lean top of scone against sandwich. Garnish with orange slice. Serve.

Cranberry Relish: In a 2-quart sauce pan, combine cranberries, sugar, vinegar, and pickling spice. Cover and heat over low, stirring occasionally, about 15 to 20 minutes until slightly thickened. Remove from heat, uncover, and set aside. Makes about 2 cups.

Note: You can use whole berry canned cranberry sauce, but omit sugar and heat it for 5 to 10 minutes with vinegar and pickling spice.

❈ *Serves 6*

Turkey Burgers with Ginger Mayonnaise

GINGER MAYONNAISE
2 tablespoons mayonnaise
$1/4$ cup sour cream
2 tablespoons sweet pickle relish
2 teaspoons lime juice
1 teaspoon minced fresh ginger root
1 clove garlic, minced
$1/8$ teaspoon salt

BURGERS
1 $1/4$ pounds ground turkey
$2/3$ cup panko bread crumbs
1 egg, lightly beaten
2 green onions, thinly sliced
2 cloves garlic, minced
3 tablespoons chopped cilantro,
   plus extra for garnish
1 teaspoon Asian sweet hot chili sauce
1 teaspoon salt
$1/2$ cup bottled teriyaki glaze
4 teaspoons honey
1 tablespoon vegetable oil,
   plus extra for hands
4 sesame seed buns, split and toasted
4 red lettuce leaves,
   washed and patted dry
1 cucumber, peeled, cut lengthwise,
   seeded, and julienned

In a small bowl mix together mayonnaise, sour cream, relish, lime juice, ginger, garlic, and salt. Adjust seasonings to taste. Cover and refrigerate.

In a large bowl, mix together turkey, panko, and egg. Add green onion, garlic, cilantro, chili sauce, and salt. Stir lightly to combine. With oiled hands, form mixture into four patties. Set aside.

In a small bowl, mix together the teriyaki glaze and honey. Set aside. Heat oil in a large non-stick frying pan over medium-high heat. Add turkey patties. Brush with teriyaki glaze. Cook 4 to 5 minutes until lightly browned and turn. Brush other side with glaze and continue to cook 4 to 5 minutes, until fully cooked through. Place toasted buns on serving platter. Top with burgers. Add lettuce and dollop of ginger mayonnaise. Garnish with cilantro and cucumber sticks. Serve.

❦ *Serves 4*

Turkey Salad on Blueberry Cornbread

INGREDIENTS
1/2 cup mayonnaise
1/2 cup plain yogurt
1/4 cup orange marmalade
2 teaspoons fresh lemon juice
1/4 teaspoon black pepper
3 cups cubed cooked smoked turkey
2 cups diced peaches
1 cup fresh blueberries
6 squares Blueberry Cornbread*
2 cups mixed salad greens,
    washed and patted dry

* Recipe on page 47

Stir together mayonnaise, yogurt, marmalade, lemon juice, and pepper in a large bowl. Add turkey and stir lightly until well coated. Add peaches and blueberries, folding gently to mix. Slice squares of cornbread in half horizontally. Place bottom half on individual plates. Add a large scoop of turkey salad. Lean upper half of cornbread against sandwich. Garnish side with salad greens. Serve.

Note: It is easier to eat this open-faced sandwich with a fork and knife.

✻ Serves 4

Smoked Salmon Salad in Toast Cups

INGREDIENTS
8 slices whole wheat bread
12 ounces cooked salmon
4 ounces smoked salmon, minced
4 plum tomatoes, seeded and diced
1/2 cup finely diced celery
2 tablespoons minced onion
1 tablespoon fresh minced basil
1/4 cup mayonnaise
1/4 cup cream cheese, softened
1/4 teaspoon salt
1/8 teaspoon black pepper
Fresh basil leaves
Very thin fresh lemon slices

Heat oven to 375°F. Trim crust from bread. Lay bread over openings of muffin tin cup. Gently work bread into cups with fingers, being careful not to tear it. Place in oven and bake 8 to 10 minutes until lightly toasted and able to retain cup shape when cooled. Remove pan to wire rack allow bread to cool in pan.

In a bowl, combine salmon, smoked salmon, tomatoes, celery, onion, and basil. Beat together mayonnaise and cream cheese. Add to salmon, stirring gently just to combine. Season with salt and pepper. Cover and chill until ready to serve. Spoon equal amounts of salmon filling into toast cups. Garnish with fresh basil and lemon slices. Serve.

❁ *Serves 4*

Warm Scallop BLT

INGREDIENTS
8 ounces thick-cut bacon
12 large sea scallops, rinsed and patted dry
Salt and freshly ground black pepper
1 cup balsamic vinegar
1 heaping tablespoon brown sugar
8 thick slices sour dough French bread, toasted
1 head Manoa or Boston lettuce, rinsed and patted dry
2 vine-ripened tomatoes, thinly sliced
Cracked black pepper

Cook bacon in a large skillet over medium heat until crisp.
Remove to paper towel to drain. Save rendered bacon fat.
Do not clean pan. Once cooled, finely chop or crumble
bacon and set aside.

Sprinkle scallops with salt and pepper. Heat 2 tablespoons
reserved bacon fat in the skillet on medium-high. Carefully
add scallops without crowding and sear for 90 seconds per
side, until slightly browned. Cook in batches if necessary.
Remove scallops and set aside. Add vinegar and sugar to pan,
stirring. Reduce heat to low, simmer 8 to 10 minutes to
reduce liquid to about 1/2 cup, and deglaze pan.

Place 2 pieces of bread on each of four plates. Add lettuce
and tomato slices. Top with 3 warm scallops each and add
crumbled bacon. Drizzle with balsamic vinegar glaze and
sprinkle with black pepper. Serve.

Note: To deglaze is to dissolve the remaining bits of sautéed or
roasted food in a pan or pot by adding liquid and heating.
This mixture often becomes the base for a sauce to accompany the food cooked in the pan.

Serves 4

Ahi Wraps

SAUCE
1/2 cup mayonnaise
1 teaspoon prepared wasabi

SLAW
2 ounces fresh snow pea pods, trimmed
*1 small head Napa cabbage, trimmed,
    washed, and shredded*
1 carrot, peeled and shredded
2 scallions, finely sliced
3 tablespoons coarsely chopped cilantro
3 tablespoons slivered almonds
1-inch piece fresh ginger root, grated
1 clove garlic, minced
1 tablespoon olive oil
1 teaspoon sesame oil
1 teaspoon granulated sugar
1 tablespoon rice vinegar
2 tablespoons fresh lime juice
Salt and black pepper

WRAPS
8 large whole wheat tortillas
12 ounces fresh tuna steak
1 teaspoon olive oil
*1 to 2 ounces enoki mushrooms,
    washed and patted dry*

In a small bowl, combine mayonnaise and wasabi, mixing well. Cover and refrigerate. Place pea pods in a small saucepan with a little water. Bring to a boil over high heat and steam 30 seconds until bright green. Drain and rinse under cold water. Remove to cutting board and slice lengthwise into thin strips. Set aside. Place cabbage in large mixing bowl. Add carrot, scallions, cilantro, and almonds and set aside.

In a small bowl combine ginger, garlic, olive oil, sesame oil, sugar, vinegar, and lime juice. Whisk together until well blended. Pour over vegetables. Toss to coat. Season with salt and pepper to taste. Spread 1 tablespoon of wasabi mayonnaise evenly over each tortilla. Do not stack but set each aside separately.

Heat a skillet over medium-high heat. Rub tuna steak with olive oil and place in hot skillet. Sear tuna, cooking each side about 2 minutes. Remove from pan. Let rest a few minutes before slicing thinly into 16 pieces. Using tongs and dividing equally, pick up vegetable slaw, shake gently to rid of excess dressing, and arrange down center of each tortilla. Top with snow pea pods, saving a few for garnish.

Arrange tuna slices on top of vegetable slaw. Top with enoki mushrooms, saving a few for garnish. Fold in sides of tortilla and roll to create a wrapped sandwich. Place seam side down on serving platter. Garnish with reserved pea pods and mushrooms. Serve.

Serves 4

Tuna with Tapenade

TAPENADE

1 long thin baguette, divided in fourths
  and split horizontally
$^1/_3$ cup pitted green olives
$^1/_4$ cup pitted kalamata olives
1 tablespoon drained capers
1 tablespoon extra-virgin olive oil
1 tablespoon fresh lemon juice
1 tablespoon fresh Italian parsley leaves
1 teaspoon lemon zest
1 anchovy, minced
Salt and freshly ground black pepper

SANDWICH

$^1/_2$ cup goat cheese
2 tablespoons Dijon mustard
Salt and freshly ground black pepper
12 to 14 ounces tuna steak
2 teaspoons extra-virgin olive oil
2 ripe red or yellow tomatoes,
  thinly sliced
1 small red onion, thinly sliced
4 romaine lettuce leaves,
  washed and patted dry

Heat grill or grill pan to medium-high heat. Grill baguette cut side down until lightly toasted, about 2 minutes. Remove and set aside. Combine green and kalamata olives, capers, oil, lemon juice, parsley, lemon zest, and anchovy in a food processor. Pulse just until the olives are finely chopped. Season with salt and pepper to taste. Scrape into a small bowl, cover, and set aside.

Stir together goat cheese and mustard in a small bowl, blending well. The tapenade and Dijon mixture can be prepared one day ahead. Keep separately, covered in refrigerator. Bring the tapenade to room temperature before using.

Rub tuna with oil. Sprinkle lightly with salt and pepper. Grill tuna to sear on the outside about 2 minutes per side. Let rest a few minutes before cutting steaks across the grain into $^1/_2$-inch thick slices.

Spread goat cheese mixture over the bottom and top of the baguette halves. Place bread bottoms on individual serving plates. Add tomato and onion slices. Arrange the tuna on top of the onions. Add generous spoonful of tapenade. Top with lettuce and other half of baguette. Serve.

※ Serves 4

Seared Tuna with Fruit Salsa

FRUIT SALSA
1 medium ripe papaya, peeled,
  seeded, and diced
1 clove garlic, minced
1 small red onion, finely diced
1/4 cup fresh lime juice
2 to 3 sprigs fresh cilantro, chopped
1/2 jalapeno pepper, minced

SANDWICH
12 ounces tuna steak
1 teaspoon olive oil
Salt and black pepper
8 slices Pineapple-Coconut Bread*
1 1/2 cups baby greens, washed and patted dry

* Recipe on page 68

Combine papaya, garlic, onion, lime juice, cilantro, and jalapeno in a non-reactive bowl, stirring to mix well. Cover and refrigerate at least 1 hour.

Heat a skillet over medium-high heat. Rub both sides of tuna steak with oil and season with salt and pepper. Place in hot pan and sear a few minutes on each side. Remove from pan and let sit a few minutes before cutting across the grain into 1/4-inch slices. Place 1 slice of bread on each of four plates. Divide greens equally. Top with 3 to 4 slices of tuna and a large spoonful of salsa. Lay second piece of bread decoratively against sandwich. Serve with extra salsa on the side.

Note: See note on non-reactive bowl on page 106. It is easier to slice tuna using a very sharp knife while slightly squeezing in sides of fish to give it firmness.

Serves 4

Soups

Vietnamese Pho

INGREDIENTS
5 pounds beef marrow or knuckle bones
2 pounds beef chuck, cut into two pieces
6 quarts water, divided
3-inch piece fresh ginger root, cut
    lengthwise and lightly bruised
2 yellow onions, peeled and quartered
1/4 cup fish sauce
3 tablespoons granulated sugar
6 whole star anise
3 whole cloves
1 tablespoon sea salt
10 ounces rice noodles
1/3 pound beef sirloin, slightly frozen
Scallions, cilantro, bean sprouts,
    herbs, chilies, lime juice, and
    black pepper

Cleanse bones and beef chuck by placing in a pot of water, bringing to a boil over high heat and boiling vigorously for 5 minutes. Transfer bones and beef chuck to a fresh soup pot filled with 4 quarts water. Bring to a boil. Reduce heat to medium-low and simmer, skimming the surface often to remove any foam and fat.

Place ginger and onions over hot grill or under broiler and char lightly. Add the charred ginger and onions, fish sauce, and sugar to soup pot. Simmer about 60 minutes. Up to two more quarts of water can be added if needed.

Lightly toast star anise in a dry pan. Wrap star anise and cloves in a spice bag or piece of cheesecloth. When the broth has been simmering for about 1 1/2 hours, add spice bag. Let infuse until the broth is fragrant, about 30 to 40 minutes.

Remove and discard both the spice bag and onions. Stir in salt. The broth will taste salty but will be balanced once the noodles and accompaniments are added. Remove one piece of chuck, drain, cut into thin slices, and set aside. Let the other piece of chuck and bones continue to simmer in the pot while the noodles are prepared and the bowls are assembled.

Cover rice noodles with cold water. Soak 20 minutes, then drain. Bring 3 cups water to a boil in a medium saucepan over high heat. Add noodles and cook 3 to 5 minutes until tender. Drain, keep warm.

Slice slightly frozen beef paper-thin across the grain. Place the cooked noodles in large preheated bowls. Place a few slices of the cooked chuck and raw sirloin on the noodles. Bring the broth to a rolling boil and ladle 2 to 3 cups of broth into each bowl. The broth will cook the raw beef instantly.

Garnish with scallions, cilantro, sprouts, herbs, chilies, lime juice, and black pepper. Serve immediately.

✿ *Serves 4 to 6*

South Pacific Soup

CHILI CREAM
1 cup crème fraiche or
  1/2 cup sour cream mixed with
  1/2 cup half-and-half
1 teaspoon ground chipotle or
  other chili powder
1/4 teaspoon salt

SOUP
2 tablespoons peanut oil, divided
4 sweet potatoes, quartered
4 ripe plantains, unpeeled
1 large onion, diced
3 stalks celery, diced
1/4 cup pure maple syrup
8 cups chicken broth
1 chicken breast, finely diced
1 cup coconut milk
1 cup half-and-half
Salt and black pepper
Chili Cream
Fresh cilantro leaves

FRIED PLANTAINS
1 green plantain,
  peeled and thinly sliced or julienned
2 cups canola oil
Salt

Combine crème fraiche and chipotle powder in a small bowl. Season with salt. Cover and chill until ready to use.

Preheat oven to 425°F. Lightly oil a baking pan using 1 teaspoon of peanut oil. Place sweet potatoes and plantains in prepared pan. Roast until potatoes are soft, and plantains skins are blackened, about 30 minutes. Remove from oven and set aside.

In a skillet, heat 2 teaspoons oil over medium heat. Add onion and celery and sauté about 5 minutes. When potatoes are cool enough to handle, peel and cut into cubes, and add to the skillet. Peel plantain, cut into pieces, and add to skillet. Add maple syrup and sauté until vegetables are coated and slightly caramelized. Place mixture in a food processor or blender with a bit of the chicken broth, and pulse until smooth. Place in a large saucepan, add remaining broth, reduce heat to low, and simmer 15 minutes to blend flavors.

Heat remaining oil in skillet over medium-high heat. Add chicken and stir-fry until thoroughly cooked. Stir in coconut milk and simmer 3 to 5 minutes. Add to soup mixture with half-and-half. Increase heat to medium and heat through. Season with salt and pepper to taste. Ladle soup into eight warm bowls. Drizzle with Chili Cream. Garnish with cilantro leaves and fried plantains if ambitious. Serve.

Fried Plantains: In a medium skillet, heat oil to 365°F. Add plantains in batches and cook until golden brown. Remove to a plate lined with paper towels and season with salt. Use as garnish.

❦ *Serves 4 to 6*

Tortilla Soup

In a large saucepan, heat oil over medium heat. Add onions, garlic, and jalapeno peppers. Sauté, stirring occasionally, until softened, about 5 minutes.

Place chicken breast between two sheets of plastic wrap. Pound with back of heavy wooden spoon or meat pounder until slightly less than $1/2$-inch thick. Cut into thin strips. Add to saucepan and sauté a few minutes. Add broth, tomatoes, chili powder, cumin, oregano, salt, and cayenne. Bring to a boil, reduce heat, and simmer 20 minutes.

Heat oven to 400°F. Place tortillas on a baking sheet. Place in oven for 5 minutes until crisp. Remove and cut each tortilla into 6 wedges. Ladle soup into bowls. Garnish with cheese, 3 or 4 tortilla wedges, avocado, and cilantro. Serve immediately.

❁ *Serves 4 to 6*

INGREDIENTS

1 tablespoon olive oil
1 large onion, chopped
2 large cloves garlic, minced
2 small jalapeno peppers,
    seeded and finely chopped
1 boneless chicken breast
3 cups chicken broth
28 ounces canned diced tomatoes
2 teaspoons chili powder
$1/2$ teaspoon ground cumin
$1/2$ teaspoon minced fresh oregano or
    $1/8$ teaspoon dried
$3/4$ teaspoon salt
$1/8$ teaspoon cayenne pepper
3 8-inch corn tortillas
2 ounces Queso Fresco or $1/2$ cup
    grated Monterey Jack Cheese
1 ripe avocado, diced
Sprigs of fresh cilantro

Hawaiian Style Fish Chowder

INGREDIENTS

1 tablespoon olive oil
1 large Maui onion, chopped
1 large sweet potato, peeled and diced
1/2 cup chopped carrot
1 teaspoon chopped fresh tarragon
1/2 teaspoon ground cinnamon
6 cups chicken broth
12 ounces boneless white fish fillet,
*   skinned and cut into 1-inch pieces*
1 cup half-and-half
Salt and freshly ground black pepper
Chopped fresh parsley or tarragon

In a large, heavy saucepan, heat oil over medium heat. Add onion and cook 5 minutes. Add sweet potato, carrot, tarragon, and cinnamon, stirring to blend well. Cook another 5 minutes. Pour in half of broth, reduce heat to low, and simmer 10 to 15 minutes until vegetables are soft. Cool a bit.

Carefully puree mixture in a food processor or blender until smooth. Return soup to clean saucepan and stir in remaining broth. Bring to a simmer over medium heat. Add fish. Continue to simmer 5 minutes until fish is tender and flakes apart easily. Add half-and-half and heat through, stirring frequently. Season with salt and pepper to taste. Ladle into warmed soup bowls. Garnish with fresh parsley. Serve.

❀ *Serves 4*

Salmon Soup

INGREDIENTS

2 tablespoons butter
1 large onion, thinly sliced
4 ounces fresh mushrooms,
*   washed and thinly sliced*
Salt and freshly ground black pepper
4 cups vegetable or chicken broth
2 pounds Yukon Gold potatoes,
*   cut in small chunks with*
*   or without skin*
1 cup milk
1/2 pound skinless Alaskan
*   salmon fillet, cut into 1/2-inch cubes*
1/4 cup chopped fresh dill or
*   1 tablespoon dried*
2 tablespoons Dijon style mustard

In a 3 to 4-quart pot, melt butter over medium heat. Add onion and sauté a few minutes until golden. Add mushrooms and season with salt and pepper to taste. Sauté 8 to 10 minutes until soft. Stir in broth and bring to a boil. Add potatoes, reduce heat to low and simmer, uncovered, 20 to 25 minutes until tender.

Add milk, stir to mix well, and heat through. Add salmon, dill, and mustard. Simmer 5 minutes to cook fish. Adjust salt and pepper to taste. Ladle into bowls. Serve.

❀ *Serves 8*

Shrimp Gazpacho

INGREDIENTS

6 large ripe tomatoes, peeled and seeded
1 large cucumber, peeled, seeded,
    and finely diced
1 green bell pepper, seeded
    and finely diced
1 small red onion, finely diced
1 1/2 cups clam-tomato juice
3 tablespoons red wine vinegar
2 tablespoons olive oil
2 tablespoons fresh lemon juice
2 tablespoons chopped fresh basil
2 tablespoons chopped fresh cilantro
    or parsley
2 1/2 teaspoons Old Bay seasoning
Salt and black pepper
8 ounces cooked shrimp,
    cut into 1/2-inch pieces

Put tomatoes in a food processor or blender. Pulse or blend until coarsely pureed. Transfer to a large bowl. Add cucumber, bell pepper, onion, tomato juice, vinegar, oil, and lemon juice. Stir to mix well. Season with basil, cilantro, Old Bay, and salt and pepper to taste. Stir to mix well. Stir in shrimp. Cover and chill until cold, at least 2 hours. Ladle into chilled bowls.

Tomatoes, cucumber, bell pepper, onion, and shrimp can be prepared the night before, and kept in separate airtight containers in refrigerator overnight. The soup can be blended together early the next morning, covered and refrigerated until serving time.

Note: To peel tomatoes, cut a small "x" on the bottom of the tomato and dip into a large pot of boiling water for 30 seconds. Drain and rinse under cold water. This makes removing the peel easier.

❧ Serves 4 to 6

Chilled Avocado Soup

SOUP
2 green onions, finely sliced
1 tablespoon olive oil
2 shallots, minced
2 cloves garlic, minced
2 large ripe avocados,
   peeled and mashed
4 teaspoons fresh lime juice
1 1/2 cups vegetable or chicken broth
1 cup half-and-half
Salt and freshly ground black pepper

LIME CREAM
1/4 cup sour cream
2 teaspoons fresh lime juice
1 small clove garlic, minced
1/4 teaspoon salt

TOPPING
4 ounces smoked salmon

Measure a heaping tablespoon of green onions and set aside for garnish. Heat oil in a saucepan over medium heat. Add shallots and garlic. Cook about 4 minutes, stirring occasionally, until softened. Remove from heat. Let cool.

Place avocado, remaining green onions, lime juice, and broth in a blender. Puree until smooth. Place in a large glass bowl. Stir in half-and-half. Season with salt and pepper to taste. Cover and chill thoroughly, about 3 hours.

Stir together sour cream, lime juice, garlic, and salt. Cover and chill. Divide soup among four chilled soup bowls. Top with a generous dollop of Lime Cream. Garnish each portion with equal amounts of salmon. Sprinkle with reserved green onions. Serve.

 Serves 4

Coriander Carrot Soup

INGREDIENTS
4 tablespoons butter
3 leeks, split lengthwise, well rinsed, and cut into 1-inch pieces
1 pound carrots, peeled and cut into 1-inch pieces
1 tablespoon ground coriander
Salt and freshly ground black pepper
5 cups chicken broth
2/3 cup thick plain yogurt, divided
2 to 3 tablespoons chopped fresh cilantro

Melt butter in a large pot over medium heat. Add leeks, carrots, and coriander. Season with salt and pepper to taste, stirring well to coat. Cover and cook about 15 minutes until vegetables are softened, stirring occasionally. Pour in broth and bring to a boil. Reduce heat to low. Cover and simmer 20 minutes until leeks and carrots are tender.

Remove from heat. Carefully pour into a food processor or blender. Puree until smooth. Return puree to cleaned pot. Add 2 tablespoons of yogurt and stir to blend well. Adjust seasoning to taste. Reheat slowly, but do not allow to boil or soup may curdle.

Ladle into soup bowls. Place a spoonful of yogurt in center of each bowl. Sprinkle with cilantro. Serve.

❀ *Serves 4*

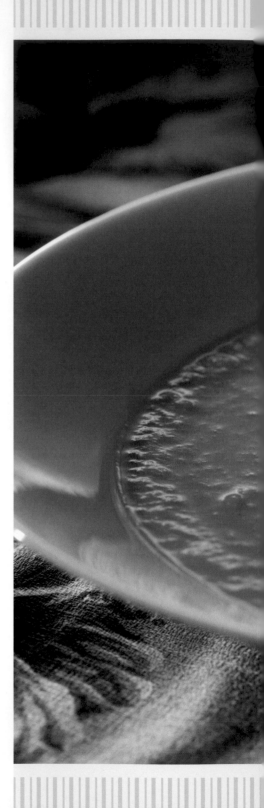

Gingered Carrot Soup

INGREDIENTS
2 tablespoons butter
1 large onion, chopped
1 stalk celery, diced
1 medium white potato, diced
2 pounds carrots, peeled and diced
1 tablespoon grated fresh ginger root
Salt and freshly ground black pepper
6 cups chicken broth
1 cup heavy or whipping cream
1/4 cup brandy
Dash or two ground nutmeg
Sprigs of fresh parsley

Melt butter in a large, heavy pot over medium heat. Add onion and celery and cook, stirring occasionally, about 5 minutes until softened. Add potato, carrots, and ginger. Season with salt and pepper. Cook another 5 minutes, stirring occasionally. Stir in chicken broth. Bring to a boil then reduce heat to low. Cover and simmer about 20 minutes.

Very carefully pour hot soup into a food processor or blender. Puree until smooth. Return soup to pan, and heat through. Turn off heat and stir in cream, brandy, and nutmeg. Adjust salt and pepper to taste. Ladle into bowls and garnish with parsley. Serve.

❀ *Serves 6*

Roasted Garlic Soup

INGREDIENTS

4 tablespoons olive oil, divided
1 bulb garlic, trimmed and peeled
1 tablespoon ground cumin
4 thick slices crusty bread, cubed
5 to 6 plum tomatoes, seeded
  and chopped
4 cups chicken, beef, or vegetable broth
8 ounces fresh spinach,
  washed and chopped
Salt and freshly ground black pepper
Fresh parsley, minced

Heat 2 tablespoons olive oil and garlic cloves in a large deep saucepan over medium heat. Cook until golden brown, stirring occasionally. Add cumin and cook, stirring, 1 minute. Remove garlic and set aside.

Reduce heat to medium-low and add remaining 2 tablespoons oil. Add bread and brown on all sides, about 5 minutes. Divide among four soup bowls. Set aside.

Add tomatoes to saucepan and cook, stirring, until softened, 3 to 5 minutes. Add broth and bring to a boil. Reduce heat and simmer for about 5 minutes. Add spinach and garlic and cook 2 to 3 minutes until spinach is wilted. Season with salt and pepper to taste. Ladle hot soup over bread in bowls. Garnish with parsley. Serve.

❀ *Serves 4*

Lentil Soup

INGREDIENTS

2 cups dried lentils, rinsed
   and picked through
8 cups chicken broth
2 slices uncooked bacon, diced
1 medium onion, diced
2 stalks celery, diced
1 large carrot, peeled and diced
1 clove garlic, minced
3 tablespoons chopped parsley
2 1/2 teaspoons salt
1/4 teaspoon black pepper
1 1/2 teaspoons dried oregano
2 cups canned diced tomatoes,
   with liquid
2 tablespoons red wine vinegar

Put lentils in a 5-quart Dutch oven. Add chicken broth and bring to boil over high heat, stirring occasionally. Reduce heat to low. Add bacon, onion, celery, and carrot, stirring to mix well. Add garlic, parsley, salt, pepper, and oregano. Simmer, covered, 1 1/2 hours, stirring occasionally. Add more broth or water if needed.

Stir in tomatoes and vinegar. Cover and simmer another 30 minutes. Adjust seasonings to taste. Ladle into soup bowls. Serve.

Note: Sausage or ham can be substituted for bacon. The meat can be omitted altogether for a vegetarian dish.

❀ *Serves 6*

Mushroom with Lemongrass Soup

INGREDIENTS

6 cups coconut milk
3 stalks lemongrass, cut into
   2-inch pieces
1/2 cup of galangal (Thai ginger) slices
4 kaffir lime leaves, thinly sliced
1 pound straw mushrooms, cut in half
2 cups cabbage, shredded
1 tomato, seeded and diced
1 tablespoon sugar
1 tablespoon salt
3 Thai bird chilies
3 tablespoons lime juice
2 tablespoons soy sauce
1 bunch cilantro, chopped

In a large saucepan, heat coconut milk over medium heat and bring to a boil, stirring constantly. Add lemongrass, galangal, and kaffir leaves to soup and continue to boil for 3 minutes. Add mushrooms, cabbage, and tomato. Season with sugar, salt, and chilies. Cook 5 minutes. Adjust seasonings to taste, and remove from heat. Stir in lime juice and soy sauce. Ladle into bowls. Sprinkle with cilantro. Serve.

❀ *Serves 4 to 6*

Savory Pear Soup with Brie

INGREDIENTS

2 tablespoons butter
2 green onions, finely chopped
6 large ripe but firm pears, peeled,
   cored, and thickly sliced
3 cups chicken broth
4 ounces Brie, cubed
Paprika
Toasted baguette slices

Melt butter in a deep skillet or large heavy pot over medium heat. Add onions and pear slices. Sauté 5 to 8 minutes until slightly tender, but do not brown. Add chicken broth, reduce heat, and simmer 10 to 15 minutes until pears are very soft. Remove from heat. Carefully pour mixture into a food processor or blender. This may have to be done in batches to accommodate all of the soup. Puree until smooth. Return to pot. Heat to a simmer.

Divide cheese among soup bowls. Ladle in hot soup. Garnish with a dash of paprika. Serve with toasted baguette slices.

❀ *Serves 6*

Creamy Red Pepper Soup

INGREDIENTS
4 large red bell peppers
2 tablespoons butter
1 medium onion, minced
2 cloves garlic, minced
1 sprig fresh rosemary
5 cups chicken broth
3 tablespoons tomato paste
1 cup heavy cream, divided
Paprika
Salt and freshly ground black pepper

Heat broiler. Place peppers under heating element. Carefully turn with long handled tongs as skin blackens. Remove peppers from broiler, place in plastic bag or bowl with lid, and seal. Leave for 15 to 20 minutes to loosen skin.

Peel the blackened skin off peppers. Do not run under water to ease removal as some of the flavor will be lost. Cut each pepper in half, remove seeds, stems, and pith. Roughly chop the flesh. Set aside.

In a deep saucepan, melt butter over low heat. Add onion, garlic, and rosemary and cook 8 to 10 minutes, stirring occasionally. Remove rosemary and discard. Add peppers and cook 2 to 3 minutes, stirring two or three times while cooking. Put into a food processor or blender with 2 cups broth and puree until smooth, adding more broth if necessary. Return to pot, stir in remaining broth, and simmer 15 minutes. Stir in tomato paste, blending until smooth. Stir in $1/2$ cup cream, and season with paprika, salt, and pepper to taste.

Ladle hot or chilled soup into bowls. Delicately swirl some of remaining cream on top. Sprinkle cream with pinch of paprika. Serve.

❋ *Serves 4*

Russet Potato Soup

INGREDIENTS

2 tablespoons unsalted butter
1 tablespoon olive oil
2 leeks, split lengthwise, well rinsed
    and cut into $1/4$-inch slices
4 medium russet potatoes,
    cut into $1/2$-inch cubes with or
    without skins
4 ounces fresh crimini or portobello
    mushrooms, thinly sliced
1 teaspoon salt
$1/8$ to $1/4$ teaspoon black pepper
$1/2$ to $3/4$ cup dry sherry
4 cups chicken broth
2 cups half-and-half
8 to 12 baguette slices, $1/4$-inch thick
12 ounces Brie, sliced $1/4$-inch thick
3 green onions, thinly sliced
2 tablespoons chopped parsley

Heat butter and oil in a heavy 4-quart saucepan over medium heat. Add leeks and sauté a few minutes, stirring occasionally. Add potatoes, mushrooms, salt, and pepper. Continue to sauté, stirring occasionally, 8 to 10 minutes.

Stir in sherry and bring to a simmer. Stir in chicken broth and bring to a boil. Reduce the heat to low and simmer 5 to 10 minutes until potatoes are soft. Mash mixture by hand until potatoes and leeks are smooth but some lumps remain. Stir in half-and-half and heat thoroughly without boiling. Adjust salt and pepper to taste.

Arrange bread slices 1-inch apart on a baking sheet. Toast in a 300°F oven for 6 to 10 minutes until golden brown. Remove and set oven to broil. Place rack at least 6-inches from broiler unit. Arrange the Brie slices over the toasted bread, covering the surface completely. Place in oven and broil 30 to 45 seconds or just until the cheese melts and is light golden brown. Remove from oven and set aside.

Ladle hot soup into warmed bowls, placing one cheese crouton on each. Sprinkle with green onions and parsley, and serve.

❦ *Serves 8*

Pumpkin Coconut Bisque

INGREDIENTS

2 tablespoons butter
1 cup chopped onion
6 cloves garlic, minced
1/2 small fresh hot red chili, minced
or 1/2 teaspoon dried crushed red
pepper flakes
1/2 teaspoon ground allspice
Dash ground cinnamon
2 teaspoons granulated sugar
2 cups chicken broth
3 cups canned solid pack pumpkin
1 1/2 cups canned coconut milk
Salt and black pepper
Shredded coconut
Ground nutmeg

Melt butter in a large, heavy saucepan over medium heat. Add onion, garlic, and chili. Sauté until onion is golden, about 8 minutes. Add allspice, cinnamon, and sugar. Cook 30 seconds, stirring to blend flavors. Scrape into a blender or food processor. Add a little of the chicken broth and puree until smooth. Add pumpkin and blend well. Return to pot. Stir in remaining chicken broth. Bring to a boil over medium-high heat. Reduce heat to medium-low, cover and simmer to blend flavors, about 30 minutes.

Just before serving, thin soup with coconut milk to desired consistency. Season to taste with salt and pepper. Heat through without bringing to a boil. Ladle soup into bowls and sprinkle with coconut and nutmeg. Serve.

Note: This soup can be made a day ahead and kept covered in refrigerator without loosing any of its richness. Coconut milk can be found in Asian specialty stores and in supermarkets that carry Asian products.

❋ *Serves 4 to 6*

Pumpkin Black Bean Soup

INGREDIENTS

1 tablespoon extra-virgin olive oil
1 medium onion, finely diced
2 teaspoons curry powder
1 teaspoon ground cumin
1/4 to 1/2 teaspoon cayenne pepper
3 cups vegetable broth
3 1/2 to 4 cups pumpkin puree,
fresh or canned
14 to 16 ounces canned, diced tomatoes
15 ounces canned black beans, drained
1 cup half-and-half
Coarse salt
Fresh chives, chopped or snipped

Heat oil in a heavy saucepan over medium heat. Add onion and sauté 5 minutes until soft, stirring occasionally. Add curry powder, cumin, and cayenne and sauté another minute or two, stirring.

Stir in broth and pumpkin puree. Add tomatoes and black beans, stirring to blend. Bring soup to a boil then reduce heat to medium-low. Stir in half-and-half and season with salt to taste. Simmer 5 minutes, but do not let boil.

Adjust seasonings to taste. Ladle into serving bowls. Garnish with chives. Serve.

❋ *Serves 4*

Summer Squash Soup

INGREDIENTS
1/4 cup olive oil
4 cloves garlic, minced
1 1/2 pounds summer squash or
    zucchini, trimmed and cut into
    1-inch cubes
1 large onion, diced
1 medium potato, cut into 1-inch cubes
4 cups chicken broth, vegetable broth,
    or water
3 sprigs fresh basil or
    1 teaspoon dried basil
15 ounces canned crushed tomatoes
15 ounces water
Salt and freshly ground black pepper
Freshly grated Parmesan
Fresh chives, cut into 1/2-inch pieces

Heat oil in a wide, deep pot over medium-high heat. Add garlic and cook a minute or two until barely golden. Remove from pot and set aside. Add squash to pot and cook 8 to 10 minutes, stirring occasionally, until squash is quite soft and slightly browned. Remove from pot and set aside.

Add onion to pot and cook 8 to 10 minutes until soft and slightly brown, stirring frequently. Add potato and broth. If using dried basil, add that now. Stir in cooked garlic and tomatoes. Add water and stir to blend well. Bring to a boil, lower heat, and simmer about 20 minutes, until potato is tender. Remove from heat. Puree in batches in a blender until smooth. Return to pot, and season with salt and pepper to taste. If using fresh basil, cut leaves into ribbons and stir them into hot soup just before serving. Ladle hot soup into warm bowls. Sprinkle with grated Parmesan and chives. Serve.

Note: Chiffonade (shihf-uh-NAHD) literally translates to "made of rags," is a French culinary term for leafy green herbs or greens that are cut into very thin strips or ribbons.

❀ *Serves 4*

Afternoon

Appetizers

Beverages

🪷 *Lanikai Afternoon, by Susan Szabo*

Appetizers

Seared Ahi with Star Fruit

INGREDIENTS

1^1/2 pounds sashimi grade ahi block
^{1}/2 cup sesame oil
1 ^{1}/2 cups mayonnaise
4 cloves garlic, passed through press
Grated zest of 2 lemons
Grated zest of 2 limes
3 tablespoons lime juice
1 teaspoon kosher salt
^{1}/2 teaspoon white pepper
2 to 3 tablespoons prepared wasabi
^{3}/4 cup black sesame seeds
^{3}/4 cup white sesame seeds
1 tablespoon coarse black pepper
1 tablespoon coarse sea salt
3 tablespoons olive oil
6 star fruit, cut into ^{1}/8-inch slices

Cut ahi into four pieces lengthwise and lay in glass baking dish. Rub with sesame oil, cover, and marinate in refrigerator 30 minutes. Put mayonnaise in blender or bowl of food processor. Add garlic, lemon and lime zest, lime juice, salt, pepper, and wasabi. Blend until smooth. Scrape aioli into a small bowl, cover, and chill.

Mix together black and white sesame seeds, pepper, and salt in a shallow dish. Roll ahi strips in seed mixture, pressing firmly so they adhere. Heat olive oil over medium-high heat in a large frying pan. Sear ahi for approximately 2 minutes on each side. Remove from heat and set aside. With sharp knife, slice ahi into ^{1}/8-inch thick pieces equal to the number of star fruit slices. Arrange star fruit on serving platter. Add a piece of ahi and dollop of aioli. Serve.

Note: "Aioli", a composite of the French words for garlic and oil, is a mayonnaise with lots of fresh garlic. A key to a successful aioli made from scratch is to work very slowly when blending the oil into the egg yolks. It is also important to have all the ingredients, including the cooking tools, at room temperature. This recipes uses a prepared mayonnaise as a base for the aioli.

❀ *Serves 8 to 12*

Bean Dip Three Ways

INGREDIENTS

12 ounces firm tofu
2 tablespoons tahini or
   creamy peanut butter
2 tablespoons fresh lemon juice
2 tablespoons fresh lime juice
1 teaspoon ground cumin
1/4 teaspoon dried chili pepper flakes
1/2 teaspoon salt
3 cloves garlic, passed through press
1 cup cooked garbanzo or white beans
1 cup cooked dark red kidney beans
1 cup cooked black beans
Paprika
2 tablespoons chopped cilantro or parsley
Carrot sticks
Celery sticks
Corn chips or toasted tortilla wedges

Drain tofu to remove excess moisture. Crumble into a food processor. Add tahini, lemon juice, lime juice, cumin, chili pepper, salt, and garlic. Puree until smooth, and scrape into bowl. Divide into thirds. Return one-third to food processor and add garbanzo beans. Puree until smooth. Scrape into one bowl of divided serving dish or into one-third of shallow bowl. Add another third of tofu puree to processor with red beans. Puree until smooth. Scrape into divided serving dish or place carefully next to white beans in shallow bowl. Add remaining third of tofu puree to processor with black beans. Puree until smooth. Scrape into divided serving dish or carefully place with red and white beans in shallow bowl. Sprinkle with paprika and cilantro. Serve with vegetable sticks or corn chips.

Note: Can be served on a bed of shredded purple cabbage instead of separate bowls surrounded by carrots, celery, and chips.

Garbanzo beans are also called chick peas.

❀ *Makes 3 cups*

Herbed Cheese and Beef Terrine

INGREDIENTS
1 pound cream cheese, softened
6 tablespoons butter, cubed
$1/2$ cup minced parsley
$1/2$ cup thinly sliced green onions
$1/2$ cup diced water chestnuts
3 tablespoons prepared horseradish
1 pound wide, thinly sliced cooked
   corned beef
1 baguette, thinly sliced
Sprigs of fresh parsley

Lightly oil a 3 x 5-inch loaf pan with 2 $1/2$-cup capacity and set aside.

Beat cream cheese and butter in a medium bowl until fluffy. Add parsley, green onions, water chestnuts, and horseradish, stirring until smooth. Neatly line prepared loaf pan with one layer of corned beef slices from end to end, extending 1 to 2 inches over each rim. Be sure to overlap bottom so cheese won't leak out. Gently spread one-half of cream cheese mixture evenly over corned beef. Layer 3 to 4 beef slices neatly onto cheese. Pat gently to eliminate air bubbles and make level. Repeat layers of cheese and corned beef. Fold extended beef pieces over last layer and pat gently to seal and make level. Wrap airtight with plastic. Chill until very firm, at least 4 hours.

Unwrap. Invert a flat plate onto top of pan. Firmly holding together, carefully turn over plate and pan, and lift off pan. Pat any loose corned beef pieces back in place. Serve with a sharp knife and bread slices. Garnish with fresh parsley. This can be made up to two days ahead.

❦ *Serves 10*

Curried Chickpea Spread

INGREDIENTS
3 tablespoons vegetable oil
1 medium onion, diced
$1/4$ teaspoon ground cumin
$1/4$ teaspoon ground cinnamon
$1/4$ teaspoon ground nutmeg
Dash or two ground cloves
1 teaspoon ground coriander
2 cloves garlic, passed thorugh press
$1/2$-inch piece fresh ginger root, grated
2 tablespoons tomato paste
$1/2$ teaspoon salt
15 to 20 ounces canned chick peas
1 tablespoon lime juice
2 ripe plum tomatoes, diced
Mini pita rounds or
  quartered 6-inch pita rounds

Heat oil in a heavy skillet over medium-high heat. Add onion and sauté, stirring occasionally, 8 minutes until tender and golden. Stir in cumin, cinnamon, nutmeg, cloves, coriander, garlic, and ginger. Cook 2 to 3 minutes. Stir in tomato paste and salt. Add chickpeas and liquid, stirring to blend. Place in food processor and pulse to coarsely puree. Place in serving bowl and stir in lime juice. Top with diced tomatoes. Serve with pita bread on the side and a small utensil for spreading.

🌸 *Makes 1 $1/2$ cups*

Layered Cheese Torta

INGREDIENTS
3 pounds cream cheese, softened, divided
1 cup chopped basil
1 cup chopped parsley or cilantro
1 tablespoon minced pine nuts
1/4 cup olive oil
Juice and grated zest of 1 lemon
1 teaspoon black pepper
1 cup slivered oil packed sun-dried tomatoes
4 cloves garlic, passed through press
2 tablespoons minced fresh rosemary
Fresh basil with flowers
Whole pine nuts

Line an 8-inch round or heart shaped cake pan with plastic wrap allowing wrap to hang over edge about 6 inches. Set aside. In a large bowl, beat 1 pound of cream cheese until smooth. In blender or food processor, combine basil, parsley, and pine nuts. Pulse a few seconds to chop. With motor running, drizzle in oil making a paste. Fold into cream cheese and beat until smooth. Scrape into prepared pan. Spread evenly over bottom, smooth top and place in refrigerator. Again, beat 1 pound cream cheese in clean bowl until smooth. Stir in lemon juice, zest, and ground pepper until blended. Make a second layer in pan by spreading lemon mixture evenly over pesto mixture, smoothing top. Return to refrigerator. Beat remaining pound of cream cheese in clean bowl. Stir in sun-dried tomatoes, garlic, and rosemary, mixing until blended. Make a final layer by spreading tomato mixture over lemon layer, smooth top. Wrap with overlapping plastic. Refrigerate until firm and well chilled, about 6 hours. Invert onto serving plate and remove plastic wrap. Garnish with fresh basil and pine nuts. Serve with crackers or thinly sliced bread.

Note: This can be made a day ahead and kept refrigerated. Try substituting goat cheese in pesto and/or tomato layer.

🌺 *Serves a crowd*

Savory Crab Cheesecake

INGREDIENTS

2 pounds cream cheese, softened

3 eggs

6 cloves garlic, passed through press

$1/2$ teaspoon salt

1 to 2 teaspoons hot pepper sauce,
   such as Tabasco

1 tablespoon fresh lemon juice

1 pound fresh packed canned crabmeat

Sprigs of fresh parsley

Heat oven to 350°F. Grease a 9-inch springform pan and set aside. Beat cream cheese in a large mixing bowl until smooth. Beat in eggs one at a time, until well blended. Stir in garlic, salt, pepper sauce, and lemon juice. Add crabmeat, mixing to blend. Pour into prepared pan and bake 45 to 55 minutes, until set. Place on wire rack to cool.

Remove from pan to serving plate, cover, and chill at least 2 hours. Remove from refrigerator 10 minutes before serving. Garnish with parsley. Serve with Ritz or Carr style crackers.

Note: Smoked or canned salmon can be used instead of crab.

❀ Makes one 9-inch cake

Gingered Crostini with Sweet Red Pepper

SWEET RED PEPPER
3 red bell peppers
1 tablespoon olive oil
1 to 2 jalapeno peppers, minced
1 teaspoon mustard seeds
1/3 cup sliced oil packed
  sun-dried tomatoes
1/4 cup minced fresh basil
1/4 cup minced fresh parsley
Salt and black pepper

CROSTINI
1 to 2 baguettes
2 tablespoons grated fresh ginger root
4 cloves garlic, passed through press
1/3 cup minced fresh parsley
1/2 teaspoon salt
2 tablespoons olive oil
Sprigs of fresh basil or parsley

Heat broiler. Place bell peppers under heating element and roast until blackened. Using tongs, carefully turn to blacken all sides. Place peppers in a heavy plastic bag, seal, and let stand 15 minutes. Remove from bag and peel blackened skin. Slit pepper and remove seeds. Put roasted pepper in food processor and puree. Let sit.

Heat oil in a skillet over medium heat. Add jalapeno and mustard seeds. Heat until seeds pop then add sun-dried tomatoes and sauté a few minutes. Add to pepper puree with basil and parsley. Puree until smooth. Season with salt and pepper to taste. Set aside.

Heat oven to 375°F. Cut baguettes into 24 1/8-inch slices. Place bread on a baking sheet. In a small bowl, mix together ginger, garlic, parsley, and salt. Stir in oil to make a paste. Spread paste thinly over bread slices using just enough to flavor bread. Bake until lightly toasted, about 8 to 10 minutes. Top each slice of bread with a dollop of pepper mixture, spreading to 1/8-inch of edge. Garnish with fresh basil. Arrange on serving tray. Serve.

❀ *Serves 6 to 8*

Eggplant Spread

INGREDIENTS
3 tablespoons olive oil
1 large eggplant, diced small
1 green bell pepper, seeded and diced
2 cloves garlic, passed through press
1 1/2 teaspoons ground cumin
1/4 teaspoon cayenne pepper
2 teaspoons granulated sugar
1/4 cup red wine vinegar
8 ounces tomato sauce
1/4 cup chopped cilantro
1 baguette, thinly sliced

Heat oil in a large frying pan over medium heat. Add eggplant and green pepper and sauté 5 minutes, stirring occasionally. Add garlic, cumin, and cayenne. Sauté a few minutes then add sugar, vinegar, and tomato sauce. Reduce heat to low, simmer, covered for 25 minutes, stirring occasionally. Uncover, remove from heat, and allow to cool. Place in serving bowl, cover and refrigerate at least 2 hours. Remove from refrigerator. Stir in cilantro. Heat oven to 400°F. Place baguette slices on a baking sheet. Toast in hot oven a few minutes until golden. Place in cloth lined basket. Serve eggplant with toasted bread.

❁ *Serves 6 to 8*

Date Walnut Spread

INGREDIENTS
1 baguette, cut into 1/8-inch slices
8 ounces cream cheese, softened
1 cup diced pitted dates
1/2 cup chopped raisins
1/2 cup finely chopped walnuts
1 firm apple, such as
  Granny Smith, grated
1 teaspoon ground cinnamon
1/4 teaspoon grated fresh ginger root
2 tablespoons Port

Heat broiler. Place bread slices on a baking sheet and toast under broiler until lightly browned. Remove to basket. Set aside.

In a medium bowl, beat cream cheese until fluffy. Stir in dates, raisins, walnuts, and apple. Sprinkle with cinnamon, ginger, and wine. Mix well. Place in glass serving bowl, cover, and refrigerate at least 1 hour. Serve with baguette slices.

Note: For Passover, use an approved wine, omit the cream cheese, and serve with matzo crackers.

❁ *Makes about 2 cups*

Sweet and Spicy Nut Mix

INGREDIENTS
1/4 cup honey
4 teaspoons Thai green curry paste
2 teaspoons macadamia oil
1 1/4 teaspoons salt
1 cup cashew halves
1 cup macadamia halves
1 cup whole almonds
1 cup pecan halves
1/2 cup shredded coconut

Heat oven to 300°F. In a large bowl, mix honey, curry paste, oil, and salt. Add nuts and coconut, stirring to mix well. Spread in a 10 x 15-inch baking pan. Place in center of oven. Bake 30 minutes, turning often with spatula, until nuts are dark gold. Watch carefully, nuts and coconut burn easily. Remove from oven. Let cool, turning nuts often. Serve warm or cooled. Store in a large shallow container. Nuts will stick together if packed too tightly in an upright container.

Note: See recipe on page 310 for homemade green curry paste.

❀ *Makes 4 cups*

Olive Tapenade

INGREDIENTS
2 cups large pitted black olives
1/2 cup chopped oil packed
   sun-dried tomatoes
2 heaping teaspoons capers
3 cloves garlic, minced
1 teaspoon anchovies
1/4 to 1/2 cup olive oil
Black pepper
Soft bread sticks or crusty bread

Place olives, sun-dried tomatoes, capers, garlic, and anchovies into a food processor and pulse until finely minced, being careful not to puree. Scrape into a bowl and combine with just enough olive oil to moisten. Season with black pepper to taste. Cover and refrigerate. Bring to room temperature. Serve with soft bread sticks or slices of crusty rustic bread.

Note: Can be served as hors d'oeuvre or mixed with additional olive oil and served with fish or pasta.

❀ *Makes about 2 cups*

Oysters with Thai Pesto

PESTO
1 bunch fresh cilantro, chopped
1-inch piece fresh ginger root,
* peeled and grated*
1 tablespoon Nam pla (fish sauce)
Juice of 1 lime
2 tablespoons olive oil
Dash or two hot pepper sauce, such
* as Tabasco*

OYSTERS
24 fresh oysters with shells
Crushed ice
or
24 fresh oyster mushrooms
24 slices toasted baguette

Place cilantro and ginger in a blender or food processor with fish sauce, lime juice, oil, and hot sauce. Puree, scraping down sides occasionally to make a paste. Scrape into a small dish. Spread crushed ice on shallow serving platter with rim. Nestle oysters in half-shells in ice. Top each with dab of pesto. Serve chilled.

Alternate: Arrange toasted baguette slices on rimmed serving platter. Grill or broil oyster mushrooms about 3 minutes. Top baguette with grilled mushrooms. Dab with pesto. Serve immediately.

Note: If oysters are in shell, ask market to shuck them, saving the shells for presentation. The oysters can be shucked a day ahead and kept flesh side up, covered, and chilled. The pesto can be made the night before, covered, and chilled.

❀ *Serves 8 to 12*

Papaya Spring Rolls

INGREDIENTS
1/2 cup chunky peanut butter
1/3 cup water
2 tablespoons rice vinegar
2 tablespoons fish sauce
2 teaspoons hot chili paste
2 large firm ripe papayas
1 long unpeeled Japanese cucumber
24 6-inch-diameter rice paper rounds
24 large fresh basil leaves
48 large fresh mint leaves
48 small fresh cilantro sprigs

In a medium bowl, whisk together peanut butter, water, vinegar, fish sauce, and chili paste. Cover and chill. Whisk again before serving. This can be made the day before. Halve papaya lengthwise, peel and remove seeds. Cut each piece in half crosswise then into 1/2-inch thick strips and set aside. Cut cucumber into 1/4-inch thick strips 2 1/2 inches long. Set aside.

Fill a shallow baking pan with warm water. Working in batches, soak 2 to 3 rice paper rounds in water until softened, about 2 minutes. Remove rounds from water and arrange in single layer on clean dish towel. Place 1 basil leaf in center of each round vein side up. Place 2 mint leaves on top of each basil leaf, again vein side up. Place 2 papaya strips, then 2 cucumber strips parallel on top of mint. Arrange 2 cilantro sprigs on top of cucumber. Fold one parallel edge (to papaya-cucumber) of each round over filling. Fold in sides and roll up rice paper rounds tightly, enclosing filling. Transfer to platter. Repeat with remaining rounds. Cover with moist paper towel, wrap in plastic, and chill. These can be made up to eight hours ahead. Keep tightly wrapped and chilled. Serve rolls with peanut sauce.

Note: Fish sauce has a very pungent, salty taste, and is an essential ingredient in many Asian dishes. In Vietnam, it is called *nuoc nam;* in Thailand, *nam pla;* and in the Philippines, *patis.* Fish sauce and rice flour wrappers known as *banh trang* are available at Asian markets and in the Asian foods section of some supermarkets.

🌸 *Makes 2 dozen*

Petite Potato Pupu

INGREDIENTS

12 small red potatoes or
   24 petite potatoes
Smoked Salmon Filling
Goat Cheese Filling
Sun-dried Tomato Filling
Sour Cream and Bacon Filling
Baby greens

SMOKED SALMON FILLING

3 1/2 ounces smoked salmon, minced
2 tablespoons sour cream
2 tablespoons minced red onion
1 teaspoon capers, drained
Black pepper

GOAT CHEESE AND SUN-DRIED TOMATO FILLING

1/2 cup goat cheese
1 tablespoon slivered sun-dried tomatoes
3 tablespoons minced black olives
2 tablespoons minced chives

SOUR CREAM AND BACON FILLING

3 hard boiled eggs
4 strips cooked bacon, crumbled
2 tablespoons sour cream
2 tablespoons mayonnaise
Paprika

Prepare the potatoes using one of the following methods:
• Scrub the potatoes and sprinkle with water, pierce with a fork. Place on a microwave-safe dish and cover with plastic wrap. Pierce with sharp knife to create vents for steam. Microwave on high for 10 minutes until somewhat tender, remove from microwave. Let stand for 2 to 3 minutes to continue cooking. Cut red potatoes into halves.
• Boil the potatoes in salted water for 15 minutes until tender. Cut red potatoes into halves and let cool.

Cut a small slice off the rounded side of each cooked potato half so they stand upright. Create a cavity by removing a scoop from the cut side with a small spoon or melon baller. Divide potatoes into three groups of eight. Fill one group with Smoked Salmon filling and garnish with a little black pepper. Fill one group with Goat Cheese filling. Fill last group with Sour Cream filling and garnish with paprika. Place a few greens on individual serving plates, arrange one potato from each group on greens, and serve.

Smoked Salmon Filling: Mix salmon, sour cream, onion, capers, and pepper in a bowl. Chill thoroughly.

Goat Cheese Filling: Mix goat cheese, sun-dried tomatoes, olives, and chives in a bowl. Chill thoroughly.

Sour Cream Filling: Peel eggs and mince. Place in a bowl, add bacon, sour cream, and mayonnaise, stirring to blend. Chill thoroughly.

Note: The potatoes and the topping may be prepared up to one day ahead and stored separately in the refrigerator.

❀ *Serves 8 as appetizer, 12 as hors d'oeuvre*

INGREDIENTS

24 won ton or gyozo pi wrappers
Extra-virgin olive oil
1 pound fresh shrimp, shelled, deveined,
* and chopped*
1 ripe mango, peeled and diced
2 cloves garlic, finely minced
1/2 cup finely chopped fresh basil
1/4 cup finely chopped fresh mint
2 tablespoons lime juice
Salt and white pepper
Tiny fresh basil or mint leaves

Shrimp in Won Ton Cups

Heat oven to 375°F. Press 1 won ton wrapper into each cup of muffin tin. Bake for 8 to 10 minutes until light brown and slightly crisp. Remove from cups and place on wire rack to cool.

Heat 1 tablespoon olive oil in a skillet over medium heat. Add shrimp and sauté a few minutes until opaque. Remove from heat and place in a bowl. Add mango, garlic, basil, mint, and lime juice, stirring to mix gently. Season with salt and pepper to taste. Spoon shrimp mixture into won ton cups. Garnish with fresh herbs. Serve.

The won ton cups can be made up to six hours ahead and once cooled, stored in an airtight container. The shrimp filling can be made ahead and kept covered in refrigerator. Assemble just before serving.

Note: Won ton wrappers are paper-thin sheets of dough used in making won tons, gyoza, pot stickers, and Chinese dumplings. Made from flour, eggs, and salt, they can be filled with a mixture of meat, seafood, or vegetables. Once filled, won tons can be boiled, deep-fried, or steamed and served as an appetizer, snack, or side dish with a variety of sauces. The wrappers come in both squares and circles and are available in various thicknesses.

✿ *Makes 2 dozen*

Grilled Vegetables with Vinaigrette

VINAIGRETTE
Olive oil
3 tablespoons balsamic vinegar
$1/2$ tablespoon soy sauce
2 teaspoons Dijon mustard
2 large cloves garlic, smashed
Freshly ground black pepper

VEGETABLES
Red and/or green pepper slices
Zucchini thick sticks
Yellow zucchini sticks
Summer squash sticks
Asparagus spears
Mushrooms
Sprigs of fresh thyme, rosemary,
*   or parsley*

In a small bowl, combine 6 tablespoons oil, vinegar, soy sauce, and mustard with a whisk until well blended. Add garlic and season with pepper, whisk to mix, and set aside. Whisk again just before serving to keep ingredients blended.

Heat grill or broiler. Rub any combination of vegetables with oil. Lightly brush grill rack with oil. Lay vegetables on rack and grill, turning as each side roasts until all sides have been exposed to heat. Grilling may have to be done in batches. Remove to serving platter. Drizzle with vinaigrette and garnish with sprigs of fresh herbs. Serve.

Note: Vinaigrette can also be used as dressing on mixed green salads.

❀ *Serves 6 to 8*

Toasted Almond Crab Spread

INGREDIENTS

1 cup slivered almonds
1 pound cream cheese, softened
3 cups shredded Swiss cheese
1 cup sour cream
$1/2$ teaspoon salt
$1/4$ teaspoon ground nutmeg
$1/4$ teaspoon black pepper
1 pound fresh crabmeat
$1/2$ cup thinly sliced green onions
$1/4$ cup minced fresh parsley

Heat oven to 350°F. Spread almonds in small baking dish. Toast lightly in oven, shaking occasionally. Remove and set aside.

Beat together cream cheese and Swiss cheese in a bowl. Stir in sour cream, salt, nutmeg, and pepper. Pick through crab and remove cartilage or shell. Mix in crabmeat, onions, and half of toasted almonds. Spread in ungreased deep decorative baking dish.

Bake for 30 minutes until very hot. Remove from oven. Sprinkle with parsley and remaining toasted nuts. Serve warm with crackers.

✿ *Makes 5 cups*

Grilled Figs on Gorgonzola Toast

INGREDIENTS

$1/4$ cup honey
6 sprigs fresh thyme
12 large ripe figs, halved
2 tablespoons extra-virgin olive oil, divided
2 teaspoons fresh thyme leaves
1 artisan-style baguette
3 ounces Gorgonzola cheese, softened

Heat honey in a small saucepan over medium heat until simmering. Add thyme sprigs, remove from heat and set aside. Heat grill or broiler. Set grill rack 4 inches from heat source. Put figs in small bowl. Sprinkle with 2 teaspoons olive oil and thyme leaves and toss lightly to mix. Cut 24 $1/2$-inch thick slices from the bread and brush both sides lightly with remaining olive oil. Lightly brush grill rack with oil. Add figs and grill until heated through but not collapsed, 1 to 2 minutes on each side. Remove to a plate. Lightly toast bread on both sides away from direct heat.

Spread cheese on toast slices and top each with a fig. Remove thyme sprigs from honey and discard. Drizzle honey over figs. Serve.

✿ *Makes 2 dozen*

Brandied Apple Crostini

INGREDIENTS
3/4 cup Calvados or brandy
3/4 cup raisins
1 baguette, cut into 1/4-inch slices
1/3 cup olive oil
Salt and black pepper
2 green apples, quartered and cored
2 tablespoons butter, softened
12 to 16 ounces goat cheese, softened

In a small glass bowl, combine Calvados and raisins. Set aside to plump raisins. Brush bread slices with oil, sprinkle lightly with salt and pepper. Place seasoned rounds on a baking sheet. Set aside.

Heat oven to low broil setting or lower oven rack with regular setting. Cut apple into thin slices, with or without peels, equal to number of bread slices. Melt 1 tablespoon of butter in a skillet over medium heat. Add half the apple slices and sauté until golden, turning gently to preserve apple shape. Strain Calvados from raisins, and sprinkle half the liquid over apple slices. Sauté until golden on both sides. Remove from pan to plate. Repeat using remaining butter, apple slices, and Calvados.

Place 1 apple slice on each seasoned bread round, mound with 1 to 2 teaspoons goat cheese. Arrange 3 to 5 raisins on cheese, pressing to secure. Arrange on baking sheet. Place baking sheet under broiler and heat until lightly browned. Watch carefully. Remove from oven. Place crostini on platter. Serve.

Note: Charlemagne (742-814 AD), King of the Franks, decided that all of the farmers in Normandy must cultivate apple trees. Eventually, there were so many apples that no one knew what to do with them. By the middle of the 16th century, several enterprising farmers used their extra apples to make brandy. Thus was the beginning of Calvados, named for the region of its distillation.

Today there are three great French brandies - Cognac, Armagnac and Calvados. But being fermented from apple juice and not from grapes really puts Calvados in a category of its own.

Serves 6

Artichoke and Mushroom Spread

INGREDIENTS

2 baguettes, cut into 1/8-inch slices
1 tablespoon olive oil
2 tablespoons butter
3 cloves garlic, minced
1 cup finely diced celery
2 pounds mushrooms,
  washed, stemmed, and diced
1 cup sliced green onions
3 cups diced marinated artichoke hearts
1 1/2 teaspoons poultry seasoning
1 teaspoon minced fresh rosemary
Salt and black pepper
1 cup shredded Parmesan
1 cup shredded Romano

Heat oven to 350°F. Lay bread slices in single layer on a baking sheet. Toast lightly in oven. Put in a cloth lined basket. Set aside.

Heat oil and butter in a large frying pan over medium heat. Sauté garlic and celery until golden. Add mushrooms and sauté until tender, about 15 minutes. Drain off any liquid from mushrooms. Add green onions, artichoke hearts, poultry seasoning, and rosemary. Stir to mix and season with salt and pepper to taste. Heat thoroughly. Remove from heat, stir in Parmesan and Romano cheese. Place in chafing dish over low flame to keep warm, or scrape into baking dish, place in oven and bake 30 minutes. Serve warm with lightly toasted bread slices.

❀ *Makes 6 cups*

Baked Brie with Macadamia Nuts

INGREDIENTS

1 round loaf sourdough bread
1 cup macadamia nuts bits
2 tablespoons butter, melted
2 tablespoons brown sugar
20-ounce wheel Brie
Wedges of apple and pear
Clusters of red and green grapes

Heat oven to 350°F. Cutting straight down, create a circle in top of bread the same size as the Brie. Carefully remove top crust and set aside to be replaced later. Remove enough bread to make a well that allows cheese to sit inside about 1/2 inch down from rim. Sprinkle macadamia nuts around well in bottom of bread.

Stir together melted butter and brown sugar. Spread on one side of Brie. Set cheese, sugar side down into bread shell on top of macadamia nuts, and replace bread top. Wrap tightly in aluminum foil. Bake 25 minutes to heat thoroughly. Remove from oven, let sit 10 minutes. Unwrap, place on serving tray. Cut into pieces with sharp bread knife. Serve warm with fruit.

❀ *Serves 12*

Brie with Crab in Puff Pastry

INGREDIENTS
1 1/2 tablespoons butter
2 large shallots, minced
4 cloves garlic, minced
4 ounces mixed mushrooms,
    washed, stemmed, and thinly sliced
8 ounces lump crabmeat,
    picked through for shells
1/4 teaspoon cayenne pepper
1 green onion, minced
Several sprigs fresh parsley, minced
2 ounces goat cheese, crumbled
2 sheets frozen puff pastry, thawed
1 pound wheel Brie
1 egg
2 teaspoons water
1 bunch watercress
Toast points

Heat oven to 400°F. Lightly oil a baking sheet or line with parchment paper and set aside. In a skillet, melt butter over medium heat. Add shallots and garlic, sauté, stirring, until soft about 2 minutes. Add mushrooms and sauté 8 to 10 minutes until tender and liquid evaporates. Stir in crabmeat, cayenne, green onion, and parsley. Sauté 2 minutes, stirring occasionally. Remove from the heat and let cool. Fold in goat cheese and set aside.

Lay out one sheet of pastry on a lightly floured surface. Press gently with rolling pin to smooth. Cut into a circle 3 inches larger than the Brie. Place on prepared baking sheet. Cut Brie in half horizontally and center one piece on the pastry on baking sheet, cut side up. Spread with crabmeat mixture and top with the remaining Brie, cut side down. Press together gently. Beat together egg and water. Brush pastry around cheese lightly with egg wash. With rolling pin, smooth other piece of pastry and cut into a circle 1 inch larger than Brie. Lay on top of filled cheese. Brush top pastry lightly with egg wash. Fold up bottom pastry to meet top, pleating, and firmly pinch edges of top and bottom together to seal. Cut several leaves or other decorative shapes from the pastry scraps and arrange on top. Lightly brush with egg wash.

Bake until the pastry is puffed and golden brown, 20 to 25 minutes. Remove from oven and let sit 5 to 10 minutes. Line a platter with the watercress and place the baked Brie on top. Surround with toast points. Serve.

❀ *Serves 10 to 12*

Chicken Wings with Pomegranate Sauce

INGREDIENTS

4 cups pomegranate juice
6 whole cloves
1 star anise
1 orange
$1/4$ to $1/2$ cup granulated sugar
    or honey
5 pounds chicken wings
Salt

Stir together pomegranate juice, cloves, and star anise in a medium saucepan over medium-high heat. Grate zest from orange over saucepan to catch oil and zest. Save orange to slice for garnish. Bring sauce to a boil. Reduce heat to medium-low and let simmer until reduced to 2 cups, about 30 minutes. Adjust sweetness to taste with sugar. Let simmer 5 to 10 minutes, remove from heat, and set aside.

Heat oven to 400°F. Cut tip section from chicken wings at joint. Save tips to make stock or discard. Rinse wings and place in single layer on rack in a large roasting pan and sprinkle with salt. Do not over-crowd, use two pans if necessary. Bake about 1 hour until well browned, basting with pan drippings every 20 minutes. Drain and discard fat from chicken wings. Place wings in serving pan or chafing dish. Cover with pomegranate sauce. Garnish with orange slices. Serve.

Note: Native to China and Vietnam, star anise is the unusual fruit of a small tree. It is star shaped, radiating between five and ten pointed rust colored seed pods about 1 $1/4$ inches long. It has a liquorice-like bouquet more pungent and stronger than anise. Pomegranate juice and star anise can be found at natural food stores.

Serves 10 to 12

Chicken Empanadas with Green Chilies

INGREDIENTS

1 $1/2$ cups all-purpose flour
1 cup masa harina
1 teaspoon baking powder
Salt
$1/2$ cup butter, melted and cooled
3 cups water, divided
8 medium tomatillos, husked
1 tablespoon olive oil
1 to 2 jalapeno peppers, minced
1 Spanish onion, minced
3 cloves garlic, minced
1 handful fresh cilantro, sliced
Juice of 1 lime
2 cups finely shredded,
    cooked dark meat chicken
1 cup crumbled Queso Fresco
1 egg, beaten
1 tablespoon water

In a large bowl, stir together flour, masa harina, baking powder, and 1 teaspoon salt. Mix in cooled butter. Gradually work in $1/2$ cup water. Add more water as needed to make a dough that is easy to handle but not sticky. Form into a ball, wrap in plastic, and chill for 30 minutes. Bring 2 cups water to a boil in a medium saucepan over high heat. Add tomatillos, reduce heat to low, and simmer for 10 minutes until soft. Drain and set aside.

Heat oil in a small frying pan over medium. Add jalapeno, onion, and garlic, sauté until tender, 5 to 8 minutes. Combine tomatillos, jalapeno mixture, cilantro, and lime juice in a blender or food processor. Add $1/4$ cup water and pulse to make a coarse puree. Season salsa verde with a generous pinch of salt. Combine the shredded chicken and Queso Fresco in a large bowl. Pour in 1 $1/2$ cups salsa verde and fold just to moisten. Set aside.

Lightly flour a rolling pin and work surface. Divide the dough in half. Roll out one half until $1/8$-inch thick. Cut out ten circles using a 4-inch cookie or biscuit cutter. Repeat with remaining dough. Spoon 2 generous tablespoons of filling into the center of each pastry circle, leaving a $1/2$-inch border. Mix beaten egg with 1 tablespoon water. Brush edges of dough with egg wash and fold in half to enclose the filling. Tightly seal edges by crimping with a fork. Chill at least 30 minutes. Heat oven to 375°F. Butter a baking sheet. Place empanadas on prepared pan and brush tops with additional egg wash. Using a fork, prick a few holes in the top of each empanada to allow steam to escape. Bake 30 minutes until the pastry is golden brown. Remove from oven. Arrange on serving platter, and serve with remaining salsa verde on the side.

🌸 *Makes 20 pieces*

Cranberry Bites

CRANBERRY BITES
2 sheets puff pastry, thawed
8 ounces goat cheese or Brie
1 $^1/2$ cups cranberry sauce

APPLE ORANGE CRANBERRY SAUCE
$^1/2$ orange
$^1/2$ cup water
1 tart apple, peeled, cored, and diced
3 cups fresh cranberries, sorted
1 cup granulated sugar
$^1/2$ teaspoon ground cinnamon
$^1/4$ teaspoon ground cloves

Heat oven to 375°F. Lightly grease the bottoms of cups of muffin tins. Cut pastry into 2-inch squares and place onto muffin tin cup bottoms, pressing to shape. Place 1 tablespoon goat cheese or 1-inch slice Brie into center of each pastry cup. Top each with a heaping teaspoon of cranberry sauce.

Bake 20 minutes until puff pastry corners are lightly browned. Cool slightly to set before removing from pan and serving.

❦ *Makes 20 pieces*

Apple Orange Cranberry Sauce: Squeeze the juice from orange half into medium saucepan. Remove the membrane and most of white pith from inside of the orange shell and discard. Cut shell into thin slivers and place in saucepan with juice. Add water, apples, cranberries, sugar, cinnamon, and cloves. Bring to a boil over medium-high heat, reduce heat to low and cover partially. Simmer gently, stirring occasionally, until sauce has thickened, apple is tender, and cranberries have burst, about 10 minutes. Transfer to bowl, let cool. Cover and refrigerate.

❦ *Makes 3 $^1/2$ to 4 cups*

Eggplant Fries with Homemade Ketchup

HOMEMADE KETCHUP

1 tablespoon vegetable oil
1 large onion, thinly sliced
1 sweet red bell pepper, seeded,
    and diced
8 large tomatoes, peeled, seeded,
    and diced
1/2 cup apple cider vinegar
1 1/2 teaspoons paprika
1/8 teaspoon ground nutmeg
1 tablespoon prepared mustard
1 tablespoon black peppercorns
1/2 teaspoon whole coriander seed
2 bay leaves
2 whole cloves
1/2 tablespoon salt
1 teaspoon black pepper
1 teaspoon hot pepper sauce, such
    as Tabasco
1/2 cup granulated sugar

EGGPLANT FRIES

2 pounds long Japanese eggplant
2 1/2 cups milk
2 cups all-purpose flour
1 tablespoon salt
2 teaspoons black pepper
Peanut oil for frying
Fresh parsley

Heat oil in a large pot over medium heat. Add onion and red pepper, and sauté a few minutes. Add tomatoes, vinegar, paprika, nutmeg, and mustard, stirring to mix well. Wrap peppercorns, coriander, bay leaves, and cloves in cheesecloth and add to pot. Reduce heat to medium low and cook, stirring occasionally for 30 to 40 minutes to reduce sauce.

Remove from heat. Remove and discard cheesecloth bag. Let ketchup cool slightly. Carefully place in a food processor or blender and puree. Return to clean pot on stove.

Season with salt, pepper, hot sauce, and sugar. Simmer about 5 minutes to dissolve sugar and blend flavors. Remove from heat and let cool. Ketchup will keep about one week, covered in refrigerator.

Note: To peel tomatoes more easily, dip them into boiling water for 30 seconds then plunge into icy cold water for a minute or two.

Eggplant Fries: Line a baking sheet with waxed paper. Trim ends from eggplant, cut in half crosswise, then cut into eighths lengthwise, making wedges. Put milk in a bowl. Whisk together flour, salt, and pepper in a shallow dish. Dip each wedge of eggplant into the milk then dredge in seasoned flour. Lay on prepared baking sheet. Heat 2 inches of oil in a large pot or deep skillet over medium heat until hot (about 335°F). Add coated eggplant wedges in batches. Fry about 4 minutes until golden brown. Remove from hot oil and drain on paper towel. Arrange on serving platter and garnish with parsley. Serve warm with ketchup.

Note: Peanut oil can be heated to high temperatures without burning, making it ideal for deep frying, but remember to ask about allergies.

❦ *Serves 4 to 6*

Stuffed Mushrooms

INGREDIENTS
36 small fresh button mushrooms
Piquant Peanut Filling
Blue Cheese Filling
Pesto Filling

PIQUANT PEANUT FILLING
4 ounces cream cheese, softened
$1/2$ cup chunky peanut butter
$1/2$ cup spicy mango chutney, diced
2 tablespoons minced parsley
$1/2$ teaspoon seasoned salt
2 tablespoons minced peanuts

BLUE CHEESE FILLING
4 ounces cream cheese, softened
2 to 3 tablespoons sour cream
$1/2$ cup blue cheese or Gorgonzola
1 tablespoon minced parsley
Sprigs of fresh parsley

PESTO FILLING
$1/2$ cup packed sliced spinach
$1/2$ cup packed sliced basil
$1/2$ cup packed sliced parsley or cilantro
3 cloves garlic, smashed
$1/3$ cup extra-virgin olive oil
$1/2$ cup chopped walnuts, toasted
$3/4$ cup crumbled Feta cheese
12 broken pieces of walnut meat

Heat oven to 400°F. Scrub and remove stems from mushrooms. Divide caps into three groups of twelve, gill side up. Using a small spoon, pack opening of twelve mushroom caps with Piquant Peanut filling. Arrange in a row on a baking sheet. With clean spoon, pack opening of second group of mushrooms with Blue Cheese filling. Arrange in a row on baking sheet. With clean spoon, pack remaining dozen mushrooms with Pesto filling. Arrange in a row on baking sheet. Place in middle of oven for 8 to 10 minutes just to heat through, watching carefully not to let fillings melt all over. Remove to serving platter. Garnish Piquant Peanut filling with sprinkling of minced peanuts. Garnish Blue Cheese filling with fresh parsley. Garnish Pesto filling with broken walnuts. Serve.

Piquant Filling: In a medium bowl, combine cream cheese and peanut butter until well blended. Add chutney, parsley, and seasoned salt. Cover and chill until ready to use.

Note: $1/2$ cup apricot jam, 1 tablespoon cider vinegar, and 2 tablespoons chopped raisins may be substituted for chutney.

Blue Cheese Filling: In a small bowl, beat together cream cheese and sour cream until smooth. Stir in blue cheese and minced parsley until well blended but still a little lumpy. Cover and chill until ready to use.

Pesto Filling: In a blender or food processor, combine spinach, basil, parsley, and garlic. Pulse a few times. With motor running, drizzle in oil and puree until somewhat smooth. Add chopped walnuts and pulse until coarsely blended. Scrape into bowl, stir in Feta. Cover and chill until ready to use.

Makes 3 dozen

Papaya Quesadillas

INGREDIENTS
2 tablespoons olive oil, divided
1 fresh jalapeno pepper, diced
  or 1 small can diced green chilies
1 large yellow onion, thinly sliced
1 ripe large papaya, peeled,
  seeded, and diced
Salt and black pepper
10 10-inch flour tortillas
4 tablespoons butter, softened
3 ounces Asiago cheese, shredded

SPICY TOMATO RELISH
6 ripe tomatoes, seeded and chopped
1 teaspoon minced fresh ginger root
4 cloves garlic, minced
1 teaspoon ground tumeric
1 tablespoon olive oil
1 1/2 teaspoons cumin seed
1/4 teaspoon fenugreek seed
1/4 teaspoon mustard seed
6 small dried hot red chilies
Salt

Heat 1 tablespoon oil in a skillet over medium heat. Add jalapeno and onion. Sauté 5 to 10 minutes until wilted and slightly golden brown. Stir in papaya. Season with salt and pepper to taste. Sauté just a few minutes. Remove from heat, transfer to a bowl. Wipe out skillet and return to stove. Heat over medium heat several minutes. Brush lightly with some of remaining oil.

Butter one side of each tortilla. Lay buttered side down in hot skillet. Cover with one-fifth of onion-papaya filling. Sprinkle with 2 tablespoons shredded cheese. Top with second tortilla, buttered side up. When browned on bottom, carefully turn quesadilla over to brown other side. Remove from pan, cut into six wedges and keep warm while preparing the remaining quesadillas. Serve warm with Spicy Tomato Relish.

Note: To prepare ahead of time, make filling and store chilled in an airtight container. Butter tortillas and place 2 buttered sides together, stack, wrap in plastic, and chill. Bring to room temperature before grilling.

❀ *Makes 30 pieces*

Spicy Tomato Relish: Place tomatoes in a large bowl. Add ginger, garlic, and tumeric, stirring to mix. In a skillet, heat oil over medium-high. Add cumin, fenugreek, mustard seeds, and chilies. Roast, stirring, about 30 seconds until they start to pop. Add tomato mixture, reduce heat to medium-low and cook 20 to 25 minutes, stirring often until thickened. Season with salt to taste. Remove from heat. Scrape in bowl, cover, and set aside. Serve at room temperature.

❀ *Makes about 1 cup*

Stilton Cocktail Puffs

INGREDIENTS
4 slices bacon
$1/2$ cup water
4 tablespoons unsalted butter
$1/2$ cup all-purpose flour
2 eggs
1 cup crumbled Stilton
2 green onions, minced
$1/4$ teaspoon black pepper

Heat a small skillet over medium heat. Add bacon and cook until crisp. Remove from pan, drain on paper towel. Let cool and crumble. Heat oven to 425°F. Lightly grease two baking sheets and set aside. Cut butter into pieces. In a small heavy saucepan, combine water and butter. Bring to a boil over high heat. Reduce heat to medium, add the flour all at once, and beat with a wooden spoon until mixture pulls away from the sides of pan and forms a ball. Remove pan from heat.

Add eggs one at a time, beating well after each addition. Stir in Stilton until blended. Add bacon and green onion, season with pepper. Drop rounded teaspoonfuls of batter 2 inches apart on prepared baking sheets. Bake in middle of oven for 15 to 20 minutes until crisp and golden. Serve immediately.

Note: The dough can be made several hours ahead, but do not bake until ready to serve.

❀ *Makes about 3 dozen*

Beverages

Measurements

Fluid Ounces = Volume Measurement
Dry Ounces = Weight Measurement

Liquid Measurement Equivalents (approximate):

1 teaspoon	=	$1/3$ tablespoon	=		=	5 ml
1 tablespoon	=	$1/2$ fluid ounce	=	3 teaspoons	=	15 ml, 15 cc
2 tablespoons	=	1 fluid ounce	=	$1/8$ cup, 6 teaspoons	=	30 ml, 30 cc
$1/4$ cup	=	2 fluid ounces	=	4 tablespoons	=	59 ml
$1/3$ cup	=	$2\,2/3$ fluid ounces	=	5 tablespoons + 1 teaspoon	=	79 ml
$1/2$ cup	=	4 fluid ounces	=	8 tablespoons	=	118 ml
$2/3$ cup	=	$5\,1/3$ fluid ounces	=	10 tablespoons + 2 teaspoons	=	158 ml
$3/4$ cup	=	6 fluid ounces	=	12 tablespoons	=	177 ml
$7/8$ cup	=	7 fluid ounces	=	14 tablespoons	=	207 ml
1 cup	=	8 fluid ounces/ $1/2$ pint	=	16 tablespoons	=	237 ml
2 cups	=	16 fluid ounces/ 1 pint	=	32 tablespoons	=	473 ml
4 cups	=	32 fluid ounces/ 2 pints	=	1 quart	=	946 ml
8 pints	=	1 gallon/ 128 fluid ounces	=	4 quarts	=	3.78 liters
1 liter	=	1.057 quarts	=			1000 ml

Glasses and Tips

Cocktail or Martini Glass
This glass has a triangle-bowl design, a long stem, and is used for a wide range of straight-up (without ice) cocktails, including martinis, manhattans, metropolitans, and gimlets.
Size: 3 - 8 ounces

Highball Glass
A straight-sided glass, used as an elegant way to serve mixed drinks, like those served on the rocks (over ice), shots, and drinks adding mixer to liquor.
Size: 8 - 12 ounces

Old-Fashioned Glass
A short, round, "rocks" glass, suitable for cocktails or liquor served on the rocks, or with a splash.
Size: 8 - 12 ounces

Collins Glass
Similar to a highball glass, only taller. The Collins glass was originally used for the Collins gin drinks, and is now also commonly used for soft drinks, alcohol/juice, and tropical/exotic mixtures such as Mai Tai's.
Size: 12 - 16 ounces

Juice Glass
A short, round glass suitable for small servings straight-up. Commonly used for juice at breakfast.
Size: 5 ounces

Cracked ice: Wrap ice cubes in a clean tea towel and place it on a firm surface. Hit it with a wooden mallet until the ice has broken into small pieces.

Crushed ice: Ice is broken more finely than cracked ice.

Fruited ice rings, decorated, colored and flavored ice cubes are sometimes used to garnish punches and cocktails.

Rule: For large parties you will always need more ice than you have. Make or buy extra in advance.

Bitter Bikini

INGREDIENTS
$^3/_4$ cup crushed ice
1 $^1/_2$ fluid ounces Campari
1 fluid ounce dry vermouth
$^1/_2$ fluid ounce triple sec

Put ice in a cocktail shaker. Add Campari, dry vermouth, and triple sec. Shake well. Strain into a rocks glass and serve.

Note: Campari, a bright red mid-proof aperitif bearing the name of its inventor Gaspare Campari, has been available since 1860. It has a bitters-like flavor and the bright red color comes from natural carmine.

 Serves 1

Pomegranate Campari

INGREDIENTS
$^1/_2$ cup crushed ice
8 fluid ounces pomegranate juice
1 tablespoon confectioners' sugar
2 to 3 fluid ounces Campari
4 lemon slices

Put ice in a cocktail shaker. Add pomegranate juice, confectioners' sugar, and Campari. Shake well. Pour into highball glasses. Garnish with lemon slices and serve.

Serves 2

Mango Mimosa

INGREDIENTS
Cracked ice
12 fluid ounces mango nectar
1 fluid ounce grenadine
1 fluid ounce fresh lemon juice
1 bottle (750 ml) chilled champagne

Fill a cocktail shaker with ice. Add mango nectar, grenadine, and lemon juice and shake well. Strain into four fluted glasses. Top with champagne and serve. Do not stir.

Can be made with passion fruit, peach, or apricot nectar.

Note: The process of fermentation is used to convert the sugar in liquids into alcohol aided by yeast. Control of the degree of fermentation determines the sweetness or dryness of wines. The terms "dry" and "sweet" are opposites and there are many degrees between these. Champagne can be dry, extra dry and brut, which is extremely dry.

Serves 4

May Sparkle

INGREDIENTS
20 fluid ounces frozen strawberry
daiquiri mix
12 fluid ounces frozen lilikoi concentrate
12 fluid ounces frozen limeade
concentrate
32 fluid ounces water
Lots of ice made from lemonade
1 orange, thinly sliced
2 limes, thinly sliced
1 pint fresh strawberries, halved
2 bottles (750 ml) chilled
brut champagne

Stir daiquiri mix, lilikoi and limeade concentrates, and water in a large pitcher. Place 3 to 4 ice cubes in each Collins type glass. Barely cover ice with juice mix. Layer in orange and lime slices and a few strawberries. Top off with champagne and serve.

Note: Can be made using seasonal ingredients or with club soda or ginger ale instead of champagne.

Serves 8 to 10

Pomegranate Royale

INGREDIENTS
4 fluid ounces pomegranate juice
1 bottle (750 ml) well chilled
  brut champagne
Pomegranate seeds

Divide pomegranate juice equally among four champagne flutes. Fill with champagne. Garnish with a few pomegranate seeds and serve.

❦ Serves 4

Raspberry Bellini

INGREDIENTS
12 ounces frozen raspberries,
  partially thawed
2 tablespoons granulated sugar
1 bottle (750-ml) chilled
  brut champagne

Set up six flute style champagne glasses. Blend the raspberries and sugar in a food processor or blender until pureed. For a finer drink, strain the raspberry puree through a sieve and discard seeds. Place 1 to 2 tablespoons of puree in each flute. Fill with chilled champagne and serve. Do not stir.

❦ Serves 4 to 6

Beachcomber

INGREDIENTS
1 fluid ounce gin
6 fluid ounces pineapple juice
1 fluid ounce Triple Sec
3/4 cup ice
Fresh pineapple chunk

Combine gin, pineapple juice, Triple Sec, and ice in a blender. Puree until smooth. Pour into a cocktail glass. Garnish with pineapple and serve.

❦ Serves 1

Evening Jasmine

INGREDIENTS
Cracked ice
1 1/2 fluid ounces gin
3/4 fluid ounce Cointreau
3/4 fluid ounce fresh lemon juice
1/4 fluid ounce Campari

Fill cocktail shaker with ice. Add gin, Cointreau, lemon juice, and Campari. Shake well. Strain into a chilled cocktail glass and serve.

Serves 1

Pink Plumeria

INGREDIENTS
1 cup cracked ice
7 1/2 fluid ounces dry London-type gin
Juice of 2 limes
1 tablespoon granulated sugar
Grenadine
Fresh pineapple chunks
Bamboo skewers

Put ice in cocktail shaker. Add gin, lime juice, and sugar. Shake vigorously for 15 seconds. Strain into chilled cocktail glasses. Add 6 drops of grenadine to each. Skewer pineapple chunks on bamboo. Garnish drinks with pineapple and serve.

Serves 4

Grapefruit Rickey

INGREDIENTS
Ice
2 fluid ounces light rum
2 fluid ounces fresh pink grapefruit juice
1 fluid ounce ginger syrup
Juise of $1/2$ lime
Soda water

GINGER SYRUP
$1/2$ cup granulated sugar
8 fluid ounces water
$1/2$ cup grated fresh ginger root

Fill a highball glass with ice. Add rum, pink grapefruit juice, ginger syrup, and lime juice. Stir to blend. Top with soda water and serve.

Ginger syrup: Combine sugar, water, and ginger in a small saucepan. Bring to a boil over high heat. Remove from heat and let cool. Strain into clean glass bottle or jar with lid. Cover and store in refrigerator.

Serves 1

Mango Daiquiri

INGREDIENTS
1 cup chopped peeled fresh ripe mango
3 fluid ounces dark rum
1 tablespoon granulated sugar
1 fluid ounce Rose's lime juice
2 cups cracked ice

Combine mango with rum, sugar, lime juice, and cracked ice in a blender. Puree, scraping down the sides occasionally, until mixture is smooth and frozen. Pour into two stemmed cocktail glasses and serve.

Serves 2

Pink Ladies

INGREDIENTS
6 fluid ounces frozen
    limeade concentrate
12 fluid ounces light rum
1/4 fluid ounce grenadine
4 cups crushed ice

Combine limeade concentrate, rum, and grenadine in pitcher. Mix well and chill. Just before serving, add crushed ice. Stir 30 to 60 seconds, depending on desired strength of cocktail. Strain into cocktail glasses and serve. Can be served in glasses filled with the crushed ice to make cocktails less strong.

The Royal Hawaiian Hotel on Waikiki Beach is affectionately known as The Pink Lady and this drink pays tribute to that place.

🌴 Serves 6

Sunset Cocktail

INGREDIENTS
Cracked ice
2 fluid ounces light rum
1 fluid ounce fresh lemon juice
3 to 4 dashes grenadine
Tonic water
Thin slice of fresh lemon

Fill a cocktail shaker with ice. Add rum, lemon juice, and grenadine. Shake, then strain into a highball glass filled with ice. Top with tonic water. Serve garnished with fresh lemon slice.

🌴 Serves 1

Frozen Ginger Margarita

INGREDIENTS
Granulated sugar
6 fluid ounces frozen limeade concentrate
4 cups crushed ice
12 fluid ounces ginger ale
6 fluid ounces tequila
2 fluid ounces Triple Sec
1 tablespoon grated fresh ginger root

Moisten edges of margarita glasses. Dip in sugar and set aside. Combine limeade concentrate, ice, ginger ale, tequila, Triple Sec, and ginger in a blender. Puree until smooth. Pour into prepared glasses and serve.

Note: Fresh ginger adds a slightly spicy flavor to the classic margarita.

🌱 *Serves 4*

Li Hing Mui Margarita

INGREDIENTS
Li hing mui powder
Granulated sugar
1 lime, cut into wedges
2 fluid ounces fresh lime juice
4 fluid ounces Triple Sec
8 fluid ounces tequila
3 cups ice cubes

Mix equal parts of li hing mui powder with sugar. Run one lime wedge around edges of margarita glasses to moisten. Dip glass edges in li hing mui mixture and set aside. Combine lime juice, Triple Sec, tequila, and ice in blender and puree until smooth. Fill prepared glasses. Garnish with lime and serve.

An alternate method is to combine lime juice, Triple Sec, tequila, and crushed ice in shaker and shake vigorously for 30 seconds before pouring into rimmed glasses.

🌱 *Serves 4*

Limoncello

INGREDIENTS
10 large limes or lemons
1 (750-ml) bottle 100-proof vodka
2 1/2 cups granulated sugar
20 fluid ounces water

Remove colored part of peel from limes in long strips using a vegetable peeler. (The white pith makes this bitter.) Reserve limes for another use. Place peels in a 1-quart jar with lid. Pour in vodka to cover. Seal with lid. Steep lime peels in vodka for one week at room temperature.

In a large saucepan over medium heat, stir together sugar and water until sugar dissolves and liquid is hot. Remove from heat and cool completely. Add infused vodka, stirring to mix. Strain into sterilized bottles, pressing on the peels to extract as much liquid as possible. Seal the bottles. Refrigerate until cold, at least 4 hours. This can be stored up to one month. Serve over ice.

Makes 1 liter

Limoncello Spritzer

INGREDIENTS
Ice cubes
1 cup fresh mint
8 fluid ounces Limoncello
8 fluid ounces club soda

Fill four Collins glasses halfway with ice. Divide mint among the glasses. Using the handle of a wooden spoon, coarsely crush the mint leaves into the ice. Pour 2 fluid ounces Limoncello into each glass. Add a splash of club soda and serve.

Serves 4

Cranberry Martini

INGREDIENTS
$^1/_2$ cup crushed ice
1 fluid ounce vodka or gin
$^1/_2$ fluid ounce Triple Sec or Cointreau
$^1/_2$ fluid ounce Rose's Lime Juice
2 to 4 fluid ounces cranberry juice
1 wedge of lime

Put ice in a cocktail shaker. Add vodka, Triple Sec, lime juice, and cranberry juice. Shake well and strain into a cocktail glass. Cut across lime wedge to form slit and place lime on rim of glass for garnish. Serve.

 Serves 1

Mango Martini

INGREDIENTS
2 cups crushed ice
7 fluid ounces vodka
$^1/_4$ fluid ounce vermouth
1 cup diced fresh ripe mango
Blueberries or raspberries

Combine ice, vodka, vermouth, and mango in a blender. Pulse to blend until smooth. Pour into cocktail glasses, garnish with berries, and serve.

 Serves 4

Sangria Blanca

INGREDIENTS

2 ripe mangoes, peeled, seeded, and
  cut into $1/2$-inch thick slices
1 small pineapple, peeled, quartered,
  and thinly sliced
2 limes, thinly sliced
1 bottle (750 ml) chilled Pinot Gris
8 fluid ounces brandy
Ice cubes made from lilikoi juice

Layer mango, pineapple, and three-quarters of the lime slices in a large pitcher. Pour in wine and brandy. Chill until cold, about 3 hours. Pour into glasses. Add a few lilikoi ice cubes. Garnish with the reserved lime slices and serve.

Note: Use a crisp dry white wine, avoid Chardonnay.

Serves 4 to 6

Chai

INGREDIENTS
20 fluid ounces water
2-inch piece cinnamon stick
8 whole cloves
1/2-inch piece fresh ginger root
3 black peppercorns
8 cardamom pods
8 fluid ounces half-and-half
3 tablespoons granulated sugar
1 heaping tablespoon loose black tea

In a medium saucepan combine water, cinnamon, cloves, ginger, and peppercorns. Using the flat side of large knife, crush cardamom pods to expose seeds. Add to the saucepan and bring to a boil over medium-high heat. Cover, turn heat to low, and simmer for 10 to 15 minutes. Stir in the half-and-half and sugar and bring back to a simmer. Add tea leaves, cover, and turn off heat. Let steep for 5 minutes. Strain into two cups and serve immediately.

Note: It takes time to make chai. Taking short cuts will not result in a quality flavor. The idea is to evaporate water from the mixture while infusing the flavor of the spices.

Serves 2

Ginger Tea

INGREDIENTS
52 fluid ounces water
$1/3$ to $1/2$ cup thinly sliced fresh ginger
4 to 8 fluid ounces honey or
   $1/2$ to 1 cup granulated sugar

In a medium saucepan, combine water and ginger. Bring to a boil over medium heat. Reduce heat to low, cover, and simmer 30 minutes. Strain into teapot. Discard ginger, sweeten to taste with honey, and serve hot.

 Serves 4

Hibiscus Infusion

INGREDIENTS
4 tablespoons spearmint leaves
3 tablespoons lemongrass
2 tablespoons hibiscus flowers
1 tablespoon rosehips
1 tablespoon granulated sugar
48 fluid ounces boiling water

Place spearmint, lemongrass, hibiscus flowers and rosehips in a large teapot. Cover with boiling water. Add sugar and let stand 45 minutes to infuse flavors. Strain and serve hot or cold.

 Serves 4

Avocado Shake

INGREDIENTS
1 large ripe avocado
3 fluid ounces sweetened
   condensed milk
3 fluid ounces milk
1 tablespoon smooth peanut butter
1 1/4 cups ice
1 to 2 tablespoons sugar, optional

Peel avocado, remove seed, dice flesh, and place in a blender. Add condensed milk, milk, peanut butter, and ice. Puree until smooth. Adjust sweetness to taste with sugar. Pour into juice glasses and serve cold.

Serves 4

Kafae Yen

INGREDIENTS
48 fluid ounces strongly brewed
   French Roast coffee, cooled
12 to 14 fluid ounces sweetened
   condensed milk
Crushed or cubed ice

In large pitcher, stir together coffee and condensed milk, mixing well. Fill highball glasses with ice. Pour in sweetened coffee and serve.

Serves 4 to 6

Light Sea Breeze

INGREDIENTS
32 fluid ounces chilled cranberry juice
32 fluid ounces chilled grapefruit juice
1/4 cup chopped fresh mint
Ice
Sprigs of fresh mint

In a large pitcher, combine cranberry juice, grapefruit juice, and chopped mint. Let stand 15 minutes in refrigerator to infuse flavors.

Fill highball glasses with ice. Pour in juice, garnish with fresh mint sprigs, and serve.

Serves 8

Masala Cider

INGREDIENTS
64 fluid ounces apple cider
1 cinnamon stick, broken into thirds
3 cardamom pods
4 whole cloves
7 saffron strands
Fresh apple slices

Combine apple cider, cinnamon, cardamom, cloves, and saffron in a large saucepan. Heat over medium heat, stirring occasionally, until cider begins to boil. Reduce heat and simmer for 30 minutes. Strain into mugs. Garnish with apple slices and serve warm.

Serves 6 to 8

Mulled Cherry Cider

INGREDIENTS
1 lemon, thinly sliced
32 fluid ounces cherry juice
16 fluid ounces apple cider
1/3 cup dried cherries
1/4 teaspoon almond extract
2 sticks cinnamon, broken

Cut two lemon slices in half and set aside for garnish.

In a large saucepan, combine cherry juice, apple cider, dried cherries, almond extract, cinnamon sticks, and remaining lemon slices. Simmer over medium heat, partially covered, for 10 minutes until very hot. Remove cinnamon sticks and lemon slices. Pour into mugs, garnish with reserved lemon slices, and serve hot.

Note: Cherry flavored cranberries can be used instead of dried cherries.

Serves 4

Spiced Cranberry Drink

Combine cranberry juice, cinnamon, cloves, and allspice in a large saucepan. Bring to a boil. Reduce heat to medium, add mint, and simmer 5 minutes. Strain and discard cinnamon, cloves, and mint. Pour into mugs, garnish with orange slices, and serve hot.

 Serves 4

INGREDIENTS

1 quart cranberry juice cocktail
2 sticks cinnamon
6 whole cloves
$1/2$ teaspoon ground allspice
3 sprigs fresh mint, or
    2 herbal mint tea bags
1 orange, thinly sliced

Summer Mint Spritzer

Combine sugar and water in a medium saucepan. Bring to a boil over medium-high heat. Continue to boil to evaporate some of the liquid, creating a simple syrup. Remove from heat and carefully stir in lemon juice and zest and orange juice and zest.

Place mint in heatproof pitcher. Pour in hot syrup. Let steep 20 minutes, strain, and refrigerate.

Place one fluid ounce chilled mint syrup in bottom of each tall thin glass. Add 4 to 6 ice cubes per glass and fill with club soda. Garnish with fresh mint and serve.

 *Serves 6 to 8*

INGREDIENTS

$3/4$ cup granulated sugar
8 fluid ounces water
Juice and grated zest of 2 lemons
Juice and grated zest of 1 orange
4 tablespoons minced fresh mint
Ice cubes
64 fluid ounces chilled club soda
Sprigs of fresh mint

Evening

Entrées
Condiments
Grains and Noodles
Vegetables

Tropical Fruit, by Roberta Goodman

Entrees

Entrees

BLT Burgers with Caramelized Onions

CARAMELIZED ONIONS

1 tablespoon olive oil
1 large Maui onion, thinly sliced
6 cloves garlic, crushed
1 tablespoon chili powder
2 tablespoons balsamic vinegar

BURGERS

2 pounds ground chuck
$^1/_3$ cup minced Maui onion
$^1/_4$ cup good red wine
2 teaspoons chili powder
1 teaspoon salt
Vegetable oil
12 slices bacon, cooked
6 soft Kaiser rolls, split
6 Manoa lettuce leaves
6 slices tomato

In a grill with a cover, prepare a medium-high fire. Heat oil in a large skillet over medium-low heat. Add onion and garlic. Cook 20 minutes, stirring occasionally, until onions are very soft and golden brown. Sprinkle with chili powder and vinegar. Cook another 5 to 10 minutes. Remove from heat and set aside.

Place beef in a large bowl. Add minced onion, wine, chili powder, and salt. Mix gently. Shape into six patties. Brush grill with vegetable oil. Place patties on hot grill rack, cover, and cook about 4 minutes. Turn and continue cooking to desired doneness. Wrap cooked bacon in foil. Place on grill to heat through. During final minutes of grilling patties, place rolls, cut side down, on outer edges of grill to toast lightly. Remove rolls from grill. On the bottom of each roll layer lettuce and a slice of tomato. Add grilled beef patty. Top with 2 slices of bacon and caramelized onions. Add bun top and serve.

 Serves 6

Sun-Dried Tomato Beef Burgers

INGREDIENTS
6 ounces Feta, crumbled
$1/4$ cup finely chopped fresh basil
$1/2$ cup chopped oil packed
   sun-dried tomatoes, well drained
2 pounds ground chuck
2 eggs, slightly beaten
1 teaspoon salt
$1/2$ teaspoon black pepper
3 cloves garlic, minced
$1/2$ cup dried Italian bread crumbs
$1/4$ cup freshly grated Parmesan
Vegetable oil
6 pieces foccacia or ciabatta bread, split
Lettuce
Thinly sliced onion, divided into rings

In a grill with cover, prepare a medium-high fire. In a small bowl, mix together Feta, basil, and sun-dried tomatoes. Divide into six equal portions, forming balls. Set aside.

In a large bowl, gently combine beef, eggs, salt, pepper, garlic, bread crumbs, and Parmesan. Do not over mix. Divide into six portions and form into balls. Using thumbs, make indentation in center of each ball and place the Feta mixture into hole. Seal and reshape into ball, compressing lightly. Gently flatten to form patty, being careful not to expose filling.

When the fire is ready, brush the grill rack with vegetable oil. Place patties on grill, cover, and cook for 4 minutes, until bottoms are brown. Turn over patties and cook an additional 4 minutes, or to desired doneness. During the last few minutes of grilling, place focaccia, cut side down, on outer edges of grill to lightly toast. Place bread bottoms on individual plates. Add patties. Garnish with lettuce and onion rings. Top with bread and serve.

 Serves 6

Thai Beef Salad

DRESSING
1/3 cup fresh lime juice
2 tablespoons packed brown sugar
1 tablespoon water
1 tablespoon fish sauce
2 to 4 cloves garlic, minced
1/4 teaspoon chili paste
1 stalk lemongrass

SALAD
1 pound flank steak
Salt and black pepper
1 head romaine lettuce
1 pint cherry tomatoes, halved
1 medium red onion, thinly sliced
1/4 cup coarsely chopped fresh mint
1/4 cup chopped cilantro

Combine lime juice, sugar, water, fish sauce, garlic, and chili paste in a bowl with a whisk, blending well. Thinly slice lemongrass and stir into dressing. Set aside.

Prepare grill or broiler. Sprinkle both sides of steak with a little salt and pepper. Place on hot grill rack. Cook 6 minutes per side. Remove from heat and let stand 10 minutes.

Wash and pat dry lettuce. Tear into bite-sized pieces. Place in a large salad bowl. Add tomatoes. Separate onion slices into rings and scatter across salad. Cut steak diagonally across the grain into thin slices. Cut slices into 2-inch pieces and add to salad. Sprinkle with mint and cilantro. Add dressing, toss to coat, and serve.

To make ahead, prepare dressing; cook and slice meat; wash and pat dry lettuce; halve tomatoes; slice onion; chop herbs; but store everything separately. Assemble just before serving.

 Serves 4

Steak and Peach Salad with Blue Cheese Dressing

BLUE CHEESE DRESSING
4 ounces blue cheese, crumbled
³/4 cup sour cream
¹/4 cup raspberry vinegar
1 tablespoon minced chives
Pinch cayenne pepper

STEAK
2 pounds London Broil
Salt and black pepper
¹/2 cup olive oil
1 teaspoon minced fresh rosemary
1 teaspoon soy sauce
1 teaspoon Worcestershire sauce
1 tablespoon honey

SALAD
4 peaches, halved and pitted
4 cups mesclun greens
2 tablespoons chopped fresh chives
3 tablespoons thinly sliced fresh basil
1 tablespoon chopped fresh tarragon
4 ounces blue cheese, crumbled
Black pepper

In a small bowl, beat half of blue cheese with sour cream. Stir in vinegar, chives, and cayenne. Cover and chill. Pat dry the steak. Season with salt and pepper and place in a shallow glass pan. In a large measuring cup, combine oil, rosemary, soy sauce, Worcestershire, and honey. Use a hand blender or whisk to mix until smooth. Pour all but 2 tablespoons over steak, cover, and refrigerate for several hours. Turn steak occasionally to coat both sides. Allow to come to room temperature before grilling. Place a ridged grill pan over moderately high heat until very hot. Season steak again with salt and pepper. Grill about 5 minutes per side for medium rare. Remove steak to cutting board and let stand 10 minutes before cutting into ¹/4-inch slices.

Brush cut side of the peaches with the reserved 2 tablespoons rosemary-oil mixture. Place cut side down on the hot grill pan for 3 minutes. Turn over and grill the other side for 1 minute to soften. Remove and cut peaches into fanned slices. Toss the greens with chives, basil, and tarragon. Divide among plates. Layer with steak and peach slices. Drizzle with blue cheese dressing, garnish with crumbled blue cheese. Season with black pepper to taste and serve.

Note: Salad can be served with just raspberry vinaigrette for those who don't care for blue cheese.

❀ *Serves 6 to 8*

Beef with Scallions and Tomatoes

INGREDIENTS
1 pound flank steak, very cold
2 tablespoons dry sherry
2 tablespoons soy sauce
2 teaspoons sesame oil
1 1/2 teaspoons cornstarch
1 teaspoon granulated sugar
1 bunch scallions
1 pound ripe Roma tomatoes
1 tablespoon chili oil
2-inch piece fresh ginger root, grated
1 tablespoon hoisin sauce
1 tablespoon water

Cut the beef against the grain into thin strips about 2 inches long by
1/4-inch thick. In a large bowl, whisk together sherry, soy sauce,
sesame oil, cornstarch, and sugar. Add the beef, mix well, and set aside.
Cut scallion green tops into 1-inch pieces and whites into 2-inch
pieces. Keep separate. Cut tomatoes into eighths and set aside. Heat a
large skillet or wok over medium-high heat. Add chili oil. When hot,
add scallion whites and beef to skillet. Spread in single layer, and cook
about 1 minute, without stirring, until well-browned on the bottom
and still pink inside. Transfer to a bowl. It is essential to only partially
cook the meat at this stage, it will finish cooking later in the sauce.

Return skillet to heat. Add ginger and cook, stirring, until fragrant,
30 seconds to 1 minute. Add scallion greens and tomatoes to hot
skillet and cook until tomato skin begins to wrinkle, about 1 minute.
Mix hoisin sauce with water. Return the beef and any collected juice
to skillet. Add hoisin and cook, stirring, until thick, about 30 seconds.
Adjust seasoning to taste. Transfer to a serving platter. Serve with rice.

Note: Slicing meat thinly can sometimes be difficult. To make slicing
easier, chill meat in the freezer until firm but not frozen.

Young ginger has a pale golden skin and a bright, fresh flavor that isn't
as assertive as an older piece.

Serves 4

Filet Mignon with Avocado Salsa

GREEN SAUCE
4 cloves garlic, minced
1/2 jalapeno pepper, minced
Juice of 1/2 lime
3 tablespoons red wine vinegar
1/2 cup olive oil
1/2 cup minced parsley
1/2 cup minced cilantro
1/2 teaspoon kosher salt

AVOCADO SALSA
1 cup celery, diced
2 avocados, peeled and diced
1/2 red onion, thinly sliced
1 cup red grape tomatoes, halved

FILET
2 filet mignon beef steaks
Kosher salt and coarse black pepper
2 tablespoons olive oil

Combine garlic, jalapeno, and lime juice in a small non-reactive bowl. Whisk in vinegar and oil. Stir in parsley, cilantro, and salt. Pour half of green sauce into a medium bowl. Cover the remaining half and set aside. Place celery, avocado, red onion, and grape tomatoes into bowl with Green Sauce. Toss gently to coat. Set salsa aside.

Season filet mignon with salt and pepper. Heat oil in a heavy skillet over medium-high heat until almost smoking. Add steaks and pan-sear for 2 minutes per side to form a crust. Place on warmed serving dish. Add a large spoonful of Avocado Salsa to side of each steak. Drizzle with some of the reserved Green Sauce. Serve.

Note: The main difference between salts is in their texture. Table salt, from underground mines, has fine granules that dissolve quickly, making it great for baking. Sea salt, recovered from evaporated seawater, can be found in both fine and coarse forms. It has a slightly briny flavor. Kosher salt, from either source, and rock salt, from evaporated salty water, are both coarse grained and add crunch. The large surface areas of the kosher salt crystals can absorb more moisture than other forms of salt. This salt is excellent for curing meats. It is used to make meat kosher, but the salt itself is not kosher. The Torah prohibits consumption of any blood so kosher meat must be slaughtered and prepared in a specific manner. A common way of removing the final traces of blood is to soak and salt the meat.

Serves 2

Beef with Asian Spices

SAUCE
1 cup mayonnaise
¹/2 cup sour cream
2-inch piece fresh ginger root, grated
1 clove garlic, passed through press
2 teaspoons sesame oil
1 tablespoon rice vinegar
5 to 6 sprigs fresh cilantro, minced

ROAST
2 tablespoons Szechwan peppercorns
1 tablespoon anise seeds
4 teaspoons coarse salt
1 teaspoon Chinese five-spice powder
1 teaspoon ground ginger
4 to 5-pound beef tenderloin roast
4 tablespoons vegetable oil, divided
Snipped fresh chives
Tarragon sprigs

Heat oven to 425°F. Stir together mayonnaise and sour cream. Add ginger, garlic, sesame oil, and vinegar, mixing well. Add cilantro and whisk together about 1 minute. Cover and refrigerate.

Heat a large heavy skillet over medium heat. Add peppercorns and anise seeds. Toast, stirring, until fragrant, about 1 minute. Remove from heat. Finely grind in an electric coffee/spice grinder or with a mortar and pestle. Sift mixture through a coarse sieve into a bowl and stir in salt, five-spice powder, and ginger.

Trim fat from roast. Tie roast with string to help keep shape. Sprinkle spice mix all over, pressing to adhere. Heat 2 tablespoons oil in a large skillet with over medium-high heat until just smoking. Add beef and brown on all sides, about 1 minute per side. Spread remaining oil in a roasting pan. Transfer seared meat to prepared pan. Roast in middle of oven 45 minutes, or until a thermometer inserted diagonally 2 inches into center registers 120°F.

Remove from oven. Let beef stand in pan on wire rack for 25 minutes. Beef will continue to cook as it stands, reaching 130° (medium-rare). Discard string and slice beef. Arrange on serving platter. Drizzle sauce down middle of slices. Garnish with chives and tarragon. Serve at room temperature with additional sauce on the side.

Serves 6 to 8

Stove Top Roast

INGREDIENTS

2 1/2 to 3 pound rump or round roast
1 tablespoon olive oil
8 cloves garlic, sliced
2 large onions, quartered
Salt and black pepper
2 tablespoon brandy
1/2 cup cream
Sprigs of fresh parsley

Rinse meat and pat dry. Heat oil in a heavy pot over medium-low heat. Add beef roast, garlic, and onions. Cook uncovered about 40 minutes, turning meat every 7 to 10 minutes to brown evenly and stirring onions occasionally. For a more well done roast, cook another 10 minutes. Season with salt and pepper to taste. Remove roast from pan and let rest on cutting board 5 to 10 minutes. Add brandy to onions in pot, stirring well. Turn off heat. Pour in cream and stir to mix well. Adjust seasonings to taste. Set aside.

Thinly slice roast and arrange on serving platter. Top with onion sauce. Garnish with fresh parsley and serve.

Note: Rather than roasting the meat in the oven, this is cooked in a heavy pot on the stove which requires a careful eye. Be sure to turn every 10 minutes so it will cook evenly.

 *Serves 6 to 8*

Short Ribs

INGREDIENTS

5 pounds beef or pork short ribs
1/2 cup all-purpose flour
2 teaspoons salt
1/2 to 1 teaspoon black pepper
2 large onions, thinly sliced
3/4 cup ketchup
2 tablespoons vinegar
2 tablespoons Worcestershire sauce
4 tablespoons soy sauce
1/2 cup granulated or packed
   brown sugar
3/4 cup water

Heat oven to 350°F. Cut ribs into 3 to 5-inch pieces. Mix flour, salt, and pepper in a shallow dish. Roll ribs in seasoned flour. Arrange in a large roasting pan. Spread onion slices over ribs. In a bowl, whisk together ketchup, vinegar, Worcestershire, soy sauce, sugar, and water. Pour over ribs. Cover with foil and bake for 3 hours until tender. Remove foil the last 30 minutes to brown meat. Remove from oven. Place on serving platter with sauce. Serve.

Note: Great with steamed rice.

 *Serves 6 to 8*

Beef Stew

INGREDIENTS

2 1/2 to 3 pound boneless
   beef chuck roast
3 tablespoons all-purpose flour
1 teaspoon ground ginger
1/2 teaspoon cracked black pepper
2 tablespoons olive oil
4 cups beef broth. divided
24 boiling onions, trimmed
   and peeled
1 pound baby carrots
1 cup pitted prunes
1/2 teaspoon salt
1/4 cup honey
1/4 cup blanched sliced almonds
1/4 cup chopped fresh parsley

Cut beef into 1 1/2-inch cubes. In a large re-sealable plastic bag, combine flour, ginger, and pepper, mixing well. Add beef. Shake to coat. Heat oil in a large heavy ovenproof pot over medium heat. Cook beef in batches 6 to 8 minutes until browned, setting cooked beef aside. When all is browned, return to pot. Add 2 cups broth.

Stove top method: Add onions. Reduce heat to low, cover, and simmer 2 hours, stirring occasionally, adding more broth as needed. Add carrots, prunes, salt, honey, and remaining broth. Cook another 20 minutes until carrots are tender and liquid has thickened. Heat a small skillet over medium heat. Add almonds and toast 5 to 8 minutes until lightly browned. Combine almonds and parsley. Sprinkle over stew. Serve.

Oven method: Add onions and carrots. Cover with foil, then lid. Bake in 400°F oven 1 1/2 to 2 hours, until beef is almost tender. Add prunes, and 1/2 cup broth if meat seems dry. Bake another 30 minutes. Remove from oven. Transfer beef, onions, carrots, and prunes to a serving bowl, using slotted spoon. Bring pan juices to a boil over medium heat. Add remaining broth, salt, and honey. Cook 10 minutes to thicken slightly, stirring occasionally to loosen any browned bits from bottom of the pot. Pour sauce over beef mixture. Combine almonds and parsley. Sprinkle over stew and serve.

Serves 4

Rosemary Lamb Chops

LAMB CHOPS
$1/2$ teaspoon white pepper
2 cloves garlic, passed through press
2 teaspoon minced fresh rosemary
8 bone-in lamb loin chops

CHERRY SAUCE
1 teaspoon olive oil
1 tablespoon butter
2 large shallots, minced
2 cloves garlic, minced
1 teaspoon grated fresh ginger root
1 teaspoon minced fresh rosemary
$1/4$ teaspoon salt
$1/2$ teaspoon white pepper
1 cup cherry jam
$1/2$ cup chopped dried cherries
2 tablespoons balsamic vinegar

In a small bowl, combine pepper, garlic, and rosemary. Rub over lamb chops. Cover and chill up to 8 hours.

In a small saucepan, heat oil and butter over medium heat. Add shallots, garlic, ginger, and rosemary and sauté until shallots are tender. Stir in salt, pepper, jam, cherries, and vinegar. Heat through. Set aside.

Heat grill. Add meat and cook 6 to 8 minutes per side, to desired doneness. Place on serving platter. Top with a little Cherry Sauce. Serve with additional sauce on the side.

Note: Fresh cherries can be used in the sauce when in season.

Serves 4

Spiced Pork with Molasses Butter

INGREDIENTS
3 tablespoons butter
2 tablespoons molasses
2 teaspoons lemon juice
6 thick boneless center loin pork chops
2 tablespoons coarse black pepper

Heat a frying or grill pan over medium-high heat. Blend butter, molasses, and lemon juice in a small bowl. Cover and refrigerate. Rub chops on both sides evenly with pepper. Cook chops 5 to 6 minutes, turn, and cook other side 5 to 6 minutes. Remove to serving platter. Top each chop with equal portions of molasses butter. Serve.

Serves 4 to 6

Hoisin Glazed Grilled Pork Chops

INGREDIENTS
1 teaspoon ground ginger
3/4 teaspoon black pepper
1/2 teaspoon salt
4 thick boneless pork chops
1 clove garlic, crushed
1/2 cup hoisin sauce
1 tablespoon cider vinegar
2 teaspoon grated fresh ginger root
Dash crushed dried red chili
   pepper flakes

Prepare medium-high fire in kettle-style grill. Stir together ginger, black pepper, and salt. Rub on both sides of pork chops. Grill over medium-high heat 5 to 7 minutes per side. Meanwhile, in a small bowl stir together garlic, hoisin sauce, vinegar, ginger, and pepper flakes. Brush on chops during last 1 to 2 minutes of grilling. Remove from heat. Place on serving platter and serve with extra sauce on the side.

Serves 4

Pork Chops with Mango Glaze

INGREDIENTS
1/2 cup red wine vinegar
1/4 cup granulated sugar
1 small hot chili, minced with seeds
1 large mango, peeled and diced
6 thick cut pork chops
6 large cloves garlic
Olive oil
Salt

Place vinegar, sugar, and chili pepper in a small saucepan and bring to a boil over medium-high heat. Reduce heat to medium-low and cook until thickened. Place mango in a blender and puree. Beat into thickened sauce. Pour into a small pitcher and set aside.

Heat grill or grill pan. Slice pork as if to butterfly each chop. Flatten garlic and place one clove into opening of each chop. Brush both sides of meat with oil and season with salt. Grill 4 to 5 minutes on each side for medium doneness. Remove to serving platter. Drizzle liberally with mango glaze. Serve.

🌸 *Serves 4*

Pork with Figs and Balsamic Vinegar

INGREDIENTS

8 thick slices center-cut pork loin
Salt and black pepper
1 1/2 tablespoons olive oil, divided
1 tablespoon butter
1/4 cup minced shallots
3 tablespoons balsamic vinegar, divided
1 cup chicken broth
6 fresh ripe figs, quartered
1/2 cup whipping cream
Sprigs of fresh parsley

Heat oven to 200°F. Sprinkle pork with salt and pepper. Heat 1 tablespoon oil in a heavy large skillet over medium-high heat. Add four pork slices and sauté until brown, 2 minutes per side. Arrange pork on serving platter. Add remaining 1/2 tablespoon oil to skillet. Sauté remaining four pork slices. Place serving platter of pork in oven to keep warm.

Melt butter in same skillet over medium-high heat. Add shallots and sauté until tender, about 2 minutes. Add 2 tablespoons vinegar. Simmer until vinegar evaporates, scraping up any browned bits on bottom of skillet, about 1 minute. Add chicken broth. Simmer until mixture is reduced by half, about 5 minutes. Add figs and whipping cream. Simmer until sauce thickens slightly, about 4 minutes. Add remaining 1 tablespoon vinegar and any accumulated juices from pork in oven. Simmer until sauce thickens enough to coat spoon, about 2 minutes longer. Season sauce with salt and pepper to taste. Spoon sauce over pork slices. Garnish with parsley. Serve.

 Serves 4

Vietnamese Style Grilled Pork

INGREDIENTS
1/4 cup granulated sugar
1 cup water, divided
2 large shallots, minced
2 tablespoons vegetable oil
2 teaspoons Nuoc Nam (fish sauce)
2 teaspoons soy sauce
Pinch salt
2 1/2 pound pork loin,
   cut into 1/4-inch thick slices

In a small saucepan, bring sugar and $1/2$ cup water to a boil over medium heat, stirring occasionally. Reduce heat and simmer, stirring occasionally, until the sauce turns deep brown, about 15 minutes. Meanwhile, heat remaining $1/2$ cup water in a small pan over high heat and bring to a boil, reduce heat to low and keep hot. When sauce reaches the desired color, stir in 4 to 5 tablespoons of hot water carefully as the hot caramel may splatter. Add enough water to make sauce thick enough to coat the back of a spoon. Set caramel sauce aside to cool.

Combine shallots, oil, fish sauce, soy sauce, salt, and caramel sauce, stirring to blend. Add pork loin to sauce. Cover and marinate 20 minutes. Heat grill or broiler. Place pork on grill and cook just until done, about 2 minutes on each side. Arrange on serving platter. Serve.

Note: The caramel is the secret to this dish.

Serves 6

Roasted Pork with Raspberry Chili Sauce

RASPBERRY CHILI SAUCE
2 tablespoons olive oil, divided
1 small onion, diced
4 cloves garlic, minced
1 teaspoon ground chipotle powder
2 cups raspberries
1/2 cup raspberry vinegar
1/2 cup granulated sugar
1/2 teaspoon salt

ROAST
2 1/2 to 3 1/2 pound boneless pork loin
1 tablespoon kosher salt
2 teaspoons black pepper
8 large cloves garlic, sliced
1 tablespoon chopped fresh rosemary
1 tablespoon chopped fresh sage
1 tablespoon chopped fresh thyme
Olive oil
1 bunch watercress

Heat 1 tablespoon oil in a medium saucepan over medium-high heat. Add onion and garlic. Sauté, stirring, until soft and slightly caramelized, about 6 minutes. Stir in chipotle powder and cook for 1 minute. Add raspberries and cook 2 to 3 minutes. Add vinegar and stir to deglaze the pan. Add sugar and salt. Bring to a boil, reduce heat to medium-low and simmer until thickened and reduced by half, about 10 minutes. Remove from heat and set aside. For a finer sauce, strain through a fine mesh sieve pressing on the solids with the back of a spoon to extract as much liquid as possible. Discard solids. Set aside.

Heat oven to 500°F. Oil bottom of a roasting pan with the remaining tablespoon oil. Season pork loin with salt and pepper. Put garlic in a food processor with rosemary, sage, and thyme. Process until smooth. Scrape into a small bowl and add enough oil to make a paste. Carefully rub the garlic-herb mixture over the pork loin. Place in oven and roast 40 to 45 minutes. Spread a few tablespoons of Raspberry Chili Sauce evenly over meat and roast another 5 minutes. Remove from the oven and tent with aluminum foil to keep warm. Let rest for 10 minutes before carving. Trim, wash, and pat dry watercress. Place on large platter. Slice the pork loin and place on watercress. Drizzle with remaining sauce. Serve.

Serves 6 to 8

Black Bean Pork Roast with Corn Relish

Corn Relish

3 $1/2$ to 4 cups corn kernels
3 tablespoons lime juice
1 tablespoon olive oil
1 teaspoon grated lime zest
2 cloves garlic, minced
1 jalapeno pepper, minced
1 teaspoon ground cumin
$1/4$ teaspoon salt
$1/2$ cup chopped cilantro
15 ounces canned black beans, drained

Roast

$1/3$ cup black bean garlic sauce
3 cloves garlic, minced
1 $1/2$ tablespoons soy sauce
1 $1/2$ tablespoons sesame oil
1 tablespoon fresh lime juice
1 tablespoon minced fresh ginger root
2 $1/2$ pounds boneless pork loin
4 baby bok choy, halved lengthwise
2 tablespoons chopped cilantro
4 lime wedges

Place corn in a large glass or plastic bowl. In a small glass bowl, combine lime juice, oil, lime zest, garlic, jalapeno, cumin, salt, and $1/2$ cup cilantro. Mix well, pour over corn; cover and chill relish at least 2 hours. Just before serving add the drained black beans.

Heat oven to 375°F. Stir together black bean garlic sauce, garlic, soy sauce, sesame oil, lime juice, and ginger in small dish. Set aside 2 tablespoons marinade. Place pork in baking dish and coat with black bean mixture. Place in oven and cook about 65 to 75 minutes, just until pork is cooked through. Let stand 5 minutes, before cutting into $1/4$-inch thick slices.

Heat grill pan over medium-high heat. Brush cut side of bok choy with reserved 2 tablespoons marinade. Grill bok choy until softened and lightly charred, 3 to 5 minutes. Arrange pork roast on serving platter. Garnish with bok choy and cilantro. Serve with Corn Relish and lime wedges.

Serves 6

Teriyaki Pork Skewers

INGREDIENTS

1 tablespoon packed brown sugar
2 teaspoons grated fresh ginger root
3 cloves garlic, passed through press
1 green onion, sliced
2 teaspoons sesame oil
$^1/_2$ cup soy sauce
$^1/_4$ cup dry sherry
2 pounds pork tenderloin
Bamboo skewers

In a medium bowl, stir together sugar, ginger, garlic, green onion, sesame oil, soy sauce, and sherry. Cut pork into 6 x $^1/_2$ x $^1/_8$-inch strips. Add pork to marinade and toss lightly to coat well. Cover and marinate in refrigerate at least 1 hour. Soak bamboo skewers in water for 30 minutes to prevent burning on grill. Drain.

Prepare medium-high fire in grill. Drain pork and discard marinade. Thread pork strips onto skewers. Grill directly over fire, turning to brown evenly, 3 to 5 minutes. Serve.

Serves 4

Glazed Pork Ribs

GLAZE
2 tablespoons olive oil
1 small onion, diced
2 cloves garlic, minced
1 cup apple juice
$1/2$ cup vinegar
$1/2$ teaspoon salt
$1/2$ teaspoon celery seed
$1/2$ teaspoon cayenne pepper
$1/2$ teaspoon black pepper
$2/3$ cup packed dark brown sugar
2 tablespoons honey
4 teaspoons Worcestershire sauce
1 tablespoon liquid smoke
2 $1/2$ cups crushed tomatoes

RIBS
4 pounds pork loin or baby back ribs
2 tablespoons granulated sugar
1 tablespoon garlic powder
1 tablespoon paprika
$1/2$ teaspoon cayenne pepper
2 teaspoons salt
$1/2$ teaspoon black pepper

Heat oil in a large saucepan over medium heat. Add onion and garlic and sauté 5 to 8 minutes until tender. Stir in apple juice, vinegar, salt, celery seed, cayenne, and black pepper. Cook 10 to 15 minutes, stirring occasionally, until liquid is reduced by half. Stir in brown sugar, honey, Worcestershire, and liquid smoke. Add crushed tomatoes, reduce heat, and cook 10 minutes until slightly thickened, stirring occasionally. Set aside.

Heat oven to 425°F. Place ribs, meaty side up, on work surface. Using a sharp knife, separate corner of thin membrane from bone. Using a paper towel, grasp and pull off entire membrane. Combine granulated sugar, garlic powder, paprika, cayenne, salt, and black pepper in a small bowl. Sprinkle two-thirds of the spices over both sides of ribs and rub into meat. Place spiced ribs on rack in roasting pan, meaty side up. Cover with foil or lid. Reduce heat to 325°F and bake 2 hours. Check for tenderness, baste with juices, and sprinkle with a little more spice mix. Cover and cook another 30 minutes. Remove cover, brush with glaze, and cook 15 minutes. Serve with remaining glaze.

❀ Serves 6

Moo Shu Pork Wraps

INGREDIENTS
3 tablespoons soy sauce
1 tablespoon cornstarch
8 pancake wrappers
$1/4$ cup hoisin sauce
1 tablespoon peanut oil
4 ounces portobello mushrooms,
    thinly sliced
2 ribs celery, finely diced
1 medium carrot, shredded
4 scallions, thinly sliced
1 small head Napa cabbage, thinly sliced
2 cups bean sprouts
8 ounces ground pork
$1/4$ cup chopped cilantro

PANCAKE WRAPPERS
3 eggs
$1 1/3$ cups whole milk
$3/4$ cups all-purpose flour
$3/4$ teaspoon salt
5 tablespoons butter, melted, divided

In a small bowl, stir together soy sauce and cornstarch. Set aside. Separate pancake wrappers into four piles of two. Spread about 1 tablespoon hoisin sauce on top wrap, flip to sandwich sauce between wraps. Stack piles together and wrap in plastic. Set aside. These will be heated in microwave prior to serving. If using oven or toaster oven, wrap in foil.

Heat oil in large wok or skillet over medium-high heat. Add all vegetables except sprouts and stir-fry 4 minutes. Stir in bean sprouts, stir-fry another minute, until softened but still crisp. Remove to a bowl. Put wrappers in microwave, heat $1 1/2$ minutes to warm. Wrap in towel upon removal. Set aside. Add pork to wok and stir-fry a few minutes to brown. Add soy sauce mixture and stir until liquids thicken. Return vegetables to wok and mix with pork. Place in a warmed serving bowl. Sprinkle with cilantro. Place warmed wrappers in cloth lined basket. Diners receive one hoisin prepared pair of pancakes at the table to separate, fill with pork mixture, and roll individually to make two wraps.

Note: The trick to stir-frying is to keep the ingredients out of the liquids that accumulate in the bottom of the wok.

Pancake Wrappers: Combine eggs, milk, flour, and salt in a blender and blend on high speed for 1 minute. If batter is lumpy, strain it through a sieve. Cover and allow to rest at room temperature for at least 1 hour. It can also be covered and refrigerated for up to one day. Bring it to room temperature before continuing with recipe.

Whisk 3 tablespoons melted butter into batter. Heat an 8-inch skillet over medium-high heat. Drop a little water in pan. If it sizzles, the pan is ready. Brush skillet with a little melted butter. Using a $1/4$-cup measure, scoop batter and pour into the hot skillet. Immediately pick up the pan and tilt and swirl so batter covers its entire bottom. Pour any excess batter back into the bowl. Loosen edges of thin pancake with a spatula. Quickly flip it over. Cook the other side until lightly golden, about 45 seconds and slide out onto a plate. Cover with waxed paper. Repeat with the remaining batter.

Serves 4

Chorizo Stuffed Chilies

INGREDIENTS

12 to 16 ounces chorizo sausage
4 cloves garlic, minced
$3/4$ teaspoon ground cumin
1 to 2 teaspoons chopped fresh oregano
$1/2$ cup diced celery
$1/2$ pound fresh spinach, rinsed
   and thinly sliced
5 ounces water chestnuts, drained
   and diced
2 cups toasted bread crumbs
2 eggs, beaten
12 fresh Anaheim chilies
1 cup shredded Monterey Jack cheese
Sour cream

Heat oven to 375°F. Heat a large frying pan over medium-high heat. Squeeze sausage from casing into hot pan. Add garlic, cumin, oregano, and celery. Stir often and thoroughly cook sausage, about 8 minutes. Drain off and discard fat. Add spinach to sausage, cover, and remove from heat. Let sit 2 to 3 minutes until spinach is limp. Put into a bowl. Add chestnuts, bread crumbs, and eggs. Mix together. Divide into 12 portions.

Oil a 9 x 13-inch baking pan, set aside. Slit chilies lengthwise and remove seeds. Gently open chili and stuff with a portion of sausage mixture, packing firmly. Lay chili, slit side up, in a single layer in prepared pan. Continue to stuff chilies and place in prepared pan. Sprinkle with cheese. Cover with foil. Bake 40 minutes to heat thoroughly and melt cheese. Serve with dollops of sour cream.

 Serves 6

Sausage with Swiss Chard

INGREDIENTS
12 ounces Italian sausage
4 cloves garlic, minced
1 onion, diced
1 cup diced celery
1/2 cup chopped Italian parsley
1 tablespoon minced fresh basil
1 teaspoon minced fresh sage
1 teaspoon minced fresh rosemary
1 1/2 pounds fresh Swiss chard
Salt and black pepper
3/4 cup shaved Parmesan

Heat a large frying pan over medium heat. Squeeze sausage from casing into pan, discard casing. Add garlic, onion, and celery. Cook, stirring often until lightly browned. Drain off fat. Stir in parsley, basil, sage, and rosemary. Lay chard on top, cover, reduce heat, and steam until chard is a bright green, about 3 minutes. Remove from heat and stir to mix well. Season with salt and pepper to taste. Transfer to serving bowl. Sprinkle with Parmesan and serve.

Note: This dish goes well with the Polenta with Gorgonzola Cream.

Serves 4 to 6

Green Chili Stew

INGREDIENTS

8 Anaheim green chilies
3 tablespoon olive oil
2 large onions, diced
8 cloves garlic, smashed
4 1/2 pounds pork shoulder
7 cups water
2 teaspoons salt
1 1/2 pounds white potatoes

Heat broiler. Set chilies on rack below heating element. As pepper skins become black and blistery, turn using long handled tongs to char on every side. When peppers are blackened, remove and place in a large bowl and cover immediately or place in self-sealing bag and close. Leave for 15 to 20 minutes. Uncover peppers. Remove charred skin and seeds. Dice and set aside.

In a heavy pot or kettle, heat oil over medium heat. Add onions and garlic and sauté a few minutes until softened. Add pork and chilies, stirring to mix. Cook a few minutes. Add water and salt. Reduce heat to low and simmer uncovered, about 2 to 2 1/2 hours until tender, adding more water as necessary to keep pork moist. Peel potatoes and cut into 1-inch pieces. Add to pot, stirring down to cover with liquid, and cook another 30 minutes until tender. Serve hot.

Serves 6 to 8

Baked Macadamia Nut Chicken

INGREDIENTS
3/4 cup chopped macadamia nuts
1/3 cup dry bread crumbs
4 tablespoons butter, melted, divided
1/2 cup all-purpose flour
6 boneless chicken breast halves
1 teaspoon celery salt
1 teaspoon paprika
1 teaspoon curry powder
1/2 teaspoon salt
1/8 teaspoon cayenne pepper
1 1/2 cups heavy or whipping cream
Fresh parsley or edible calendula petals

Heat oven to 350°F. Spread macadamia nuts in a small baking dish. Toast lightly in oven, shaking occasionally. Be sure to keep an eye on the nuts so they don't burn. Remove from oven and mix with bread crumbs and 1 tablespoon of melted butter. Set aside.

Place flour in a shallow bowl or plastic bag. Add chicken pieces, tossing to coat, then arrange in a shallow 3-quart baking dish. In a bowl, mix remaining butter with celery salt, paprika, curry powder, salt, and cayenne. Drizzle over chicken. Pour cream around chicken. Bake uncovered for 45 minutes. Sprinkle macadamia nut mixture over chicken and bake uncovered for 5 to 8 minutes until golden. Garnish with parsley and serve.

❀ *Serves 6*

Chicken and Pine Nuts with Lemon Pasta

INGREDIENTS
12 ounces fresh fettuccine
3/4 pound boneless chicken breasts
2 tablespoons olive oil, divided
4 cloves garlic, passed through press
4 ounces snow peas, julienned
1/4 cup pine nuts, toasted
1/4 cup chopped fresh Italian parsley
1 tablespoon lemon zest
3 tablespoons fresh lemon juice
1 1/2 tablespoons Dijon mustard
Salt and black pepper

Cook pasta in a large pot of boiling salted water until tender but still a little firm to bite. Drain well and transfer to a large bowl. Set aside.

Cut chicken into thin strips. Heat 1 tablespoon oil in a large skillet over medium-high heat. Add garlic and chicken and sauté until cooked and golden, 3 to 5 minutes. Add snow peas and pine nuts and sauté 2 minutes until snow peas are bright green but still crisp. Add to pasta in bowl. Sprinkle with parsley and lemon zest. Whisk together lemon juice and mustard in a small bowl. Pour over pasta-chicken mixture. Toss to coat. Season with salt and pepper to taste.

Note: Can be made up to three hours ahead if kept covered in refrigerator. Bring to room temperature and toss before serving.

❀ *Serves 4 to 6*

Chicken Scaloppini with Artichoke Hearts

INGREDIENTS
4 boneless chicken breasts
Salt and black pepper
1 tablespoon olive oil
1 tablespoon butter
3 cloves garlic, minced
1/4 cup vermouth
Juice and grated zest of 2 lemons
1/2 cup chicken broth
2 tablespoons all-purpose flour
1 1/2 cups half-and-half
1/2 cup grated Parmesan
2 cups chopped marinated
    artichoke hearts
1/2 bunch fresh parsley
Coarse black pepper
Very thin lemon slices

Place chicken breasts between waxed paper or plastic wrap. Pound until thin with meat pounder. Season with salt and pepper. Set aside.

Heat oil and butter in a large, nonstick skillet over medium heat. Add garlic and sauté a few minutes. Add seasoned chicken and sauté until golden on both sides. Remove chicken from pan, arrange in overlapping layers on warmed serving platter, cover to keep warm, and set aside.

Add vermouth, lemon juice, and lemon zest to pan. Stir, scraping the bottom of the pan to loosen any browned bits. Increase heat to medium-high and cook to reduce liquids a bit. Whisk in broth. Whisk together flour and half-and-half then add to hot broth, whisking constantly to keep lumps from forming. Allow the sauce to thicken then season with salt and pepper to taste.

Add the Parmesan and whisk until incorporated. Allow sauce to thicken a little more. Gently stir in artichoke hearts and heat until warmed through. Pour sauce down middle of warm chicken. Garnish with parsley, coarse black pepper, and lemon slices. Serve.

Serves 4

Chicken with Apricot Sauce

INGREDIENTS
2 pounds boneless chicken breast
3 tablespoons olive oil, divided
1 large onion, diced
1 cup chopped dried apricots
1/2 cup apricot jam
2 tablespoons rice vinegar
1/2 cup coarsely chopped pistachio nuts
1/2 cup chopped fresh parsley

Cut chicken into $1/2$-inch thick strips. Set aside.

In a small saucepan, heat 1 tablespoon oil over medium heat. Add onion and sauté until golden. Add apricots, jam, and vinegar, stirring to mix well. Remove from heat and set aside.

In a large frying pan or wok, heat 1 tablespoon oil over medium-high heat. Add half the chicken and sear until golden brown all over and cooked through, about 4 to 5 minutes. Do not over crowd or juices will boil meat and not sear it. Arrange on warmed serving platter. Add remaining oil and sear second batch of chicken. Add to serving plate. Cover with sauce. Sprinkle with pistachios and parsley. Serve.

If made ahead, keep meat and sauce separate. Heat both gently in microwave, then assemble, and serve.

 Serves 6

Chicken with Spinach in Phyllo Cups

INGREDIENTS

$^1/4$ cup walnut pieces or pine nuts
4 tablespoons butter, melted, divided
3 sheets phyllo dough
Salt and black pepper
2 boneless chicken breasts
2 tablespoons olive oil
3 cloves garlic, minced
1 medium onion, thinly sliced
$^1/2$ cup thinly slivered oil packed
   sun-dried tomatoes
1 $^1/2$ pounds spinach, thinly sliced
8 ounces Feta

Heat oven to 375°F. Spread walnuts on a small baking dish. Place in oven and bake about 5 minutes until lightly toasted, being careful not to burn. Remove from dish and set aside. Increase heat to 400°F. Brush six large ramekins or over-sized muffin cups lightly with some of the melted butter. Set aside.

Brush one sheet of phyllo dough with melted butter. Top with second sheet. Brush with butter. Season with salt and pepper. Top with final sheet of phyllo. Cut in half lengthwise, then into thirds making six pieces. Gather up corners of each piece and carefully lay in prepared cups. Allow extra phyllo to create folds and spill over rim of cups. Gently brush inside of pastry cups with remaining butter. Bake until golden, 5 to 8 minutes. Remove from oven. Let cool in pan.

Cut chicken into thin strips and set aside. Heat oil in a skillet over medium heat. Add garlic and onion. Sauté until tender. Add chicken and sauté until cooked through. Season with salt and pepper. Stir in sun-dried tomatoes. Lay spinach on top. Cover and reduce heat. Allow steam to cook spinach just until wilted. Stir to mix well. Remove from heat. Spoon into phyllo cups. Sprinkle with Feta. Garnish with toasted nuts. Serve.

Note: Garbanzo beans (chickpeas) can be substituted for the chicken to make a vegetarian version.

❧ *Serves 6*

Coconut Crusted Chicken Nuggets

INGREDIENTS

1 1/2 pounds skinless,
  boneless chicken breasts
1 teaspoon paprika
1/2 teaspoon ground cumin
1/4 teaspoon ground turmeric
1/4 teaspoon cayenne pepper
3 cloves garlic, passed through press
2 tablespoons lime juice
2 tablespoons dark rum
1 tablespoons packed dark brown sugar
1 cup all-purpose flour
2 teaspoons baking powder
1/2 teaspoon salt
1 cup club soda
Vegetable oil
3 cups shredded coconut

PEANUT SAUCE

2 jalapeno peppers
1 tablespoon peanut oil
1 medium Ewa sweet onion, diced
1 large clove garlic, passed through press
1 large tomato, diced
1/2 cup coconut milk
1 cup chopped peanuts
1/2 teaspoon cracked black pepper

Rinse and pat dry chicken breasts. Cut into 1 1/2 x 1 1/2-inch pieces. Mix together paprika, cumin, turmeric, cayenne, and garlic. Rub onto chicken pieces. Place in a glass bowl and toss with lime juice, rum, and sugar. Cover with plastic wrap and chill for 2 to 6 hours.

In a medium bowl, sift together flour, baking powder, and salt. Whisk in club soda. Let stand for 10 minutes. Remove chicken from marinade. In a deep heavy skillet, heat 1 1/2 inches of oil over medium heat. Place one-third of coconut on shallow plate, replace as needed. Working with a few pieces of chicken at a time, dip into batter, letting the excess drip off. Roll in coconut, pressing firmly to adhere. Place in hot oil, frying in batches about 4 to 5 minutes, until crisp and golden. Drain on paper towels. Serve with Peanut Sauce.

❁ *Serves 6*

Peanut Sauce: Place jalapenos under broiler unit and roast, turning until they start to blister. Remove, let cool, then seed and mince. Heat oil in a heavy skillet over medium heat. Add onion and garlic. Sauté 5 minutes, stirring occasionally. Stir in tomato, jalapeno, and coconut milk. Cook 10 minutes or until soft, stirring frequently. Stir in peanuts and pepper. The sauce can be stored in a covered container in refrigerator up to one week.

Note: Omit coconut milk and serve as a topping on braised greens or as a pureed spread on pita bread.

❁ *Makes about 1 cup*

Thai Yellow Curry

INGREDIENTS
3 stalks lemongrass
3 kaffir lime leaves
2 1/4 pounds pumpkin
2 pounds boneless chicken breast
2 teaspoons peanut oil, divided
1 tablespoon yellow Thai curry paste
14 ounces coconut milk
1 1/2 cups chicken broth
3 tablespoons fish sauce
2 tablespoons granulated sugar
1/2 teaspoon turmeric
Bok choy, thinly sliced
Juice of half to whole lime
Fresh cilantro

Cut lemongrass into 1-inch pieces. Bruise by pressing with side of a large knife. Cut kaffir leaves into thin strips. Peel and cut pumpkin into large bite-sized pieces. Cut chicken into thin strips. Set all aside.

In a large saucepan or casserole over medium heat, heat 1 teaspoon oil with the curry paste until sizzling. With a whisk or wooden spoon, stir in coconut milk until combined. Still stirring, gently add the chicken broth, fish sauce, sugar, lemongrass, lime leaves, and turmeric. Bring to a boil and add pumpkin. Simmer until the pumpkin is tender, about 15 minutes. The curry can be prepared up to this point and left to sit, covered.

Five minutes before serving, return curry sauce to a simmer. Heat remaining oil in a wok or skillet. Add chicken strips and stir-fry until cooked through, about 3 minutes. Add chicken and bok choy to simmering curry. Cook until bok choy is wilted. Add lime juice, stirring to blend. Adjust seasonings to taste. Remove pan from heat and transfer into a large serving bowl. Sprinkle with cilantro. Serve with sticky or jasmine rice.

Note: Most of the standard Thai curries are a combination of herbs and seasonings that are pounded together in a mortar and pestle to form a specific curry paste. The sauce can be either water-based or coconut milk-based. Cooks can make their own paste but most are now available in ready-to-use form in local markets. There are many variations of curry paste. *Gaeng massaman* (*masamam*), *gaeng phanaeng* (*panang*), *gaeng phet* (red), *gaeng leuang* (yellow), and *gaeng phet* or *gaeng kiow wahn* (green curry) are the more popular curries.

Serves 4 to 6

Chicken with Orange Essence

INGREDIENTS

2 pounds boneless chicken thighs
   or breasts
Salt and black pepper
3/4 cup panko flakes
1 1/2 tablespoons olive oil, divided
4 cloves garlic, passed through press
1/4 cup fresh lime juice
1/4 cup fresh orange juice
2 tablespoons white vinegar
1 1/2 tablespoons granulated sugar
2 teaspoons grated lime zest
2 teaspoons grated orange zest
1 small orange, thinly sliced

Wash and pat dry chicken. Rub with salt and pepper. Coat with panko. Heat 1 tablespoon of oil in a skillet over medium heat. Add chicken. Do not overcrowd, cooking may have to be done in batches. Sauté until lightly browned. Turn and continue to sauté until cooked through. Lay chicken in a serving dish. Set aside and keep warm.

Heat remaining oil in a small saucepan. Add garlic and sauté until tender. Add lime juice, orange juice, vinegar, and sugar. Heat over medium, stirring occasionally, until hot and sugar dissolves. Stir in 1 teaspoon each of lime and orange zests. Pour sauce over chicken. Sprinkle with remaining lime and orange zests. Garnish with orange slices. Serve.

Serves 4

Chicken Long Rice

INGREDIENTS
One 3 to 4 pound whole chicken, cut up
6 tablespoons soy sauce, divided
1 tablespoon sesame oil
2 tablespoons minced fresh ginger root
3 cloves garlic, minced
1 1/2 teaspoons granulated sugar
Dash black pepper
1/2 cup water
10 ounces long rice noodles
2 tablespoons vegetable oil
8 ounces mushrooms, sliced
4 green onions, sliced
3 carrots, shredded
Sesame seeds

Heat oven to 350°F. Rinse and lay chicken pieces in a large baking pan. Combine 2 tablespoons soy sauce, sesame oil, ginger, garlic, sugar, and pepper in a small bowl. Pour over chicken. Add water, cover, and bake 1 1/2 hours.

Place long rice noodles in a medium bowl. Add enough cold water to cover and soak for 20 minutes. Drain and set aside.

Heat vegetable oil in a large skillet or wok over medium-high heat. Add mushrooms, green onions, and carrots. Sauté 3 minutes. Remove chicken from oven. Place meat in a deep dish, leaving juices in pan. Add sautéed vegetables, rice noodles and remainder of soy sauce to pan juices, stir to mix. Spoon over chicken. Sprinkle with sesame seeds and serve.

Serves 4 to 6

Pineapple Chicken

INGREDIENTS
1 large ripe fresh pineapple
4 to 6 boneless chicken breasts or thighs
Salt
1 tablespoon vegetable oil
1 tablespoon butter
1 large onion, finely diced
1 small red bell pepper, seeded and thinly sliced
1/2 cup pineapple orange juice concentrate
1/2 cup white wine
2 tablespoon Dijon style mustard
1/2 teaspoon cornstarch
1/2 teaspoon black pepper
1/2 cup chopped fresh basil

Twist crown from pineapple. Cut pineapple in half lengthwise. Carefully cut out pineapple meat, keeping shells intact to use for presentation. Cube pineapple and place in a bowl. Set aside.

Cut chicken into 1-inch pieces. Season with salt and set aside. Heat oil and butter in a large skillet over medium heat. Add onion and sauté until tender. Add chicken and sauté until nicely browned and cooked through. Place in a bowl. Add pineapple to skillet and sauté until lightly browned. Add red pepper to skillet and sauté, stirring occasionally, until softened. Add to chicken in bowl.

Combine juice concentrate, wine, mustard, and cornstarch in skillet. Stir until blended, deglazing pan. Bring to a boil over medium-high heat, stirring occasionally. Cook until thickened. Add sautéed pineapple and chicken. Heat thoroughly. Season with pepper. Mound into pineapple shells. Place on serving platter. Garnish with chopped basil and serve.

Serves 4 to 6

Teriyaki Chicken

INGREDIENTS

5 pounds chicken parts
1 1/2 cups soy sauce
1/2 cup water
1 cup packed brown sugar
1/4 cup honey
6 cloves garlic, passed through press
5-inch piece fresh ginger root
1 bunch green onions, sliced
1/2 bunch cilantro, sliced
2 tablespoons mirin (sweet Japanese
    rice wine), optional
Dash crushed red chili pepper flakes,
    optional

Wash and pat dry chicken. Layer in a large pan. In bowl, stir together soy sauce, water, brown sugar, honey, and garlic. Peel ginger, julienne and add to sauce. Put aside a few green onions for garnish. Add remaining green onions, cilantro, mirin, and chili pepper flakes. Pour over chicken. The chicken can be cooked in four different ways.

• Arrange in single layer in several skillets, cover with sauce, and bring to a boil over medium-high heat. Reduce heat to low and simmer 50 minutes, until done.

• Arrange in single layer in a baking pan, cover with sauce and bake at 375°F about 1 1/2 hours until very tender.

• Place sauce and chicken in a crock pot and cook for 4 to 6 hours until very tender.

• Or, marinate chicken overnight in the sauce, covered, in the refrigerator, and grill over hot coals, using sauce to baste meat until very tender.

Garnish with reserved green onions. Serve.

Note: This is best when marinated overnight. If unable to marinate overnight, omit water and marinate for as long as possible. Sauce is great over steamed rice.

❀ *Serves 1 big family*

Five-Spice Chicken Wings

INGREDIENTS
Vegetable oil
1 ¹/2 teaspoons minced garlic
1 ¹/2 teaspoons Chinese
* five-spice powder*
1 ¹/4 teaspoons salt
1 ¹/2 teaspoons soy sauce
3 pounds chicken wings

Set oven rack at least 8 inches from heating unit. Heat broiler and oil rack of a broiler pan. Stir together garlic, five-spice powder, salt, and soy sauce in a large bowl. Cut off and discard tips from chicken wings, then halve wings at joint. Pat dry and add to spice mixture, tossing to coat. Arrange wings in single layer on prepared rack and broil, turning over once, until browned and cooked through, about 20 minutes total.

Note: In Chinese cooking, it is important to incorporate the principal of the yin and the yang, balancing the heat element of a dish equally with cooling ingredients. Five-spice powder blends not only the pungent with the sweet but includes sour, bitter, and salty encompassing all five of the taste senses.

❀ *Serves 4*

Roasted Chicken with Chili-Sage Glaze

CHICKEN
One 4 to 5 pound whole chicken
8 whole fresh sage leaves
Salt and coarse black pepper
1 cup dry white wine

CHILI-SAGE GLAZE
1 tablespoon butter
3 tablespoons chopped fresh sage
3 large shallots, minced
2 to 3 tablespoons chili powder
1 cup dry white wine
5 tablespoons apple chutney or jelly

Heat oven to 400°F. Remove giblets from chicken cavity and discard. Rinse and place chicken in a roasting pan. Starting at neck end, gently slide fingers between skin and meat to loosen skin. Place 4 whole sage leaves decoratively under skin on each breast. Sprinkle with salt and pepper. Pour in 1 cup wine. Roast 1 hour.

Meanwhile melt butter in a small, heavy saucepan over medium heat. Add chopped sage and shallots and sauté until tender. Add chili powder. Stir in wine and apple chutney. Reduce heat and simmer until glaze is slightly thickened, about 10 minutes. Baste chicken with pan juices, then drizzle on some of the Chili-Sage Glaze. Return to oven. Cook another 30 to 45 minutes until tender, basting every 10 minutes. Remove chicken from oven. Let stand 5 minutes. Transfer to serving platter. Drizzle with remaining glaze. Serve.

❀ *Serves 4 to 6*

Maui Lavender Spiced Cornish Hens

INGREDIENTS

6 Cornish game hens or
   one large roasting chicken
1 cup dry white wine
$^1/4$ cup Cognac or brandy
1 teaspoon Worcestershire sauce
1 teaspoon hot pepper sauce, such
   as Tabasco
2 tablespoons fresh thyme
1 tablespoon dried lavender flowers
1 tablespoon celery salt
1 teaspoon white pepper
3 cloves garlic, minced
Sprigs of fresh thyme and lavender

Rinse and pat dry game hens. Pack in a single layer in a non-reactive deep pan or plastic container. Combine wine, Cognac, Worcestershire, and hot sauce. Pour over hens. Cover and refrigerate at least 6 hours or overnight, turning or basting occasionally.

Heat oven to 425°F. In a spice mill, food processor, or small bowl, combine thyme, lavender, celery salt, pepper, and garlic. Whirl or mash together to blend. Drain hens, discarding marinade. Rub each hen with some of the herb mixture. Arrange in roasting pan. Place in center of oven and bake 1 $^1/2$ hours, basting occasionally (if using large roasting chicken, bake about 2 hours), until juices run clear. Remove from oven, let stand 5 to 10 minutes before serving. Garnish with fresh thyme and lavender.

Note: Lavender is grown in the uplands of Maui along the slopes of Haleakala. Edible lavender flower buds can be ordered from Maui but are also available at natural food stores.

Serves 6

Turkey Cakes

INGREDIENTS
1 pound ground turkey
2 eggs, divided
1 cup soft bread crumbs
$1/4$ cup chopped fresh basil
$1/2$ teaspoon salt
$1/8$ teaspoon black pepper
1 tablespoon water
$3/4$ cup ground walnuts
2 tablespoons chopped parsley
2 tablespoons butter
1 tablespoon oil

WARM TOMATO CHUTNEY
3 large ripe tomatoes
1 tablespoon olive oil
2 teaspoons grated fresh ginger root
1 tablespoon minced garlic
$1/2$ teaspoon cayenne pepper
$1/8$ teaspoon ground cinnamon
$1/4$ cup currants
2 tablespoons apple cider vinegar
$1/2$ teaspoon salt
2 tablespoons packed brown sugar
$1/4$ cup toasted chopped pistachios

In a bowl, combine turkey, 1 egg, bread crumbs, and basil. Add salt and pepper. Shape into four round patties about 1-inch thick. In a shallow bowl, beat remaining egg with water. In another shallow bowl, combine walnuts and parsley. In a large skillet over medium heat, melt butter in oil. One at a time, dip turkey patties into egg wash and coat with ground nuts. Place in hot skillet. Cook 3 to 5 minutes per side until meat is no longer pink. Place on warmed platter. Serve with Warm Tomato Chutney.

🪷 *Serves 4*

Warm Tomato Chutney: Peel and dice tomatoes. Set aside. Heat oil in a small heavy skillet over medium-high heat. Add ginger, garlic, cayenne, and cinnamon. Sauté about 1 minute before adding tomatoes and currants. Cook uncovered 10 to 12 minutes, stirring occasionally, until most of the liquid is evaporated. Stir in vinegar, salt, and sugar. Bring to a boil, reduce heat and simmer until thick, about 8 to 10 minutes. Remove from heat and stir in pistachios. Put into serving dish. Serve warm.

🪷 *Makes about 1 cup*

Bok Choy with Crab

INGREDIENTS
2 tablespoons olive oil, divided
1/4 cup minced basil
3 cloves garlic, minced
2 green tomatoes, diced
1 cup dry white wine
8 baby bok choy
6 ounces crabmeat, cooked
Fresh sprigs of basil
Freshly ground black pepper

Heat 1 tablespoon oil in a deep saucepan over medium-high heat. Add basil, garlic and tomatoes and sauté until tomatoes are tender. Add wine, reduce heat to medium-low and let liquid reduce by half, about 10 minutes. Remove from heat, but keep warm.

Heat remaining tablespoon oil in skillet or wok over high heat. Add bok choy and stir-fry, tossing frequently until tender and bright green in color. Place bok choy in serving dish, place sauce down center, top with crabmeat. Garnish with sprigs of basil and sprinkle of black pepper. Serve.

Serves 4 to 6

Baked Scallops

INGREDIENTS
2 pounds fresh bay scallops
1/2 cup butter
3 cloves garlic, minced
3 tablespoons minced fresh parsley
2 teaspoons minced fresh basil
1 teaspoon salt
1/4 teaspoon black pepper

Heat oven to 350°F. Rinse scallops in cold water. Drain and pat dry with paper towel. Arrange in a single layer on bottom of a shallow baking dish. In small saucepan, heat butter with garlic, parsley, and basil until melted. Pour over scallops. Season with salt and pepper. Place in oven and bake for 15 to 20 minutes until scallops are opaque and tender.

Serves 6

Scallops with Pineapple

INGREDIENTS

1 teaspoon sesame oil
1 tablespoon butter
1 pound fresh sea scallops
2 teaspoons soy sauce
1/8 teaspoon chili powder
1 clove garlic, minced
1 cup diced fresh pineapple
1/3 cup chopped fresh basil
1 teaspoon grated, peeled fresh
    ginger root
1 tablespoon water
1 teaspoon cornstarch
Sprigs of fresh basil
2 cups hot cooked jasmine rice

Heat oil in a nonstick skillet over medium-high heat. Add butter, scallops, soy sauce, chili powder, and garlic. Cook, stirring frequently, for 3 to 4 minutes until scallops are opaque. Gently remove scallops, leaving seasonings. Add pineapple, basil, and ginger to skillet and stir well to combine with seasonings. Stir together water and cornstarch. Add to pineapple mixture, stirring. Bring to a boil and cook until thickened, stirring constantly. Pour into a shallow serving dish. Arrange scallops on top of pineapple. Garnish with sprigs of basil and serve with rice.

Serves 4

Spicy Shrimp

INGREDIENTS

12 thick slices French bread
2 lemons, thinly sliced
3 dozen large shrimp, peeled
1/2 cup butter
4 anchovy fillets, minced
4 cloves garlic, minced
1 teaspoon minced fresh rosemary
2 teaspoons Dijon-style mustard
2 teaspoons Worcestershire sauce
1/2 teaspoons hot pepper sauce, such
    as Tabasco
1 cup diced tomatoes
Sprigs of fresh parsley

Adjust rack to highest position in oven. Heat broiling unit. Arrange bread on a baking sheet. Place under broiler and toast lightly. Remove from oven. Place two pieces of bread on each serving plate.

Layer lemon slices on bottom of a large metal baking pan. Carefully score back of shrimp to butterfly and remove vein. Arrange as a single layer on lemon slices. Melt butter in a saucepan over medium heat. Stir in anchovies, garlic, and rosemary. Sauté a few minutes. Stir in mustard, Worcestershire, hot sauce, and tomatoes, mixing well. Bring to a boil. Remove from heat and pour over shrimp. Place shrimp in hot oven and broil, without turning, until opaque and cooked through, about 5 minutes. Top bread with lemon slices and a scoop of spicy shrimp. Garnish with parsley sprigs. Serve.

Serves 6

Ginger Grilled Shrimp

INGREDIENTS
4 to 6 bamboo skewers
1 1/4 pounds large shrimp
3 tablespoons extra-virgin olive oil,
    plus extra
2 teaspoons grated fresh ginger root
Sea salt
1 large papaya, diced
2 firm ripe yellow or red tomatoes, diced
4 green onions, finely diced
1 to 2 serrano peppers, seeded and diced
2 tablespoons chopped fresh basil
Juice of 2 limes
Fresh basil

Lay bamboo skewers in a shallow dish. Cover with water and let soak until ready to use. Peel shrimp leaving the tails on. Remove vein. Toss shrimp with oil, ginger, and a pinch of salt in a glass or non-reactive bowl. Cover and let stand for at least 15 minutes in the refrigerator. Combine papaya, tomatoes, green onions, peppers, basil, lime juice, and a pinch of salt in mixing bowl. The more pepper, the spicier the relish, so adjust accordingly. Cover and set aside.

Heat grill or grill pan. Divide shrimp equally into fourths. Place on skewers. Remaining shrimp may be placed on extra skewers. Lightly brush grill rack with oil. Arrange skewers on hot grill. Cook about 2 minutes until shrimp become opaque. Turn and cook other side. Place heaping spoonful of papaya relish on four plates. Lay skewered shrimp along side. Garnish with basil and serve.

Note: The papaya and tomatoes balance the heat of the chili and zing of the ginger.

❀ *Serves 4*

Prawns with Garlic and Black Bean Sauce

Ingredients

1 head Manoa lettuce
1 1/2 pounds Tiger prawns
6 cloves garlic, minced, divided
3 tablespoons peanut oil, divided
White pepper
1 teaspoon black bean paste
1/2 teaspoon water
2 tablespoons granulated sugar
2 tablespoons oyster sauce
1/2 cup soy sauce
2 tablespoons sherry
3 to 4 drops chili oil
1/2 cup chopped green onions
1/2 bunch cilantro, minced
Juice of 1 lemon
1 lemon, sliced

Wash, pat dry lettuce, and arrange on serving platter. Shell and devein prawns. Mix prawns with half the garlic and 2 tablespoons peanut oil. Sprinkle with white pepper. In a small bowl, mix bean paste with water. Add sugar, remaining garlic, oyster sauce, soy sauce, sherry, and chili oil. Heat remaining tablespoon peanut oil in wok over medium-high heat. Add prawns and garlic and stir-fry until pink. Sprinkle with green onions and cilantro. Add lemon juice and black bean mixture. Continue to stir and simmer for 2 minutes. Place on bed of lettuce. Garnish with lemon slices. Serve.

Serves 4

Shrimp and Scallop Satay

INGREDIENTS

10 wooden skewers
20 button mushrooms, washed
    and stemmed
1 pound medium shrimp,
    peeled and deveined
1 pound sea or jumbo scallops
3 tablespoons butter
3 tablespoons olive oil
6 large cloves garlic, minced
$1/2$ teaspoon ground cumin
$1/2$ teaspoon ground coriander
1 bunch green onions, sliced, divided
2 tablespoons tomato paste
$1/4$ cup dry white wine
Salt and white pepper
Olive oil
$1/3$ cup chopped fresh parsley

Lay skewers in a shallow pan. Cover with water and soak at least 30 minutes. Arrange mushroom caps, shrimp, and scallops in a large glass baking dish. Melt butter in olive oil in a small saucepan over medium heat. Add garlic, cumin, coriander, and half the green onions and sauté 2 to 3 minutes until soft. Stir in tomato paste and wine until blended. Bring almost to a boil, remove from heat, and pour over mushroom-seafood mixture. Cover and marinate in refrigerator at least 2 hours, stirring occasionally.

Heat grill. Drain skewers and pat dry. Thread four skewers with a shrimp-mushroom-scallop-mushroom-shrimp pattern. Thread four skewers with a scallop-mushroom-shrimp-mushroom-scallop pattern. Arrange any remaining mushrooms, shrimp, and scallops on remaining skewers. Season with salt and pepper to taste. Lightly brush grill rack with oil. Lay skewers over coals. Cook 2 to 3 minutes per side, until opaque and lightly browned. Remove to four plates giving guests one of each style of seafood pattern. Sprinkle with chopped fresh parsley. Serve immediately.

Note: Satay means triple stacked. It is an Indonesian favorite consisting of strips of marinated meat, poultry, or seafood grilled on skewers. Often it is served with a spicy peanut sauce for dipping.

Serves 4

Aiea Paella

Ingredients
1 tablespoon paprika
2 teaspoons dried oregano
1 teaspoon Hawaiian sea salt
1 teaspoon black pepper
2 pounds boneless chicken thighs
3 cups medium-grained rice
5 to 6 cups water
15 ounces canned diced tomatoes
1/4 cup chopped parsley
1 pound Portuguese sausage, thickly sliced
2 Ewa sweet onions, diced
6 garlic cloves, crushed
1 pound jumbo shrimp, peeled and deveined
1 pound sea scallops
1 cup frozen green peas, thawed
Lemon wedges

Mix together paprika, oregano, salt, and pepper in a small bowl. Cut chicken into 1-inch pieces. Place chicken in a glass bowl, sprinkle with spices, and rub in. If time permits, cover, and marinate for 1 hour in refrigerator.

In a large pot, combine rice and water. Bring to a boil over high heat, reduce heat to low, cover, and cook 20 minutes until tender. Stir in tomatoes and parsley. Set aside.

Heat a large skillet over medium heat. Add sausage and cook until browned. Drain fat. Remove to a large bowl and set aside. Add chicken and cook until browned. Remove and set aside with sausage. Add onions and garlic. Sauté 5 to 8 minutes until soft. Stir shrimp and scallops into onions. Cook 3 minutes stirring and tossing until opaque. Add peas and cook 1 minute. Remove from heat. Gently stir sausage and chicken into rice. Spoon shrimp and scallops over rice and gently fold in with a few swift strokes. Garnish with lemon and serve.

Note: True paella is made in one large paella pan on the stove with ingredients slowly added as it cooks.

There are only 12 letters in the Hawaiian alphabet: a, e, h, i, k, l, m, n, o, p, u and w. And 18 sounds a, e, i, o, u, ä, ë, ï, ö, ü, h, k, l, m, n, p, w, and w with a v sound. The ʻokina (ʻ) is a glottal stop like the sound between the nos in "no-no". In order to clarify pronunciation, the ʻokina is often used on words such as Hawaiʻi.

Serves 6 to 8

Udon with Seafood

INGREDIENTS

1 pound medium shrimp
8 ounces firm white fish
3/4 pound small hard shelled clams
2 tablespoons canola oil
4 cloves garlic, smashed
1 tablespoon minced fresh ginger root
1/2 cup sliced shiitake mushrooms
1 cup shredded bok choy
1 cup diced Roma tomatoes
1 quart dashi broth
2 tablespoons butter
14 ounces fresh udon noodles
Fish cake, thinly sliced
Salt and white pepper

Peel and devein shrimp and set aside. Cut fish into 2-inch pieces and set aside. Scrub clams well and set aside.

Heat oil in a large skillet over high heat. Add garlic, ginger, and shiitake. Stir fry 1 to 2 minutes. Add bok choy and tomatoes. Cook until limp. Add dashi broth and butter, cover, and bring to a boil. Add shrimp, fish, and clams. Return to a boil and cook 2 minutes then add noodles. Cook 3 more minutes until fish is opaque and clams open, but do not over cook noodles. Ladle into serving bowls. Top with slices of fish cake. Season with salt and pepper to taste. Serve.

Note: Dashi is a soup stock made with dried bonito tuna flakes and dried kelp used in Japanese cooking.

Serves 4

Grilled Mahi-Mahi

MAHI-MAHI
1 cup Chardonnay or Pinot Grigio
$1/2$ teaspoon ground cumin
1 tablespoon sea salt
Freshly ground black pepper
Juice of 4 limes
4 skinless mahi-mahi fillets

PINEAPPLE CHUTNEY
4 tablespoons olive oil, divided
$1/2$ red bell pepper, finely diced
$1/2$ red onion, finely diced
4 to 6 cloves garlic, minced
1 tablespoon chili powder
1 tablespoon curry powder
1 medium pineapple, peeled,
  cored, and diced
$1/2$ cup Chardonnay or Pinot Grigio
$1/4$ cup orange juice
$1/3$ cup packed brown sugar
1 teaspoon cinnamon
1 teaspoon salt

Stir together wine, cumin, salt, pepper and lime juice. Place mahi-mahi in a non-reactive dish and pour in marinade. Cover and refrigerate overnight, if possible.

Heat 2 tablespoons oil in a medium skillet over medium-high heat. Add bell pepper and onion. Sauté 5 minutes until soft. Add garlic and chili and curry powders. Sauté 1 to 2 minutes. Measure out 2 cups diced pineapple and add to skillet with wine, orange juice, sugar, cinnamon, and salt. Reduce heat to medium and simmer until liquid is reduced by half. Remove and cool chutney to room temperature.

Heat coals until medium hot. Lightly brush grill rack with some of remaining oil. Lay fish over hot coals and grill about 4 minutes per side. Remove to serving platter. Top each fillet with a spoonful of Pineapple Chutney.

Serves 4

Jerk Seasoned Mahi-Mahi

MELON SALSA
1/2 cantaloupe melon
1 medium onion, diced
1/3 cup chopped fresh cilantro
2 tablespoons fresh lime juice
3/4 teaspoon grated lime peel
Salt and black pepper

MAHI-MAHI
Olive oil
1 avocado, peeled and seeded
1 tablespoons fresh lime juice
Salt and black pepper
4 thick mahi-mahi fillets
1 tablespoon olive oil
3 tablespoons Jamaican jerk seasoning

Cut cantaloupe into $1/2$-inch cubes and place in a medium bowl. Add onion, cilantro, lime juice, and lime zest. Lightly stir together. Season with salt and pepper to taste. Set aside.

Heat grill to medium-high. Lightly brush grill rack with oil.

In a small bowl, mash avocado. Add lime juice and season with salt and pepper. Set aside. Brush fish with oil. Sprinkle with jerk seasoning, coating well. Place on grill. Cook fish until just opaque in center, about 4 minutes per side. Remove to serving platter. Top with generous spoonful of Melon Salsa. Place dollop of avocado on the side and serve.

Note: Jamaican jerk seasoning; a blend of chilies, thyme, garlic, onion, and spices; gives the grilled fish a beautiful dark color and spicy flavor. Look for it in the spice aisle.

 Serves 4

Panko Crusted Moi

PAPAYA SAUCE
3 tablespoons olive oil
1 Maui onion, diced
1 jalapeno pepper, minced
4 cloves garlic, minced
$1/4$ cup dry white wine
2 ripe papayas, diced
2 tablespoons honey
Salt and black pepper

MOI
1 $1/2$ cups rice flour
Salt and black pepper
3 eggs, beaten
3 tablespoons milk
1 cup panko flakes
4 6-ounce pieces moi or catfish
3 tablespoons vegetable oil
Sprigs of fresh cilantro
Lime wedge

Heat olive oil in a medium saucepan over medium heat. Add onion, jalapeno, and garlic. Stir and cook until soft. Stir in wine and cook until reduced by half, about 10 minutes. Add papaya and cook, mashing slightly, until nicely blended. Add honey and season with salt and pepper to taste. Set papaya sauce aside.

Place rice flour in a medium bowl and season with salt and pepper. Mix eggs and milk in a large bowl. Place panko in a medium bowl. Season fish with salt and pepper, coat with rice flour, dip into egg mixture, and finish with panko. Heat vegetable oil in a large skillet until almost smoking. Sauté fish until golden brown on both sides. Transfer to serving platter. Garnish with cilantro and lime wedges. Serve with Papaya Sauce.

🌸 *Serves 4*

Dilled Salmon

INGREDIENTS

3 to 4 pound salmon fillet
Garlic salt
1 cup mayonnaise
1 cup sour cream
1 medium cucumber
1/4 cup finely chopped onion
2 teaspoons minced capers,
    drained well
Juice of 1/2 lemon
2 teaspoons dried dill

Heat oven to 350°F. Lightly oil an 8 x 12-inch baking pan. Arrange fish in prepared pan. Sprinkle lightly with garlic salt. Mix mayonnaise and sour cream in a small bowl. Halve cucumber lengthwise. Remove seeds. Thinly slice cucumber crosswise. Add to mayonnaise with onion, capers, lemon juice, and dill. Adjust seasonings to taste. Spread mayonnaise mixture over fish. Cover with foil and bake for 25 minutes. Serve.

Note: A very flexible recipe. The fish can weigh as much as is needed for the number of people being served. Adjust the sauce ingredients proportionately.

Serves a crowd

Salmon Salad with Leek and Potato

INGREDIENTS

1 tablespoon olive oil
1/2 teaspoon chopped caraway seed
2 leeks, split lengthwise, well rinsed,
    and cut into 1-inch pieces
2 large red skinned potatoes, scrubbed
    and cut into 1/4-inch cubes
1 pound salmon fillet, boned
3 cups baby spinach, rinsed and
    patted dry
1/2 cup sweet mustard relish
1/4 cup plus 1 teaspoon
    chopped fresh dill, divided
1/2 cup crème fraiche or sour cream
2 tablespoons dried currants
Sea salt and black pepper
1 ounce salmon roe

Heat oil in a frying pan over medium heat. Add caraway and lightly toast. Add leeks and potatoes, cook until tender, 10 to 15 minutes. Place in mixing bowl. Add salmon to frying pan and cook until fish is opaque. Gently break up fish and add to sautéed vegetables in bowl.

Scatter spinach on a serving platter. In a small bowl, combine mustard relish, 1/4 cup dill, crème fraiche, and currants, stirring until blended. Season with salt and pepper to taste. Gently fold into leek-salmon mixture. Mound on greens and garnish with remaining dill and salmon caviar. Serve.

Note: May be served warm or chilled.

Serves 4

Seared Salmon with Ginger-Lime Sauce

GINGER-LIME SAUCE

1 teaspoon minced garlic

3 Thai chilies, minced

3 tablespoons granulated sugar

3 tablespoons minced fresh ginger root

3 tablespoons fish sauce

3 tablespoons lime juice

3 tablespoons water

SALMON

2 tablespoons vegetable oil

4 6-ounce skinless salmon fillets

4 cloves garlic, sliced

GARNISH

3 Japanese cucumbers, peeled

1/3 cup chopped Thai basil

3 tablespoons chopped, roasted peanuts

Combine garlic, chilies, sugar, ginger, fish sauce, lime juice, and water in a small bowl and stir well. Set aside for 30 minutes before serving to let flavors develop.

Heat oil in a large non-stick frying pan over medium heat. Cook salmon fillets until golden and just done, 3 to 4 minutes on each side depending on the thickness. About 2 minutes before salmon is done, add sliced garlic. Remove salmon and garlic and drain on paper towels.

Cut cucumbers in half lengthwise, remove seeds, and julienne. Combine cucumber and basil in a small bowl. Divide in half. Place equal amounts from one half on four individual plates. Cover each with salmon fillet, top with equal amounts of remaining cucumbers. Sprinkle with basil and a few pieces of the cooked garlic. Drizzle with 2 tablespoons of Ginger-Lime Sauce, top with peanuts, and serve immediately.

Note: A wonderful dish during the warm summer months.

 Serves 4

Salmon with Tomato Relish

TOMATO RELISH
$^1/4$ cup rice vinegar
1 tablespoon grated fresh ginger root
1 tablespoon soy sauce
2 teaspoons granulated sugar
3 pints red and/or yellow
   cherry tomatoes, quartered

SALMON
Vegetable oil
1 tablespoon extra-virgin olive oil
2 to 3 pound salmon fillet with skin
1 teaspoon salt
$^1/2$ teaspoon black pepper
3 tablespoons fresh thyme
Lime wedges
Sprigs of fresh thyme

Combine vinegar, ginger, soy sauce, and sugar in a glass bowl. Add tomatoes. Cover and set aside.

Heat grill. Brush generously with vegetable oil. Brush both sides of salmon fillet with olive oil. Sprinkle with salt and pepper. Sprinkle fresh thyme leaves on skinned side. Grill salmon fillet skin side up over medium heat, 4 to 5 inches from heat source, 8 to 10 minutes until lightly browned. Using two large metal spatulas carefully turn salmon. Grill 10 minutes more or until fish flakes easily with a fork. Transfer to serving platter. Garnish with lime wedges and thyme sprigs. Serve with Tomato Relish.

Note: To make ahead prepare Tomato Relish, cover and refrigerate overnight. Prepare and cook salmon, cooling fillet completely. Cover with plastic wrap and refrigerate up to 6 hours. Let salmon and relish stand at room temperature 30 minutes before serving.

Serves 6 to 8

Coconut Crusted Snapper

INGREDIENTS
2 tablespoons oil
1 cup flour
1 egg
$1/3$ cup milk
3 cups shredded coconut
4 red snapper fillets
4 teaspoons fresh lime juice
4 fresh Thai chilies, minced
Salt

Heat oil in a frying pan over medium heat. Place flour in a shallow dish. Beat egg with milk in a medium bowl. Place coconut in a shallow dish. Dust each fish fillet in flour, dip in egg-milk mixture letting excess drip off, and place in coconut, pressing lightly to adhere. Lay coated fish in hot pan. Sauté 4 minutes, then turn. Continue to sauté 4 to 6 minutes, until fish flakes easily with a fork. Remove to serving platter. Sprinkle with lime juice, chilies, and salt. Serve.

Note: Thai chilies are available in specialty produce sections or at Asian markets.

 Serves 4

Sole with Hoisin Glazed Scallions

SOLE
$1/4$ cup miso
$1/4$ cup mirin
$1/4$ cup sake
$1/4$ cup packed brown sugar
3 tablespoons rice vinegar
3 tablespoons soy sauce
1-inch piece fresh ginger root, sliced
2 cloves garlic, minced
4 sole fillets
2 tablespoons olive oil

GLAZED SCALLIONS
16 scallions or green onions
2 tablespoons macadamia nut oil
Salt and black pepper
$1/4$ cup hoisin sauce

In a small bowl, combine miso, mirin, sake, sugar, vinegar, and soy sauce stirring to blend well. Add ginger and garlic. Layer sole in a 9 x 9-inch glass pan. Add sauce, cover, and marinate in refrigerator about 30 minutes.

Heat grill or grill pan. Trim scallions, rinse, and pat dry. Brush with macadamia nut oil then sprinkle lightly with salt and pepper. Grill scallions, turning once just until lightly charred and cooked through. Brush with hoisin sauce. Cut into 3-inch pieces. Lay on serving platter. Set aside.

Heat olive oil in a large frying pan over medium heat. Add the sole fillets and cook about 4 minutes per side until opaque and cooked through. Arrange on top of Glazed Scallions. Serve.

 Serves 4

Grilled Swordfish with Pesto

PESTO
4 tablespoons butter, softened
1 cup fresh basil
1 cup spinach
1/2 cup fresh parsley
2/3 cup olive oil
1/4 cup sun-dried tomatoes
3 cloves garlic, smashed
1/2 cup walnuts
1/2 cup grated fresh Parmesan

SWORDFISH
Olive oil
4 thick swordfish steaks
Salt and black pepper
4 whole walnuts
Sprigs of fresh parsley

Heat grill to medium. Place softened butter in a medium bowl and set aside. Place some of the basil, spinach, and parsley in a food processor or blender. With motor running, drizzle in oil. Continue to add leaves until have a smooth paste. Add sun-dried tomatoes, garlic, and walnuts, process until smooth. Add pesto to butter and stir to mix well. Blend in cheese.

Rub swordfish with a little oil, and season with salt and pepper to taste. Grill fish over medium heat for 4 to 5 minutes per side until fish is flaky. Place on warmed serving platter. Top with a dollop of Pesto. Garnish with whole walnuts and parsley. Serve with extra Pesto on the side.

Note: Pesto gets its name from the process used to create it. *Pestare* is the Italian verb meaning to stomp on or crush.

Serves 4

253

Seared Tuna with Pineapple Sauce

PINEAPPLE SAUCE
6 cups pineapple juice
2 tablespoons olive oil
2 Maui onions, diced
4 cloves garlic, minced
1 teaspoon ground chipotle or hot chili powder
1 to 2 tablespoons honey
Salt

TUNA
1 tablespoon coarse black pepper
1 teaspoon cayenne pepper
1 teaspoon ground chipotle powder
4 6-ounce tuna steaks
Olive oil
Salt
Mixed baby salad greens
Diced papaya

Place pineapple juice in a medium saucepan over medium heat. Cook to reduce to 3 cups, about 20 minutes. Heat oil in a medium saucepan over medium heat. Add onions and garlic. Sauté until soft. Add chipotle. Cook for 2 minutes. Add the reduced pineapple juice and bring to a boil. Continue to cook until reduced to 2 cups. Place mixture in a blender and carefully blend until smooth. Return to pan and add honey. Cook for 5 minutes over medium heat. Season with salt to taste.

Mix together black pepper, cayenne, and chipotle in a flat bottomed bowl. Brush tuna on each side with oil and season with salt. Dredge one side of each tuna steak in the spice mixture. Heat 1 tablespoon of oil in a heavy skillet over medium-high heat until almost smoking. Add 1 tablespoon oil. Add tuna spice-side down. Sear for 2 to 3 minutes, to form a crust. Turn over. Continue cooking for 1 to 2 minutes for rare. Arrange salad greens on platter. Top with seared tuna. Drizzle ribbon of pineapple sauce across each fillet. Garnish with papaya and serve.

Serves 4

Seared Tuna Tartar with Rice Noodles

TUNA

1 pound fresh tuna,
    cut into 1-inch cubes
3 tablespoons Asian sweet chili sauce
1 tablespoon sesame oil
2 cloves garlic, crushed
1-inch piece fresh ginger root

DRESSING

1 teaspoon granulated sugar
1 tablespoon rice vinegar
2 tablespoons fish sauce
2 tablespoons soy sauce
Juice of 1 lime

NOODLES

10 ounces rice thread noodles
1 tablespoon sesame oil
1 bunch choi sum, thinly sliced
1 small bunch mizuma, thinly sliced
$1/2$ cup bean sprouts
1 large carrot, shredded
1 sweet red pepper, finely julienned
Black sesame seeds
Sprigs of fresh cilantro

Place tuna in a medium glass bowl. Add chili sauce, oil, and garlic. Peel and julienne ginger. Add to sauce, stir to coat. Cover and chill for 2 hours.

Mix together sugar, vinegar, fish sauce, soy sauce, and lime juice. Cover and set aside.

Place noodles in a large bowl and cover with water. Let soak 20 minutes. Drain and set aside. Heat oil in a wok or a large frying pan over high heat. Add tuna with marinade and stir-fry for 30 seconds to sear. Remove from the pan and set aside. Add choi sum, mizuma, bean sprouts, carrot, and red pepper to the pan and stir-fry for 1 minute or until just cooked and still crunchy. Return tuna and add noodles. Toss well. Pour dressing over all and arrange on serving plates. Sprinkle with black sesame seeds and cilantro. Serve immediately.

Serves 4

Wahoo Fish Tacos

PINEAPPLE CHILI SALSA
2 cups pineapple, minced
1 small onion, finely minced
1/2 cup finely chopped green onion
1 to 2 serrano chili peppers,
  finely minced
1 to 2 jalapeno peppers, finely minced
2 tablespoons rice vinegar
1/2 teaspoon salt

FISH
2 cups buttermilk
1 to 1 1/2 tablespoons hot pepper sauce,
  such as Tabasco
1 teaspoon Hawaiian sea salt
1 tablespoon fresh lime juice
1 1/2 pounds wahoo, tilapia or
  mahi-mahi, cut into 1-inch
  thick strips

TACOS
12 corn tortillas
4 cups shredded cabbage or lettuce
2 cups all purpose flour
2 teaspoons baking powder
2 teaspoons Hawaiian sea salt
1/2 teaspoon black pepper
Vegetable oil
Lime wedges

In a bowl, combine pineapple, onion, green onions, serrano and jalapeno chilies, vinegar, and salt. Stir to mix well. Cover and refrigerate at least 30 minutes to blend flavors.

In a large bowl, mix buttermilk, pepper sauce, salt, and lime juice. Add fish and toss to coat. Cover and marinate in refrigerate at least 1 hour, but no longer than 3 hours.

Heat oven to 300°F. Wrap tortillas in foil and place in oven to warm. Line a baking sheet with paper toweling. Place cabbage in serving bowl, cover, and set aside.

Whisk together flour, baking powder, salt, and pepper in a medium bowl. Heat 1-inch oil in a large skillet over medium-high heat. Working in batches, remove fish from marinade and dredge in flour mixture. Carefully add fish to hot oil (about 350°F) in skillet. Fry until golden brown, turning occasionally, about 4 minutes. Transfer to prepared baking sheet to drain. Keep warm in oven while cooking remaining fish. Place on warmed serving platter.

Bring salsa, cabbage, tortillas, and fish to the table. Allow diners to make tacos as follows: Put a small amount of cabbage in the middle of each tortilla. Top with a few pieces of fish and 1 to 2 teaspoons salsa. Add a squeeze of lime, fold, and eat.

Serves 4

Wahoo in Banana Leaf

HERB PASTE
1 1/2-inch piece fresh ginger root,
   peeled and minced
5 cloves garlic, minced
1 fresh hot green chili, minced
1/2 cup shredded coconut
3 cups fresh cilantro
1/3 cup fresh mint
1/4 cup white wine vinegar
1 teaspoon granulated sugar
1/4 teaspoon salt

WAHOO
6 12 x 10-inch pieces banana leaf
6 thick 6-ounce pieces wahoo fillets
Salt and pepper
6 24-inch pieces kitchen string
Shredded coconut or dried coconut chips
Banana chips

In a grill, prepare a medium fire. Put ginger into a food processor with garlic, chili, and coconut. Pulse to combine. Add cilantro and mint. Process until somewhat smooth. Add vinegar, sugar, and salt. Blend well to make paste.

Arrange banana leaves in a stack with a short side nearest you. Season fish fillets on both sides with salt and pepper. Spread one slightly rounded tablespoon of Herb Paste on top of each fillet. Invert, placing paste side down, crosswise, onto center of a banana leaf. Spread plain side with another slightly rounded tablespoon of herb paste. Fold bottom edge of leaf over fish. Fold in sides over fish. Fold package away from you, enclosing fish. Tie package in both directions with kitchen string. String may be tied with bow for easier opening. Repeat with remaining fillets, Herb Paste, and banana leaves. Grill fish packets, turning over once, until cooked through, 8 to 10 minutes. Do not overcook. Untie one package to check doneness. Place packets on a serving plate. Sprinkle with coconut and banana chips. Serve.

Note: String can be cut before serving. Banana leaves are inedible, but make a nice presentation.

❀ *Serves 4 to 6*

Eggplant with Corn and Chiles

INGREDIENTS

3 Anaheim chilies
2 large round eggplant
Juice of 1 lime
2 tablespoons olive oil, plus extra
4 cloves garlic, minced
2 large ripe tomatoes, diced
1 cup fresh or canned corn kernels
$^1/4$ cup sour cream
1 cup shredded Parmesan
Salt and black pepper
Sprigs of fresh parsley

Heat broiler. Lay chilies in a baking pan. Place under heating element. Roast chilies until skin blisters and blackens. Remove from oven, cover, and let sit until cool enough to handle. Peel, seed, and finely dice. Set aside.

Heat oven to 350°F. Trim and halve eggplant lengthwise. Hollow out flesh of eggplant leaving a $^1/4$-inch shell. Mince pulpy flesh and set aside. Rub the eggplant shells with lime juice and then coat with a bit of oil. Lay shells on a lightly oiled baking sheet, cut side up. Place in center of oven and bake for 40 minutes, until shells are tender but still retain their shape. Overcooking will collapse the shells.

Heat 2 tablespoons oil in a large frying pan over medium heat. Add minced eggplant and cook 5 minutes. Add garlic, tomatoes, and roasted chilies, cook 3 to 5 minutes to soften. Stir in corn. Cover, reduce heat to low, and cook 8 to 10 minutes until tender and well blended, stirring occasionally.

Remove from heat and stir in sour cream and Parmesan. Season with salt and pepper to taste. Fill baked shells with eggplant mixture. Return to oven and bake an additional 20 minutes to heat through. Garnish with fresh parsley and serve hot.

Note: May be served with a homemade tomato sauce.

Serves 4

Sweet Japanese Eggplant

INGREDIENTS
4 Japanese eggplant
1 tablespoon oil
1 large onion, minced
1 small red chili pepper, minced
8 ounces ground pork, optional
1 tablespoon curry powder
1 tablespoon minced fresh ginger root
3 tablespoons packed dark brown sugar
1 cup cooked white beans
2/3 cup tomato sauce
1 cup vegetable or chicken broth
Salt
1/2 cup sliced almonds

Heat oven to 350°F. Grease a 9 x 9-inch baking pan. Set aside. Make a deep slit lengthwise in each eggplant but don't cut all the way through. Set aside.

Heat oil in a skillet over medium heat. Sauté onion and chili pepper 5 minutes. Add pork and continue to cook, stirring occasionally. Mix in curry powder, ginger, and sugar. Let cook 1 to 2 minutes. Add white beans, tomato sauce, and broth, stirring to blend. Simmer 3 to 5 minutes. Season with salt to taste. Remove from heat. Spread a layer of sautéed vegetable mixture on bottom of prepared pan. Arrange eggplant on top. Gently fill slit of each eggplant with remaining vegetables. Sprinkle with almonds. Cover with foil and bake 40 minutes. Uncover and bake 20 minutes more until eggplant is tender. Serve.

Note: Accompany with rice or other grains.

Serves 4

Grilled Portobello with Corn Cake

PEPPER SAUCE
2 red bell peppers
$^1/_2$ to 1 teaspoon ground chipotle chili
$^1/_3$ cup extra-virgin olive oil
$^1/_4$ teaspoon salt

MUSHROOMS
8 medium portobello mushroom caps
$^1/_3$ cup extra-virgin olive oil
4 large cloves garlic,
    passed through press

CORN CAKE
1 cup corn kernels
1 cup all-purpose flour
1 cup cornmeal
1 tablespoon granulated sugar
$^1/_2$ teaspoon salt
$^1/_2$ teaspoon chili powder
$^1/_2$ teaspoon baking powder
$^1/_2$ teaspoon baking soda
1 $^1/_4$ cups buttermilk
1 tablespoon olive oil
2 green onions, finely sliced
Fresh parsley

Heat broiler. Place bell peppers under heating element and roast until blackened. Using tongs, carefully turn to blacken all sides. Place peppers in a heavy plastic bag. Seal and let stand 15 minutes. Remove from bag and peel blackened skin. Slit peppers and remove veins and seeds. Put roasted peppers in a food processor and puree. Add chili powder. Slowly add oil, processing until smooth. Stir in salt. Set aside. This sauce can be made one to two days ahead. Cover and store in refrigerator.

Wash and pat dry mushroom caps. In a small bowl, combine oil and garlic. Brush onto mushroom caps. Let stand about 20 minutes.

Heat oven to 400°F. Grease a 9 x 9-inch pan. Place corn in food processor and pulse until partially pureed. Set aside.

In a large bowl, combine flour, cornmeal, sugar, salt, chili powder, baking powder, and baking soda. Mix well. In a medium bowl, combine pureed corn, buttermilk, oil, and green onions, blending well. Add to dry ingredients, stirring just until moistened. Spread batter evenly in prepared pan. Bake 20 to 23 minutes or until firm to the touch.

Grill or broil mushroom caps until tender, turning once. Cut corn cake into eight rounds with 2 $^1/_2$-inch cutter and place on individual serving plates. Top each with a grilled mushroom, gill side down. Drizzle with Pepper Sauce. Garnish with parsley. Serve.

Note: Can be served as an appetizer as well.

❀ *Serves 8*

Portobello Wild Rice Purses

INGREDIENTS
1 1/2 cups water
1/2 cup wild rice
Olive oil
1 cup chopped green onion
4 portobello mushrooms,
    stemmed and diced
1/4 cup finely diced celery
4 ounces cream cheese or goat cheese
1 teaspoon thyme
Salt and black pepper
8 sheets phyllo dough
4 to 6 long fresh chives

CUCUMBER SAUCE
1/2 cup sour cream or plain yogurt
1 teaspoon fresh dill
1 shallot, minced
1/2 cucumber, peeled, seeded, and
    finely diced

Bring water to boiling over high heat. Stir in rice, reduce heat to low, cover, and cook about 45 minutes until tender. Heat 1 tablespoon oil in a skillet over medium heat. Add green onion and mushrooms, sauté 5 minutes. Add celery and sauté another 3 minutes until soft. Stir in cooked rice, cream cheese, and thyme. Season with salt and pepper to taste. Remove from heat. Set aside.

Heat oven to 350°F. Lightly oil a baking sheet. Separate phyllo into four piles of two sheets. Divide rice mixture equally among phyllo, placing in center or each. Gather up corners of pastry to completely enclose filling, creating a frilly effect on top. Pinch tightly. Tie with chive. Place on prepared baking sheet. Bake 25 minutes until golden.

In a small bowl, combine sour cream, dill, and shallot. Stir cucumber into sauce. Cover and chill. Remove purses from the oven and set on serving plates. Drizzle with Cucumber Sauce. Serve hot.

Note: Chinese black rice may be substituted for wild rice but cooks more quickly so keep an eye on it. Smaller purses can be made to serve with cocktails.

Serves 4

Crispy Quesadillas

PESTO

1 bunch fresh cilantro
2 teaspoons minced garlic
1/4 teaspoon crushed red chili
    pepper flakes
1 teaspoon ground coriander
1/2 cup olive oil
Salt and black pepper

DRESSING

1/4 cup fresh lime juice
1/2 cup olive oil
Salt and black pepper

SAUCE

1 ripe mango, peeled and sliced
1 jalapeno pepper, minced
1 tablespoon honey
Pinch salt

QUESADILLA

4 large flour tortillas
12 ounces Queso Asadero, or
    Oaxaca, shredded
1 tablespoon butter, quartered
1 head Boston lettuce,
    washed and dried
1 head red leaf lettuce,
    washed and dried

Place cilantro in a food processor with garlic, pepper flakes, and coriander. With the processor running, add oil in a slow stream. Add salt and pepper and pulse to combine, making a pesto. Adjust seasonings to taste. Set aside.

Pour lime juice into the cleaned bowl of the processor. Add 1 tablepoon pesto and, with the processor running, add oil in a slow stream. Process until the dressing emulsifies. Add salt and pepper to taste, and pulse. Set dressing aside. Place mango, jalapeno, honey, and salt into the cleaned bowl of the processor. Puree until smooth. Set aside.

Heat broiler. Set out a baking sheet. Spread a generous amount of pesto on each tortilla spreading to the edges. Sprinkle with a generous amount of the queso. Heat a large skillet over medium-high heat. Add one piece of butter and melt, do not let burn. Slide in one tortilla, cheese side up. Cook, shaking occasionally, for 1 to 2 minutes until bottom is golden brown. Transfer tortilla to baking sheet. Repeat with remaining tortillas. Place the baking sheet under broiler for 3 to 5 minutes to slightly brown cheese.

Tear lettuce into bite-sized pieces and combine in a large bowl. Add half the dressing. Arrange salad on four plates. Remove the quesadillas from the oven and slice each into four pieces. Arrange on salad. Drizzle with mango sauce. Serve. Offer extra dressing and mango sauce on the side.

❀ *Serves 4*

Squash Quesadillas

INGREDIENTS

3 tablespoons extra-virgin olive oil,
    divided
1 small Kobucha pumpkin
Coarse salt and black pepper
Pinch crushed red chili pepper flakes
1 large onion, thinly sliced
1 jalapeno pepper, minced
8 ounces goat cheese, crumbled
8 12-inch flour tortillas
4 tablespoons chopped fresh cilantro
4 teaspoons fresh lime juice
Sprigs of cilantro

Heat oven to 375°F. Drizzle 1^1/2 tablespoons oil over the bottom of a 9 x 13-inch baking dish. Set aside. Halve and seed pumpkin. Cut into ^{1}/2-inch slices. Place in prepared pan. Season with salt and pepper to taste and add red pepper flakes. Roast in oven until fork-tender, about 40 minutes. Remove and let cool. Peel pumpkin and set aside.

In a large frying pan, heat 1 teaspoon oil over medium heat. Add onion and jalapeno. Sauté 5 to 8 minutes until tender. Remove and set aside. Sprinkle goat cheese evenly over four tortillas. Sprinkle each with 1 tablespoon cilantro. Arrange pumpkin slices on top. Scatter on onion-jalapeno mixture. Sprinkle with lime juice. Cover each with a plain tortilla. Reheat skillet over medium-high heat and brush with some of remaining oil. Add one filled quesadilla and cook until golden in color, about 2 minutes per side. Remove from heat and cut each quesadilla into quarters with kitchen scissors or a knife. Garnish with a few sprigs of cilantro. Serve.

Note: To turn quesadilla more easily, try sliding onto a dinner plate; cover with another plate, turn over, and slide back into the pan, uncooked side down.

Serves 4

Summer Squash with Lentils

INGREDIENTS
3 tablespoons olive oil, divided
1 cup dried yellow lentils
2 cups water
4 medium sized yellow squash
1/2 teaspoon salt
1 medium onion, diced
1/4 cup finely diced celery
1 teaspoons grated fresh ginger root
1 teaspoon cumin seeds
1 teaspoon curry powder
Fresh dill

Heat 1 tablespoon oil in a saucepan over medium heat. Add lentils, sauté a few minutes. Add water and bring to a boil. Reduce heat, cover, and cook until tender, about 15 to 20 minutes, stirring occasionally. Trim and halve squash lengthwise. Scoop out seeds, making an indentation for filling. Heat 1 tablespoon oil in a large skillet over medium heat. Place squash cut side down and sauté until edges turn golden brown, about 5 minutes. Do not overcrowd. May have to cook in two batches. Turn each piece and cook rounded side 2 minutes or until tender. Remove to serving platter and sprinkle with salt.

Remove lentils from heat and drain any remaining water. Heat remaining tablespoon oil in skillet. Add onion, celery, ginger, cumin seeds, and curry. Sauté a minute or two before adding lentils. Cook, stirring occasionally, about 5 minutes. Spoon filling into squash boats. Garnish with fresh dill. Serve.

Serves 4 to 6

Roasted Sweet Potato Chili

INGREDIENTS

1 1/2 pounds sweet potatoes, peeled
    and cut into 1-inch cubes
1 large onion, thinly sliced
1 cup fresh pineapple chunks
1 bell pepper
1 large Granny Smith apple
2 teaspoons olive oil
3 cloves garlic, minced
1 jalapeno pepper, minced
1 tablespoon chili powder
1 teaspoon ground cumin
1/2 teaspoon salt
1/2 teaspoon ground cardamom
4 cups fresh tomato puree
1 cup water
2 cups fresh roasted corn kernels
15 ounces canned kidney beans
15 ounces canned black beans

Place oven rack at least 8 inches from heating element. Heat broiler unit. Place sweet potoato in a shallow metal baking pan with onion, pineapple, bell pepper, and apple. Place under broiler to brown slightly. Be careful not to burn. Remove from oven and set aside.

Heat oil in a large pot over medium heat. Add garlic and jalapeno. Cook, stirring occasionally, about 3 minutes. Season with chili powder, cumin, salt, and cardamom, stirring to blend. Heat a minute or two to release flavors. Stir in tomato puree, water, and corn. Add kidney beans, black beans, and roasted fruit and vegetables. Bring to a boil, cover, reduce heat to medium-low, and simmer about 45 minutes, stirring often until sweet potatoes are tender.

Note: Canned tomatoes, corn, and pineapple can be used when fresh ingredients are not in season. Remember to drain off any liquid before measuring.

Serves 4 to 6

Rice Paper Wrapped Vegetables

ORANGE-CHILI SAUCE
$1/2$ cup freshly squeezed orange juice
3 tablespoons granulated sugar
3 tablespoons soy sauce
2 teaspoons lime juice
1 tablespoon sesame oil
1 tablespoon balsamic vinegar
1 teaspoon crushed red chili pepper flakes
1 teaspoon kosher salt

WRAPS
2 cups very warm water
1 package rice paper wrappers
$1/4$ cup cilantro
$1/2$ cup julienned red bell pepper
$1/2$ cup julienned yellow bell pepper
1 cup julienned snow peas
$3 1/2$ ounces enoki mushrooms
1 cup bean sprouts
Seasoned Soba Noodles
$1/4$ cup pickled ginger
Kosher salt and black pepper
2 tablespoons black sesame seeds

SEASONED SOBA NOODLES
1 teaspoon sesame oil
1 teaspoon rice wine vinegar
1 cup cooked soba noodles

Whisk together orange juice, sugar, soy sauce, lime juice, sesame oil, vinegar, chili pepper flakes, and salt in a mixing bowl. Allow Orange-Chili Sauce to stand for 30 minutes.

Put warm water in a 9 x 9-inch baking dish. Add one rice paper wrapper at a time and soak about 20 seconds until soft. Lay wrapper out on a tea towel to absorb excess water. Remove to work surface. Working one-third from the bottom of wrapper, create a 3-inch long row using $1/6$ of cilantro. Top with $1/6$ red pepper, yellow pepper, snow peas, mushrooms, bean sprouts, soba noodles, and ginger. Season with salt and pepper to taste. Sprinkle exposed top third of rice wrapper with sesame seeds. Carefully fold the bottom of the rice paper wrapper over the vegetables. Turn in the sides and roll up completely. Set aside.

Continue to make six rolls, using all the vegetables. Slice each roll in half on a bias. Place one half on salad plate. Stand other half cut edge up next to or leaning against first half. Serve with Orange-Chili Sauce.

Seasoned Soba Noodles: In a medium bowl, whisk together oil and vinegar. Add noodles and toss to coat.

🌼 *Serves 4 to 6*

Linguine with Dill Mushroom Sauce

INGREDIENTS

2 tablespoons unsalted butter
2 tablespoons olive oil
6 to 8 shallots, minced
12 ounces mixed mushrooms,
    thinly sliced
$^1/_2$ cup Madeira sherry
$^1/_2$ cup vegetable broth
$^3/_4$ cup half-and-half
4 quarts water
1 pound fresh linguine
$^1/_4$ cup chopped fresh dill or
    2 tablespoons dried
Salt and black pepper
Feta cheese

Heat butter and oil over medium-low heat in a large heavy skillet. Add shallots and sauté stirring occasionally. Add mushrooms. Cook, stirring occasionally, for 15 minutes, until mushrooms are very tender.

Add Madeira and broth and heat mixture, stirring occasionally, until liquid is reduced by half. Reduce heat, stir in half-and-half, and simmer until slightly thickened. Meanwhile, in a large saucepan bring water to a boil. Add linguine and cook to al dente. Drain. Stir dill into cream sauce and season with salt and pepper to taste. Toss the linguine with sauce coating well. Sprinkle with Feta and serve.

Serves 4

Spicy Soba with Tofu

DRESSING
1/3 cup soy sauce
2 tablespoons packed brown sugar
1 small hot red chili, minced
1 tablespoon minced fresh ginger root
1 tablespoon minced garlic
1 tablespoon molasses
3 tablespoons sesame oil
3 tablespoons tahini
3 tablespoons chili oil
3 tablespoons balsamic vinegar
Salt

NOODLES
8 ounces fresh soba
1/2 bunch scallions, thinly sliced
8 ounces firm tofu
1 tablespoon olive oil
1 small red chili, minced
4 cloves garlic, minced
1/2 cup minced fresh parsley
2 tablespoons fresh lemon juice
Salt and black pepper

Heat soy sauce in a saucepan over medium heat. Add sugar, chili, ginger, and garlic. Bring to a boil. Reduce heat to low. Stir in molasses. Heat through. Remove from heat. Place in a small bowl. Beat in sesame oil, tahini, chili oil, and vinegar with whisk to combine. Season to taste with salt. Set aside.

Bring a large pot of salted water to a boil. Add soba. Bring back to a boil. Cook, stirring occasionally, about 3 minutes. Soba noodles can overcook very quickly. Prepare a large bowl of iced water.

Drain noodles. Plunge into ice water. Place in a colander. Drain well. Combine noodles and dressing. Add scallions. Toss well. Cover. Chill or set aside.

Drain tofu. Pat dry. Gently crumble. Set aside. Heat oil in a skillet over medium heat. Add chili and garlic. Cook 1 to 2 minutes. Increase heat to medium-high. Add crumbled tofu. Stir fry a few minutes to sear tofu. Remove from heat. Place in a small bowl. Sprinkle with parsley and lemon juice. Season with salt and pepper to taste. Sprinkle over prepared noodles and serve, or cover and chill to serve cold.

Serves 4

Shanghai Noodles

INGREDIENTS
1 chicken bouillon cube
2 1/2 cups boiling water, divided
5 large fresh shiitake mushrooms
2 carrots
1 small head green cabbage
3 green onions
1 pound tofu
12 ounces fresh chow mein noodles
3 tablespoons soy sauce
1 tablespoon balsamic vinegar
1 teaspoon sesame oil
1 teaspoon oyster sauce
2 teaspoons peanut oil
4 cloves garlic, minced

Prepare all ingredients before cooking. Dissolve boullion cube in 1/2 cup boiling water. Wash mushrooms, remove stems, and thinly slice. Julienne carrots. Thinly shred cabbage. Thinly slice green onions. Cut tofu into 1-inch cubes. Cover noodles with remaining 2 cups boiling water for 1 to 2 minutes until soft. Drain. In a small bowl, stir together broth, soy sauce, vinegar, sesame oil, and oyster sauce.

In a large non-stick skillet or wok, heat peanut oil over medium-high heat. Working quickly, stir-fry garlic and mushrooms 1 to 2 minutes. Add tofu. Cook a few minutes until golden. Add carrots, cabbage, and green onions. Cook 2 to 3 minutes. Add broth mixture and softened noodles. Stir thoroughly to mix well. Heat through. Serve immediately.

Note: This is an easy one-dish meal for the family, even fussy toddlers eat this one.

Serves 4

Condiments

Five-Spice Apples

INGREDIENTS
2 tablespoons vegetable oil
1 small onion, finely diced
3 Granny Smith apples,
   peeled, cored, and diced
1 $1/2$ teaspoons Chinese five-
   spice powder
1 tablespoon packed brown sugar
1 cup apple juice
Salt and black pepper
1 tablespoon butter

Heat oil in a medium skillet over medium heat and swirl to coat the bottom of the pan. Add onion and sauté, stirring occasionally, until golden, about 8 to 10 minutes. Add apples with five-spice powder and sugar, stirring to mix. Sauté a few minutes, then stir in juice. Season with salt and pepper to taste. Cook 10 to 12 minutes until liquid is reduced by half. The apples should retain their shape and some liquid should remain in the pan. Do not overcook. Stir in butter and adjust seasonings to taste. Serve warm.

Note: A nice condiment for grilled meat. Try substituting li hing mui for five-spice powder.

⚜ *Makes about 2 cups*

Pineapple Peppercorn Relish

INGREDIENTS

3 1/2 cups fresh pineapple, diced
3/4 cup minced red onion
1/4 cup fresh lime juice
1 1/2 tablespoons green peppercorns
   in brine, drained
Salt

In a bowl, combine pineapple, onion, lime juice, and peppercorns. Season with salt to taste. Cover and chill at least 2 hours before serving.

Note: Serve this with roasted poultry or fish.

✿ *Makes about 4 cups*

Plum-Ginger Relish

INGREDIENTS

6 red or black plums, peeled and diced
1 sweet red pepper, seeded and diced
2 green onions, thinly sliced
2 tablespoons minced red onion
2 tablespoons minced cilantro
2 tablespoons minced pickled ginger
3 tablespoons rice vinegar
1 tablespoon granulated sugar
1 tablespoon safflower oil
1 tablespoon lime juice
1 teaspoon soy sauce
1/2 teaspoon sesame oil

Combine plums, pepper, green onions, red onion, cilantro, and ginger in a bowl. Stir to mix. Add vinegar, sugar, safflower oil, lime juice, soy sauce, and sesame oil. Stir to mix. Cover and chill several hours to blend flavors. Serve at room temperature.

Note: Great with grilled meat, fish or poultry. Can be used as dipping sauce with potstickers.

✿ *Makes about 1 cup*

Sambal Cerise

INGREDIENTS

1 large Ewa Sweet or Maui onion,
    thinly sliced
2 cups fresh cherries, pitted and
    finely chopped
1 tablespoon packed brown sugar
1/3 cup fresh lime juice
4 small fresh hot red chilies

Caution: Wear rubber gloves to prepare hot chili or thoroughly wash hands after handling and do not touch your eyes.

Place onion and cherries in a medium non-reactive bowl. Sprinkle with sugar and lime juice and stir to mix. Cut each chili in half lengthwise. Add the seeds from one chili to bowl. Discard remaining seeds. Julienne each chili and add to bowl. Stir to mix. Cover and let stand at least 1 hour before serving.

When off season, try using a mixture of chopped dried sweet cherries, dried sweetened cranberries, and golden raisins in place of the fresh cherries. Soak 10 minutes in 1 1/4 cups warm berry juice to plump.

Note: Serve as a condiment to poultry or pork.

Makes about 4 cups

Grains

Barley Mushroom Pilaf

INGREDIENTS
2 tablespoons butter
1 medium onion, thinly sliced
2 cloves garlic, minced
1 teaspoon fresh thyme
1/4 teaspoon black pepper
8 ounces mushrooms, thinly sliced
1/4 teaspoon sea salt
2 1/2 cups chicken broth
3/4 cup pearl barley
Chopped fresh parsley

In a heavy medium saucepan, melt butter over medium-high heat. Add onion, garlic, thyme, and pepper, and sauté, stirring occasionally, for 5 minutes. Stir in mushrooms. Sprinkle with salt and cook, stirring occasionally, for 5 to 8 minutes until tender. Bring broth to a boil over high heat. Stir barley and hot broth into mushrooms. Bring to a boil. Reduce heat to low, cover, and simmer for 30 to 35 minutes until the barley is tender and most of the liquid is absorbed. Remove from heat and let stand, covered, for 5 minutes. Place in a warmed serving bowl. Garnish with chopped parsley. Serve.

Note: Pilafs are not always made with rice. It is a style of cooking that originated in the Mediterranean area.

❀ *Serves 4*

Bulgur with Spinach and Bacon

INGREDIENTS
2 tablespoons olive oil
1 large onion, diced
3 cloves garlic, minced
1 1/2 cups coarse bulgur
3 cups chicken broth
2 cups water
8 ounces baby spinach, washed
8 ounces bacon, diced large
2/3 cup grated Parmesan
Salt and black pepper

Heat oil in a 2-quart heavy saucepan over medium heat. Add onion and sauté, stirring occasionally, 8 to 10 minutes until softened. Add garlic and cook, stirring, 1 minute. Add bulgur, broth, and 1 1/2 cups water. Bring to a boil, reduce heat to low and simmer, covered, until bulgur is tender and creamy like risotto, about 20 minutes. Add a little more water as needed. Stir in spinach.

Heat a small skillet over medium. Add bacon and cook, stirring occasionally, until crisp. Remove and drain on paper towels. Set aside. Discard fat.

Stir half the bacon into bulgur. Season with salt and pepper to taste. Place in serving bowl. Sprinkle with Parmesan and remaining bacon and serve.

❀ *Serves 6 to 8*

Apricot Almond Couscous

INGREDIENTS
$^1/_2$ cup slivered almonds
2 $^1/_2$ cups water
2 tablespoons butter
$^1/_2$ cup sliced dried apricots
10 to 12 ounces couscous
Salt and black pepper
1 tablespoon chopped fresh cilantro

Heat a small skillet over medium-high heat. Add almonds and toast, shaking pan frequently, until lightly golden. Remove from pan and set aside. Heat water and butter in a medium saucepan over high until boiling. Stir in apricots and couscous. Cover, remove from heat, and let stand 5 to 10 minutes until most of the water has been absorbed. Stir occasionally with a fork to separate grains. Season with salt and pepper to taste. Place in a serving bowl. Sprinkle with cilantro. Serve.

❀ Serves 8

Couscous with Currants

INGREDIENTS
1 cup vegetable broth
$^1/_2$ cup couscous
1 tablespoon oil
1 green onion, sliced
1 clove garlic, crushed
$^1/_8$ teaspoon ground cumin
$^1/_3$ cup seeded, diced plum tomato
$^1/_4$ cup garbanzo beans
2 tablespoons currants
1 tablespoon chopped fresh parsley
2 tablespoons lemon juice
$^1/_4$ teaspoon black pepper

Bring broth to a boil over high heat in a medium saucepan. Stir in couscous. Cover, remove from heat, and let stand for 5 minutes until couscous is tender and liquid is absorbed. Fluff with a fork and set aside.

Heat oil in a medium skillet over medium-high heat. Stir in green onion, garlic, and cumin, sauté 1 minute. Add tomato, garbanzo beans, currants, and couscous. Cook, stirring occasionally until heated through, about 2 minutes. Remove from heat and stir in parsley, lemon juice, and pepper. Place in a serving bowl and serve.

❀ Serves 2

Kasha with Onion Confit

CONFIT
1 tablespoon butter
2 tablespoons olive oil
1 medium red onion, thinly sliced
2 large Maui onions, thinly sliced
4 shallots, thinly sliced
1 tablespoon sugar
$1/2$ teaspoon sea salt
$1/4$ teaspoon black pepper

KASHA
2 cups chicken broth
1 cup kasha
2 tablespoons butter
$1/4$ teaspoon black pepper
$1/2$ teaspoon sea salt
3 tablespoons chopped fresh chives
Chive flowers

In a large heavy skillet, melt butter in oil over medium heat. Add red and Maui onions and shallots. Sauté for 10 minutes. Reduce heat to low and continue to cook another 25 to 30 minutes until onions are soft and nicely colored. Stir often to keep onions from sticking to bottom of pan. Sprinkle with sugar, salt, and pepper. Turn off heat, and let confit sit 5 minutes.

Bring chicken broth to a boil in a saucepan over high heat. Heat a heavy medium skillet over medium heat. Add kasha to skillet and cook for 2 to 3 minutes, scraping bottom of pan constantly, until the grains are dry, separate, and have a toasted smell. Stir in hot broth, butter, pepper, and salt. Bring to a boil. Reduce heat to low, cover, and simmer 15 to 20 minutes, until kasha is tender and most of the liquid is absorbed. Place in a warmed serving bowl, top with onion confit. Sprinkle with chives. Garnish with chive flowers and serve.

Note: A confit historically refers to meat submerged in flavorful rendered fat and cooked slowly until very tender. However, it also can mean something cooked slowly to melt flavors together.

❀ *Serves 4 to 6*

Quinoa Timbales

INGREDIENTS

1 tablespoon olive oil
1 small onion, minced
1 teaspoon ground cumin
$^1/_2$ teaspoon ground cinnamon
$^1/_4$ teaspoon turmeric
1 cup quinoa, rinsed
1 cup chicken broth
$^2/_3$ cup water
$^1/_3$ cup dried currants
$^1/_4$ cup diced tomato
$^1/_2$ teaspoon salt
3 tablespoons minced fresh parsley
Sprigs of parsley

Heat oil in a heavy medium saucepan over medium-high heat. Add onion and sauté, stirring, until soft, about 5 minutes. Stir in cumin, cinnamon, and turmeric, and cook for 30 seconds. Add quinoa and cook, stirring, for 1 minute. Stir in broth, water, currants, tomato, and salt. Cover, reduce heat to medium-low and simmer for 15 minutes until the liquid is absorbed. Remove from heat. Let stand, covered, for 5 minutes. Stir in minced parsley.

Firmly pack one-sixth of quinoa mixture into a $^1/_2$-cup ramekin or measuring cup. Invert, tapping gently, onto a platter. Make six. Garnish with sprigs of parsley. Serve.

Note: Quinoa is available at natural foods stores and specialty food sections of grocery stores.

❀ *Serves 6*

Polenta with Gorgonzola Cream

INGREDIENTS

2 $^1/_4$ cups water
1 teaspoon salt
$^3/_4$ cup polenta or yellow cornmeal
2 ounces Gorgonzola cheese
$^3/_4$ cup half-and-half
$^1/_4$ teaspoon black pepper
Pinch ground nutmeg
2 tablespoons minced fresh chives

In a heavy medium saucepan, bring water to boiling over high heat. Remove from heat, stir in salt and add polenta in a slow, steady stream, whisking constantly. Beat until smooth. Return to stove. Reduce heat to low and cook, stirring frequently and vigorously with a wooden spoon, 15 to 20 minutes until very dry and smooth.

Crumble cheese and add, beating until well blended. Stir in half-and-half. Season with pepper and nutmeg. Place in warmed serving bowl. Sprinkle with chives. Serve.

Note: In Northern Italy, polenta is a staple and can be fried, baked, or served soft and creamy. An American equivalent is Southern grits.

❀ *Serves 6*

Polenta Florentine

INGREDIENTS

$^1/_4$ cup raisins

$^1/_2$ cup boiling water

3 $^1/_2$ cups water

$^1/_2$ teaspoon salt

1 cup polenta or cornmeal

2 tablespoons butter

$^1/_4$ cup grated Parmesan

3 tablespoons olive oil

8 scallions, thinly sliced

2 cloves garlic, passed through press

2 $^1/_2$ pounds fresh spinach, washed, stemmed, and chopped

$^1/_4$ cup pine nuts

Salt and ground mixed peppercorns

Lightly oil an 8 x 8-inch baking pan. Set aside. Put raisins in a small bowl and cover with $^1/_2$ cup boiling water. Set aside.

In a medium saucepan, bring 3 $^1/_2$ cups water to a boil over high heat. Add salt. Gradually sprinkle in polenta, stirring constantly with a wooden spoon. Reduce heat to low. Cook, stirring frequently, until polenta begins to thicken and pull away from the sides of the pan, about 20 to 25 minutes. Remove from heat. Stir in butter and cheese. Spread on bottom of prepared pan. Set aside.

In a skillet, heat oil over medium-low. Add scallions and garlic, sauté about 5 minutes, stirring occasionally. Drain raisins and add with spinach and pine nuts. Sauté another 3 to 5 minutes, stirring occasionally, until spinach is wilted and tender. Season with salt and pepper to taste.

Cut polenta into 2 $^1/_2$-inch circles or squares. Arrange on warmed serving platter. Top each with spinach mixture and serve.

Note: Pine nuts can turn rancid quickly so buy them in small quantities and store in refrigerator.

❀ *Serves 6*

Basmati Rice with Figs

INGREDIENTS
2 tablespoons butter
2 teaspoons mustard seeds
1 large onion, minced
1 jalapeno pepper, minced
2 cups basmati rice
¹/2 teaspoon salt
3 ³/4 cups water
6 fresh Kadota figs
1 tablespoon minced crystallized ginger

Melt butter in a heavy bottomed saucepan over medium heat. Add mustard seeds, onion, and jalapeno. Sauté, stirring occasionally, until softened, about 5 minutes. Add rice and sauté, stirring frequently, about 3 minutes. Add salt and water. Bring to a boil over medium heat. Reduce heat to low, cover, and cook 10 minutes, stirring occasionally.

Cut figs into eighths. Stir into rice with ginger. Remove from heat. Keep covered and let steam another 10 minutes until tender. Place in serving dish, and serve.

Note: Dried figs can be substituted for fresh, just double the amount called for in the recipe.

❋ *Serves 6*

Note: Throughout the world, rice is categorized as long or short-grained. The US recognizes a third size, medium-grained. Short-grain rice is plump and almost round with the length and width nearly equal. It becomes very soft when cooked and clings together making it great for sushi dishes. Medium-grain rice is two to three times longer than it is wide. It cooks up moist with a tendency to cling together and is used in risottos and puddings. Long-grain rice has a length that is four to five times longer than its width. It is light and fluffy when cooked with the grains remaining rather distinct.

Chinese Black and Red Rice Stack

INGREDIENTS
1 1/2 cups Chinese black rice
1 1/2 cups red rice
6 cups water, divided
2 cups coconut milk, divided
1 ripe mango, finely diced
3 cloves garlic, passed through press
1 cup shredded coconut
1 hot chili, minced
Fresh mint or basil leaves

Put Chinese black rice and red rice in separate pots. Add 3 cups water to each and bring to a boil over high heat, stirring occasionally. Reduce heat to medium-low and cook, covered, about 30 minutes until tender and most of water is absorbed. Stir occasionally to keep rice from sticking to bottom of pots. Add 1 cup coconut milk to each, stirring to mix well. Continue to cook until most of liquid has been absorbed. Stir mango and garlic into Chinese black rice. Stir shredded coconut and chili into red rice.

Form timbales by pressing 1/4 cup black rice into bottom of a timbale mold or ramekin. Top with 1/4 cup red rice. Press firmly to shape, keeping separate layers. Place on warmed serving platter. Remove from mold. Continue to use all of rice. Garnish with mint and serve.

Note: This dish can be kept in warm oven or reheated just before serving.

❦ *Makes 2 dozen*

Cinnamon Rice

INGREDIENTS
3 tablespoons butter, divided
$^1/2$ cup diced carrot
$^1/2$ cup diced celery
$^1/2$ cup diced onion
1 $^1/2$ cups long-grain rice
$^1/2$ teaspoon salt
1 $^1/2$ teaspoons ground cinnamon
1 teaspoon ground cumin
$^1/4$ teaspoon crushed red chili pepper flakes
3 $^1/4$ cups water
$^1/2$ cup dried currants
Salt and black pepper

Melt 2 tablespoons butter in a deep saucepan over medium heat. Add carrot, celery, and onion. Sauté, stirring occasionally, for 5 minutes.

Add rice, salt, cinnamon, cumin, and chili pepper flakes. Sauté a few minutes then add water and bring to a boil over high heat. Reduce heat to low, cover, and cook for 25 to 30 minutes, stirring occasionally, until rice is tender. Mix in currants and remaining butter, season with salt and pepper, and serve.

Note: This is a great side dish with roasted meat.

❁ Serves 6

Garlic Ginger Rice

INGREDIENTS
2 tablespoons vegetable oil
6 cloves garlic, minced
1 tablespoon grated fresh ginger root
1/4 teaspoon black pepper
2 cups Jasmine rice
2 cups coconut milk
1 1/4 cups water
1 to 2 tablespoons soy sauce
3 tablespoons shredded coconut
Fresh parsley

Heat oil in a saucepan over medium-low heat. Add garlic, ginger, and pepper. Sauté about 2 minutes.

Rinse rice until water runs clear. Drain well and add to pan. Stir to mix and sauté 1 to 2 minutes. Stir in coconut milk, water, and soy sauce. Bring to a boil. Stir, cover, reduce heat to low, and simmer 15 minutes until liquid is absorbed and rice is tender.

Remove from heat, stir in shredded coconut and let sit covered about 5 minutes. Fluff with fork, and garnish with fresh parsley before serving.

❀ *Serves 4 to 6*

Rice with Green Herbs

INGREDIENTS

2 cups long-grain rice
$1/2$ cup water
8 ounces fresh spinach, washed well
$1/2$ cup chopped fresh parsley
$1/2$ cup chopped fresh cilantro
$1/2$ cup diced onion
3 cloves garlic, minced
2 tablespoons olive oil
3 cups chicken broth
Salt
3 ounces canned chopped green chilies

Place rice in sieve. Rinse. Set aside to drain. Bring water to a boil over high heat. Add spinach, cover, remove from heat, and let sit 5 minutes. Place water and spinach in blender. Add parsley, cilantro, onion, and garlic. Puree until smooth. Set aside.

Heat oil in a skillet over medium-high heat. Add rice and sauté for 5 minutes until golden. Add spinach puree and cook 2 minutes. Add chicken broth. Bring to a boil, reduce heat to low, cover, and simmer about 20 minutes until rice is tender. Remove from heat and let stand covered for 10 minutes. Season with salt to taste. Serve garnished with chopped green chilies.

❀ *Serves 4 to 6*

Lemon Rice

INGREDIENTS
1 ¹/₂ cups rice
¹/₈ teaspoon turmeric
¹/₄ teaspoon salt
1 tablespoon oil
1 green chili, minced
¹/₄ teaspoon mustard seeds
¹/₂ teaspoon fenugreek seeds
1 teaspoon curry powder
¹/₄ cup cashew nuts
10 kaffir lime leaves
Juice of 1 lemon
1 tablespoon shredded coconut

Place rice in sieve and rinse two or three times in fresh water. Place in bowl and soak, covered with water, for 30 minutes.

Bring water equal to 1 ¹/₄ times the volume of rice to a boil in a saucepan over medium-high heat. Add rice, turmeric and salt. Reduce heat to medium-low, cover, and cook 8 to 10 minutes, until all the liquid is absorbed. Remove rice and spread in a flat dish or pan to cool and dry out. Leave for 30 minutes.

Heat oil in a wok or frying pan over medium-high heat. Stir-fry chili for 1 minute, then add mustard seeds, fenugreek seeds, curry, cashew nuts, and lime leaves and stir-fry for 30 seconds. Stir in the cooked rice mixing well but carefully with a flat spatula so as not to mash the rice. Sprinkle with lemon juice. Heat thoroughly. Place in warmed serving dish. Garnish with coconut and serve.

✤ *Serves 4*

Sticky Rice

INGREDIENTS
1 pound (about 2 ¹/₂ cups) sticky rice
Water

Put rice in a bowl. Cover with cold water and soak for at least 3 hours, or overnight if possible. Drain and rinse thoroughly.

Line steamer basket with double thickness muslin or cheesecloth. Add rice. Fill bottom pot of steamer with water. Put on stove over medium heat and bring to a boil. Cover with top basket and steam rice about 30 minutes until tender, adding water as needed. Turn into serving bowl. Serve.

Note: Sticky Rice can be found in Asian markets and natural food stores. Cooking baskets and steamers are also becoming more available.

✤ *Serves 6 to 8*

Pad Thai

SAUCE
$^1/_4$ cup fish sauce
$^1/_4$ cup tamarind juice
$^1/_4$ cup rice vinegar
3 tablespoons granulated sugar
2 tablespoons soy sauce
14 ounces dried rice noodles

PAD THAI
4 tablespoons peanut oil, divided
8 ounces tofu, cubed
3 eggs, well beaten
4 cloves garlic, minced
1 $^1/_2$ pounds shrimp,
  peeled, with tails on
1 teaspoon Thai hot chili sauce
4 cups bean sprouts
1 cup chopped peanuts
1 bunch green onions, sliced
$^1/_4$ cup chopped Thai basil
$^1/_4$ cup cilantro
Lime wedges

In a medium bowl, combine fish sauce, tamarind juice, vinegar, sugar, and soy sauce, stirring until sugar is dissolved. Set aside. Soak noodles in hot water 15 minutes until slightly limp. Drain and set aside. Prepare and measure all of the other ingredients before beginning to cook.

Heat 3 tablespoons oil in a wok or large skillet over medium-high heat. Add tofu and stir-fry until somewhat crispy on outside. Remove from wok and set aside. Add beaten eggs. Swirl to coat bottom of pan, working up the sides to make a thin omelet. Cook until set. Roll up and place on cutting board. Cut into thin slices. Set aside.

Increase heat to high. Add remaining oil to wok. Working quickly, add garlic and shrimp and toss until shrimp are about halfway done. Add chili sauce and toss to combine. Add noodles and toss well. Add bean sprouts and cooked tofu, and toss. Add peanuts, green onions, basil, and cilantro and toss.

When shrimp is just cooked through, add sauce. Heat 30 seconds and remove from stove. Turn into large serving bowl. Garnish with shredded eggs and lime wedges. Serve.

Note: This can be made with chicken breast instead of shrimp or with just the tofu.

❁ Serves 6 to 8

Pasta with Pistachios

SAUCE
2 tablespoons olive oil
1 large onion, finely diced
4 cloves garlic, minced
1 tablespoon flour
1 1/2 cups dry white wine
1 cup oil packed sun-dried tomatoes,
   thinly sliced
1 tablespoon minced fresh basil
1 tablespoon minced fresh oregano
4 tablespoons minced fresh parsley

PASTA
1 pound fresh angel hair pasta
1 cup pistachios
1 cup grated Parmesan

Heat oil in a large skillet over medium heat. Add onion and sauté 8 to 10 minutes, stirring occasionally, until golden. Add garlic and sauté 1 minute. Stir in flour using whisk and cook a few minutes. Slowly stir in wine blending well with whisk. Heat, stirring frequently, until mixture comes to a boil and thickens slightly. Stir in sun-dried tomatoes, basil, oregano, and parsley and heat through. Cover and remove from heat. Keep sauce warm.

Cook pasta in boiling water 3 to 5 minutes, just until tender (note package directions). Drain. Add hot pasta to warm sauce. Place in warmed serving bowl. Sprinkle with pistachios and cheese. Toss lightly. Serve.

❈ *Serves 4 to 6*

Soba Noodles with Edamame

INGREDIENTS
1 chicken bouillon cube
1/2 cup water
3 tablespoons tahini
1 1/2 tablespoons rice vinegar
1 tablespoon soy sauce
1 tablespoon grated fresh ginger root
2 teaspoons granulated sugar
1 teaspoon chili paste
1 carrot, julienned
8 ounces fresh soba noodles
2 cups shelled soybeans
1 sweet red pepper, julienned
4 green onions, thinly sliced
1 tablespoon black sesame seeds

Dissolve bouillon cube in 1/2 cup water in a small saucepan over medium-high heat. Add tahini, vinegar, soy sauce, ginger, sugar, and chili paste to broth using whisk. Bring to a boil, reduce heat to low, and simmer 5 minutes. Remove from heat. Add carrot, cover, and set aside.

Bring a large pot of water to a boil. Add soba, stirring gently. Cook 2 to 3 minutes, stirring occasionally. Stir in soybeans. Cook another 2 to 4 minutes until soba is cooked and soybeans are warmed through.

Drain well. Put in warmed serving bowl. Toss with sauce. Sprinkle with pepper, green onions, and sesame seeds. Serve.

❈ *Serves 6*

Soba with Caviar and Sour Cream

INGREDIENTS
2 tablespoons unsalted butter
12 ounces fresh soba noodles
1/2 cup sour cream
2 tablespoons snipped fresh chives
2 ounces red caviar or salmon roe

Heat butter in a large skillet until golden brown. Add soba and cook for 3 to 5 minutes. Add half the sour cream, half the chives and half the caviar. Arrange on serving plates. Top with remaining sour cream and caviar. Sprinkle with remaining chives. Serve.

❋ *Serves 6*

Udon with Peanut Ginger Pesto

PEANUT GINGER PESTO
2 tablespoon minced crystallized ginger
1 to 2 jalapeno peppers, minced
4 cloves garlic, minced
1 cup toasted peanuts, divided
1 1/2 cups fresh basil
1/2 cup fresh cilantro or mint
2 tablespoons peanut oil
1 tablespoon sesame oil
1 tablespoon fish sauce
1 tablespoon rice vinegar
1 tablespoon soy sauce

NOODLES
14 ounces fresh udon noodles
1 tablespoon peanut oil
8 ounces fresh green beans, or
 4 ounces snow peas, julienned
3 carrots, julienned
8 ounces mixed mushrooms,
 thinly sliced

Place ginger, jalapeno, garlic, 1/2 cup peanuts, basil, and cilantro in a blender or food processor. Slowly add peanut oil while motor is running. Turn off motor, scrape down sides and pulse until somewhat blended. Mix in sesame oil, fish sauce, vinegar, and soy sauce. Scrape into bowl and adjust flavorings and set aside. Chop remaining peanuts and set aside.

Bring 2 quarts water to a boil in a large pot. Add noodles and cook 2 to 4 minutes. Drain well. Add Peanut Ginger Pesto and toss to coat.

Heat oil in skillet over medium heat. Add green beans, carrots, and mushrooms. Sauté 5 minutes until almost tender but still firm. Add vegetables to noodles and mix lightly. Sprinkle with remaining peanuts and serve.

❋ *Serves 6*

Vegetables

Grilled Asparagus with Pomegranate Seeds

INGREDIENTS
2 tablespoons fresh lemon juice
1 medium shallot, minced
1 tablespoon minced chervil or flat leaf parsley
¹/2 teaspoon kosher salt
¹/4 teaspoon cracked black pepper
5 tablespoons extra-virgin olive oil, divided
1 medium pomegranate
2 pounds asparagus

In a medium bowl, whisk together lemon juice, shallot, chervil, salt, and pepper. Gradually whisk in 3 tablespoons oil, blending. Set aside. Separate pomegranate seeds and place in a bowl. Set aside. Trim ends from asparagus and blanch. Lay asparagus on plate and brush with remaining 2 tablespoons oil.

Heat grill to medium-high. Working in batches, grill asparagus, turning, just until tender and lightly browned, about 4 minutes. Arrange on serving plate. Whisk dressing for 30 seconds and drizzle over asparagus. Garnish with pomegranate seeds and serve.

❧ *Serves 4 to 6*

Asian Spring Asparagus

INGREDIENTS
1 pound asparagus, trimmed
1 tablespoon peanut oil
1 teaspoon grated fresh ginger root
1/4 teaspoon black pepper
1 tablespoon soy sauce
1/3 cup coarsely chopped pistachios

Slice asparagus on a sharp diagonal into 3-inch lengths. Heat oil in a large skillet over medium-high heat. Add asparagus, ginger, and pepper. Stir-fry for 2 minutes. Add soy sauce and stir-fry 1 more minute. Sprinkle with pistachios, toss briefly just to heat through, place in serving bowl, and serve.

❧ Serves 2 to 4

Asparagus with Walnut Vinaigrette

INGREDIENTS
4 pounds asparagus, trimmed
2 tablespoons apple cider vinegar
1 tablespoon sherry
1/3 cup walnut oil
1 teaspoon coarse mustard
1/2 teaspoon granulated sugar
1/4 cup thinly sliced fresh chives
   or green onions
Coarse black pepper
Coarse salt
1/2 to 3/4 cup chopped walnuts

In a large deep skillet bring 1 1/2 inches of salted water to a boil over high heat. Add asparagus and cook 2 to 3 minutes, until the stalks are bright green – do not overcook. Drain well and arrange on serving platter. In a bowl whisk together vinegar, sherry, oil, mustard, and sugar, blending well. Whisk in chives. Season with pepper to taste. Pour the dressing over the asparagus, tossing lightly to coat. Sprinkle lightly with salt. Top with walnuts. Serve.

Note: Walnut oil is available at natural food shops and some supermarkets. Try using macadamia oil and macadamia nuts as an alternative.

❧ Serves 8

Beets with Zesty Cream

INGREDIENTS
8 medium beets
1 1/2 tablespoons olive oil
1 1/2 to 2 tablespoons red wine vinegar
1 teaspoon granulated sugar
Salt and black pepper
1 cup chopped watercress
3/4 cup sour cream
1 teaspoon grated orange zest
Sprigs of watercress

Heat oven to 400°F. Wash beets. Place on sheet of aluminum foil, wrap, and seal tightly. Bake for 1 1/2 to 2 hours until tender but firm when tested with knife. Cool slightly. Peel beets, slice into 1/4-inch rounds, then into 1/4-inch thin strips. Place in a bowl.

In a small bowl, whisk together oil, vinegar, and sugar. Season with salt and pepper. Drizzle over beets, toss to mix. Spread chopped watercress in shallow serving dish and top with beets. In a small bowl, mix together sour cream and orange zest. Place in dollops on top of beets. Garnish with sprigs of watercress, and serve.

Note: If making ahead, do not top beets with sour cream until ready to serve. The beet juice will bleed into the sour cream making it pink.

❧ *Serves 6 to 8*

Braised Beet Greens

INGREDIENTS
1/3 cup raspberry vinegar
2 cloves garlic, minced
1 teaspoon granulated sugar
2 pounds beet greens,
  washed and chopped
1/4 cup water
Cayenne pepper
2 tablespoons sesame seeds

In a medium saucepan, heat vinegar, garlic, and sugar over medium heat. Add beet greens and water, reduce heat, and cook gently to evaporate liquid and wilt greens. Place greens on warmed serving platter, sprinkle with cayenne and sesame seeds, and serve.

❧ *Serves 4*

Bok Choy with Black Mushrooms

INGREDIENTS

2 tablespoons soy sauce
2 tablespoons sherry
1 tablespoon cornstarch
1 teaspoon sesame oil
12 fresh shiitake mushroom caps
3 scallions, cut into 1-inch pieces
1 tablespoon minced fresh ginger root
1 tablespoon peanut oil
6 to 8 baby bok choy
Thinly sliced scallion

Stir together soy sauce, sherry, cornstarch, and sesame oil in a large bowl until smooth. Add mushroom caps, scallions, and ginger. Toss to coat. Marinate at room temperature, stirring occasionally, 30 minutes. Heat peanut oil in a wok over medium-high heat. Swirl to coat sides. Trim ends from bok choy, halve lengthwise, and rinse well. Pat dry. Add bok choy to wok and stir-fry until leaves are bright green and just limp, 1 to 2 minutes. Stir in marinated mushroom caps and stir-fry until sauce is slightly thickened, about 1 to 2 minutes. Place in serving dish and garnish with thinly sliced scallion. Serve.

 Serves 4

Broccoli with Adzuki Beans

INGREDIENTS

3/4 cup adzuki beans
3 cups water
1 1/2 tablespoons olive oil
1 large onion, thinly sliced
2 cloves garlic, minced
1 1/2 pounds broccoli,
  cut into small pieces
2 large ripe tomatoes, diced
1 teaspoon grated fresh ginger root
1 to 2 tablespoons miso
1 teaspoon sesame oil

Place adzuki beans and water in a medium saucepan. Bring to a boil over medium-high heat. Reduce heat to medium-low. Cover and cook about 1 hour until tender, adding water as needed. Drain. Heat oil in a large skillet over medium heat. Add onion and garlic. Sauté until golden. Add broccoli, stirring to mix. Cover and let steam, stirring occasionally, 2 to 3 minutes until broccoli is bright green. Stir in tomatoes, adzuki beans, and ginger. Cook a few minutes to heat through. Season with miso and sesame oil, stirring to blend. Place in a serving bowl and serve.

 Serves 4 to 6

Lemon Broccoli

INGREDIENTS

1 pound broccoli, cut into $^1/_2$-inch pieces
$^1/_2$ cup water
2 tablespoons butter
2 to 3 anchovies
$^1/_4$ teaspoon black pepper
2 teaspoons olive oil
4 cloves garlic, passed through press
1 tablespoon grated lemon zest
2 tablespoons fresh lemon juice

Combine broccoli and water in a medium saucepan. Cover and bring to a boil over high heat. Cook 2 to 3 minutes until bright green and crisp-tender. Drain, put in a dish, and set aside. Reduce heat to medium. Dry pan and return to heat. Add butter, anchovies, pepper, oil, and garlic to pan. Cook about 2 minutes, stirring frequently. Return broccoli and toss to coat. Sprinkle with lemon zest and lemon juice, toss again. Place in serving dish and serve.

❀ *Serves 4*

Ginger-Sesame Broccoli

INGREDIENTS

1 $^1/_2$ pounds broccoli
2 teaspoons sesame seeds
2 teaspoons sesame oil
3 tablespoons tamari
2 teaspoons grated fresh ginger root
2 teaspoons packed brown sugar
2 tablespoons water

Slice broccoli stalk thinly on the diagonal. Separate florets. Set aside. Heat a frying pan over medium heat. Add sesame seeds and lightly toast, shaking accasionally. Remove from pan and set aside. Return frying pan to heat. Add sesame oil. Add broccoli to hot oil and sauté 5 to 7 minutes until crisp tender. Combine tamari, ginger, sugar, and water. Sprinkle over broccoli. Remove from heat. Place in serving dish, sprinkle with sesame seeds, and serve.

Note: Shoyu is the Japanese word for soy sauce. It is made from soybeans, roasted wheat, sea salt, and koji. This is an all-purpose cooking sauce and condiment with the ability to harmonize and enhance the flavors of other food.

Tamari means liquid pressed from soybeans. It is richer and more intense in flavor than shoyu. Originally it was the dark thick liquid found in casks of fermenting miso. Today it is brewed in a similar manner to shoyu but without the wheat, making it popular with those who have wheat allergies.

❀ *Serves 4*

Brussels Sprout and Potato Duet

INGREDIENTS
1 tablespoon butter
1 tablespoon olive oil
1 large potato, peeled, and diced
*   into $1/2$-inch cubes*
1 onion, diced
1 bay leaf
1 pound Brussels sprouts
1 sweet red pepper, diced
$1/2$ cup chicken broth
1 teaspoon whole grain mustard
$1/4$ teaspoon black pepper
2 tablespoons minced fresh parsley

In a large skillet, melt butter in oil over medium heat. Add potato, onion, and bay leaf. Cook stirring often until onion is soft. Wash, trim, and halve Brussels sprouts. Add with red pepper, sauté 5 minutes. Add broth and mustard, lower heat, and simmer 5 minutes. Remove bay leaf. Season with pepper. Place in serving dish. Sprinkle with parsley and serve.

Note: The Brussels sprout, a member of the cabbage family, is native to northern Europe. When selecting sprouts, look for firm, heavy, compact bright green heads without blemishes. The smaller young sprouts have a sweeter flavor than the older sprouts or those with yellowed leaves.

❀ *Serves 4 to 6*

Sautéed Brussels Sprouts

INGREDIENTS
8 ounces bacon, large dice
1 $1/2$ teaspoons caraway seed
1 pound Brussels sprouts
$1/4$ cup white wine vinegar
2 teaspoons soy sauce
$1/4$ teaspoon black pepper

In a medium frying pan, cook bacon until crisp over medium-low heat. Remove and place on paper towel. Drain fat from pan saving a little for sautéing. Return pan to stovetop, increase heat to medium. Add caraway seeds and heat a few minutes until lightly toasted. Remove and set aside. Wash, trim, and halve Brussels sprouts. Add Brussels sprouts to pan, and a little bacon fat if needed to keep from sticking. Sauté sprouts until tender. Add vinegar, soy sauce, and pepper. Heat a few minutes to reduce liquid. Place in serving dish. Top with crispy bacon and toasted caraway seeds. Serve.

❀ *Serves 4*

Baby Carrots with Dill and Capers

INGREDIENTS

1 pound baby carrots
$^1/_2$ cup water
4 tablespoon unsalted butter
$^1/_4$ cup chopped fresh dill
1 $^1/_2$ tablespoons capers, minced

Trim tops from carrots and peel. Place in a medium saucepan with water. Bring to a boil over medium-high heat and cook 3 to 5 minutes until crisp-tender. Reduce heat to low. Drain carrots and return to heat. Add butter and dill, stirring often until butter melts. Add capers and toss to mix. Place in warm serving dish and serve.

Note: Baby carrots aren't really babies at all. They are a variety bred to grow long and slender, to be peeled and cut into 2-inch pieces. First introduced in 1989, they are the most popular variety of carrots in the marketplace.

❦ *Serves 4 to 6*

Carrot Parsnip Swirl

INGREDIENTS

1 pound parsnips
1 pound carrots
1 pound potatoes
2 cloves garlic, minced
6 tablespoons butter, divided
$^1/_2$ cup heavy cream, divided
3 tablespoons grated Parmesan
1 teaspoon grated fresh ginger root
2 tablespoons pure maple syrup
Salt and white pepper
Ground paprika
Black sesame seeds

Peel parsnips and cut into 1-inch pieces. Place in a large pot. Peel carrots and cut into 1-inch pieces. Place in another large pot. Peel potatoes and cut into 1-inch pieces. Add half the potatoes to parsnips and the other half to carrots. Add enough water to cover vegetables. Bring to a boil, reduce heat to medium and cook until vegetables are soft, 15 to 20 minutes. Drain. Add garlic to the parsnips and mash, adding 3 tablespoons butter and $^1/_4$ cup heavy cream. Stir in Parmesan and season with salt and pepper to taste. Mound parsnips on one side of a warm shallow serving dish. Press to create a crescent. Garnish with paprika.

Add ginger to the carrots and mash, adding 3 tablespoons butter and $^1/_4$ cup heavy cream. Stir in maple syrup, season with salt and pepper to taste. Add carrots to remaining space in dish. Garnish with sesame seeds. Serve.

❦ *Serves 8*

Carrots with Star Anise

INGREDIENTS
1 1/2 pounds carrots
1/2 cup water
3 star anise
1 tablespoon granulated sugar
Pinch salt
2 tablespoons butter, cut into small pieces

Peel carrots, trim ends, and cut into 1/4-inch slices. Put carrots and water in a medium saucepan. Add star anise, sugar, and salt. Bring to a boil over high heat. Reduce heat to medium, cook, turning a couple of times, until the water boils away and carrots just start to sizzle, 8 to 10 minutes. Add butter and stir until melted. Remove from heat. Place in serving bowl and serve.

❊ *Serves 6 to 8*

Cauliflower Béchamel

INGREDIENTS
1 large head cauliflower
1/2 cup water
1 tablespoon butter
2 tablespoons all-purpose flour
2 cups milk
1 tablespoon Dijon-style mustard
Ground nutmeg
Salt and black pepper
3/4 cup shredded smoked Gouda cheese
1 tablespoon minced parsley

Heat oven to 375°F. Butter a 2-quart shallow baking dish and set aside. Cut cauliflower into small florets. Place in a medium saucepan with water. Bring to a boil over high heat. Cook 2 to 3 minutes until just tender. Drain and put in prepared baking dish. Melt butter in a medium saucepan over medium heat. Using a whisk, stir in flour to make a smooth paste and cook 2 minutes, stirring occasionally. Add milk in a steady stream stirring constantly with whisk. Blend in mustard. Cook until sauce thickens, 5 to 8 minutes, whisking frequently. Season with nutmeg, salt, and pepper. Pour over cauliflower. Sprinkle with cheese. Place in oven for 25 to 30 minutes until lightly golden and hot. Sprinkle with parsley and serve.

Note: Béchamel sauce can be served with steamed vegetables, potatoes, eggs, or pasta. Grated Parmesan and finely minced herbs such as basil or parsley can be added.

❧ *Serves 4 to 6*

Cauliflower with Goat Cheese

INGREDIENTS
1 head cauliflower
Salt
2 tablespoons whipping cream
2 tablespoons unsalted butter
2 tablespoons freshly grated Parmesan
2 tablespoons goat cheese

Cut cauliflower into small florets. Place in a large pot with 2 inches of water and a pinch of salt. Bring to a boil over high heat. Reduce heat to medium and cook, covered, until completely tender, 10 to 15 minutes. Pour into a colander and drain well. Press cauliflower gently but firmly to remove all water. Toss the cauliflower and continue pressing. This step is very important to the texture of the dish. Transfer the cauliflower to a food processor. Add cream and puree until very smooth. For a chunkier texture, mash by hand, adding the cream after the cauliflower is mashed. Return to the pot. Just before serving, heat over low heat, stirring constantly. Add butter, Parmesan, and goat cheese. Stir to blend well, adjust salt to taste. Place in serving bowl and serve.

❋ *Serves 4 to 6*

Sizzling Celery

INGREDIENTS
2 cups water
10 ribs fresh celery
1 teaspoon salt
1 teaspoon granulated sugar
1 tablespoon vegetable oil
1 small red hot chili, minced
$1/2$ cup chopped water chestnuts
2 green onions, thinly sliced
Freshly ground black pepper

In a medium pot over high heat, bring water to a boil. Trim ends from celery. Cut into 1-inch pieces on the diagonal. Add celery to boiling water, cover, turn off heat and simmer 2 to 3 minutes until celery is tender but still crunchy. Drain, place in a bowl, and sprinkle with salt and sugar. Return pan to stove. Heat oil over medium heat. Add chili and water chestnuts, sauté 2 minutes to soften. Stir in celery and sauté a minute or two, tossing to mix well. Do not overcook, or undercook. Put in warmed serving dish. Add green onions and season with black pepper. Stir lightly to mix and serve warm or at room temperature.

Note: Originating in Southeast Asia, water chestnuts are the tuberous roots of an aquatic plant that grows in slow moving, nutrient-rich freshwater ponds, marshes, and lakes.

❋ *Serves 4 to 6*

Choi Sum with Enoki and Sprouts

INGREDIENTS
1 tablespoon extra-virgin olive oil
1 bunch choi sum, rinsed and cut into
   3-inch pieces
1 1/2 ounces mung bean sprouts, rinsed
3 cloves garlic, sliced
Pinch of crushed dried hot chili
   pepper flakes
1 ounce enoki mushrooms,
   rinsed and trimmed
Pinch of sea salt

Heat oil in a large skillet or wok over high heat. Working quickly, add choi sum, and toss. Add bean sprouts, garlic, and chili pepper flakes. Continue to toss to prevent burning. Heat 2 to 3 minutes until greens are slightly wilted and bright green. Do not overcook. Remove to serving bowl. Add mushrooms to pan. Toss quickly but gently. Heat through. Arrange across top of greens. Sprinkle with salt and serve.

Note: Choi sum has lovely little yellow flowers that add to the presentation of this dish. The greens have a pungent flavor and are used in Italian as well as Chinese cooking. Choi sum is also called broccoli rabe and rapini.

❀ *Serves 4*

Corn Custard with Relish

INGREDIENTS
4 cups corn kernels, divided
6 ounces cherry tomatoes, diced
1/3 cup minced red onion
1 tablespoon minced fresh basil
2 teaspoons extra-virgin olive oil
1 teaspoon red wine vinegar
Salt and black pepper
1 1/2 cups whole milk
2 eggs
1/2 teaspoon salt
1/8 teaspoon cayenne pepper

Stir together 3/4 cup corn, tomatoes, onion, and basil in a bowl. Stir in oil and vinegar. Season with salt and pepper. Cover and chill. Preheat oven to 350°F. Lightly oil four 6-ounce ramekins and set aside.

Put remaining corn in a saucepan with milk and heat over medium just until boiling, stirring occasionally. Lower heat and simmer 10 minutes. Remove from heat and place in a blender or food processor. Carefully puree until somewhat smooth. Pour through sieve into a bowl. Beat in eggs, salt, and cayenne until blended. Divide mixture among prepared ramekins, place in a large roasting pan, and add 1-inch of water. Place in oven and bake just until set, about 40 minutes. Remove ramekins from water bath and let sit a few minutes. Run a knife around edges to loosen. Invert on plates. Add spoonful of relish and serve.

❀ *Serves 4*

Thai Eggplant with Basil

INGREDIENTS
$1/2$ cup coconut milk

2 tablespoons oil

16 small green Thai eggplant, trimmed
and quartered

2 cloves garlic, minced

1 to 2 teaspoons green curry paste,
homemade or prepared

2 tablespoons fish sauce

1 teaspoon granulated sugar

$1/2$ cup broth or water

2 kaffir lime leaves

20 basil leaves

GREEN CURRY PASTE
2 long green chilies, minced

10 small green chilies, minced

1 tablespoon chopped lemongrass

3 shallots, minced

2 tablespoons minced garlic

1-inch piece galangal or fresh
ginger root, minced

1 tablespoon minced cilantro

1 teaspoon ground coriander seed

$1/2$ teaspoon ground cumin

$1/2$ teaspoon ground white pepper

1 teaspoon chopped kaffir lime leaves

2 teaspoons shrimp paste

1 teaspoon salt

In a small saucepan, gently warm coconut milk over medium-low heat, do not allow to boil. Set aside.

In a frying pan or wok, heat oil over medium-high heat until it starts smoking. Add eggplant and garlic. Fry until golden. Add curry paste and stir-fry a few seconds. Add warmed coconut milk and stir until thickened. Add fish sauce, sugar, and broth. Reduce heat and simmer 3 to 4 minutes, stirring occasionally. Add lime leaves and basil, stir and cook 1 minute. Place into serving dish. Serve hot.

Green Curry Paste: Using a mortar and pestle or spice grinder, blend all ingredients together to form a smooth paste. Keep refrigerated.

Note: Galangal is a Thai ginger root.

 Serves 4

Grilled Green Beans with Gorgonzola Vinaigrette

Green Beans
1 cup water
Salt
1 pound green beans, trimmed

Gorgonzola Vinaigrette
1 tablespoon olive oil, divided
3 tablespoons balsamic vinegar
$1/3$ cup crumbled Gorgonzola cheese,
   plus extra
1 tablespoon packed brown sugar
4 cloves garlic, minced
1 green onion, thinly sliced
1 teaspoon minced fresh thyme
1 teaspoon minced fresh basil
Salt and black pepper

In a medium saucepan over medium-high heat, bring water and a dash of salt to a boil. Add green beans and cook 2 minutes until bright green but still crisp. Remove from heat, drain, and set aside.

In a small saucepan over medium-low heat, combine $1\,1/2$ teaspoons oil with vinegar, Gorgonzola, sugar, garlic, green onion, thyme, and basil. Cook gently to blend flavors, about 5 to 7 minutes. Remove vinaigrette from heat. Toss green beans with remaining $1\,1/2$ teaspoons oil then season lightly with salt and pepper. Lightly grill the beans on barbecue or grill pan about 1 to 2 minutes, turning to keep from burning. Remove from grill and place on serving platter. Drizzle with warm vinaigrette. Sprinkle with some Gorgonzola and serve.

❧ Serves 4

Minted Green Beans

INGREDIENTS

6 hard-cooked eggs
6 tablespoons extra-virgin olive oil
6 tablespoons minced fresh mint, divided
Sea salt and coarse black pepper
1/2 cup water
2 pounds green beans, cut into
    2-inch pieces
1 tablespoon macadamia nut oil
2 cloves garlic, minced
5 large vine-ripened Kula tomatoes,
    diced
Whole mint leaves

Using the coarse shredding side of a hand held grater, shred eggs into a bowl. Add olive oil and 4 tablespoons chopped mint. Season with salt and pepper to taste. Gently stir just to blend. Set aside. In a medium saucepan over medium-high heat, bring water to a boil. Add green beans to boiling water and cook for 2 to 3 minutes until tender but still crisp and bright green. Put into colander to drain. Place on serving platter.

In a large saucepan, heat macadamia nut oil and garlic over medium-high heat, just until garlic starts to sizzle. Add diced tomatoes and remaining 2 tablespoons chopped mint. Sprinkle lightly with salt and sauté a few minutes to wilt tomato. Remove from heat and lay down center of green beans on serving platter. Gently sprinkle egg dressing down the middle of tomatoes. Garnish with mint leaves and serve.

 Serves 6

Greens with Lime and Cilantro

INGREDIENTS

3 tablespoons olive oil
1 large onion, chopped
3 large cloves garlic, minced
1 teaspoon ground coriander
1 pound mixed greens
1/2 teaspoon salt
1/2 teaspoon black pepper
16 ounces canned
    whole hominy, drained
1/2 cup chopped fresh cilantro
2 to 3 tablespoons fresh lime juice

In a heavy skillet, heat oil over medium heat. Add onion, garlic, and coriander and cook, stirring frequently, for 5 minutes. Add several handfuls of greens, cover, and cook until wilted, 3 to 5 minutes. Stir well and repeat until all the greens have been added. Uncover, season with salt and pepper. Stir in hominy and heat through. Remove from heat, stir in cilantro and lime juice. Place in a warmed serving bowl and serve.

Note: Mixed greens can be a combination of kale, collards, mustard, spinach, and chard.

 Serves 4

Steamed Greens with Honey Sesame Dressing

INGREDIENTS

1 ¹/2 pounds spinach, baby bok choy,
   or choi sum
2 tablespoons soy sauce
1 tablespoons rice wine vinegar
1 tablespoon honey
1 teaspoon sesame oil
1 ¹/2 teaspoons toasted sesame seeds

Pour enough water into a wok to measure 1 inch and bring to a boil over high heat. Put greens into a bamboo steamer and cover. Put steamer into wok and steam vegetables about 5 minutes or until just tender. Meanwhile, make dressing by combining soy sauce, vinegar, honey, oil, and 1 teaspoon sesame seeds in a small bowl. Place cooked greens on a serving platter, drizzle with dressing, and toss well to coat. Garnish with remaining sesame seeds and serve immediately.

❋ *Serves 4 to 6*

Stir-Fried Greens with Oyster Sauce

INGREDIENTS

2 tablespoons oyster sauce
1 tablespoon soy sauce
2 pinches of granulated sugar
Juice of 1 lime
1 pound mixed Chinese greens
3 tablespoons walnut oil
1 tablespoon sesame oil
1-inch piece fresh ginger root, thinly
sliced
4 scallions, julienned
Salt and black pepper

In a small bowl, mix oyster sauce, soy sauce, sugar, and lime juice. Set aside. Trim and remove any blemished stalks from greens. Cut into 3-inch pieces. If using spinach, put it aside to add to pan at the last minute, as it cooks very quickly. Plunge other greens into boiling water for about 1 ¹/2 minutes until just tender. Drain well.

Heat walnut and sesame oils in a wok or large pan over medium-high heat. Add ginger and cook about 30 seconds. Add scallions, greens, and sauce. Stir, add spinach, and toss to coat with sauce. Heat to reduce sauce. Season with salt and pepper to taste. Place in serving bowl and serve immediately.

❋ *Serves 4*

Wilted Greens

INGREDIENTS

2 cloves garlic, minced
1 hot chili pepper, julienned
1-inch piece fresh ginger root, minced
5 green onions, thinly sliced
4 teaspoons fish sauce
Juice of 1 lime
2 teaspoons granulated sugar
1 tablespoon soy sauce
1 tablespoon mirin
2 tablespoons rice wine or sherry
1 bunch choi sum
1 bunch mizuna

Combine garlic, chili, ginger, and green onions in small bowl. Sprinkle with fish sauce, lime juice, sugar, soy sauce, mirin, and rice wine. Set aside.

Wash and trim choi sum and mizuna. Place in large saucepan, add 1 inch of water, and cook over high heat just until wilted. Drain, place in serving bowl, sprinkle with sauce, and serve.

❀ *Serves 6*

Braised Kale

INGREDIENTS

1 pound red potatoes, cut into
    1-inch cubes
1 tablespoon olive oil
8 ounces crimini mushrooms, stemmed
    and thinly sliced
2 medium shallots, minced
8 cloves garlic, minced
Salt and black pepper
1 pound kale, thinly sliced

Place potatoes in a medium saucepan, cover with water, and bring to a boil. Reduce heat and cook just until tender, 15 to 18 minutes. Drain. Set aside.

In a large skillet, heat oil over medium heat. Add mushrooms, shallots, and garlic. Cook, stirring often until tender, about 5 minutes. Season with salt and pepper. Add kale to skillet, continue to cook, stirring often, until kale is bright green, about 5 minutes. Add potatoes, heat through, and serve warm.

❀ *Serves 4 to 6*

Lima Beans Kamuela

INGREDIENTS
20 to 24 ounces frozen lima beans
1 cup water
1 large onion, diced
2 teaspoons fresh oregano
$^1/4$ cup chopped fresh parsley
1 large Kamuela tomato, diced
1 teaspoon salt
Pinch dried red chili pepper flakes
3 green onions, cut into 1-inch pieces
1 sweet red pepper, thinly sliced
2 tablespoons extra-virgin olive oil

In a medium saucepan, combine lima beans and water. Cook over medium heat, about 5 minutes, checking water and adding as necessary. Add onion, oregano, parsley, and tomato. Stir to mix well. Season with salt and chili pepper flakes. Continue to cook until beans are soft and sauce thickens, about 10 minutes.

Stir in green onions and sweet red pepper. Remove from heat, place in serving bowl, and drizzle with olive oil. Serve.

Note: Can be served with fresh rosemary bread or over steamed rice.

❀ *Serves 4*

Lima Beans with Dill and Coconut

INGREDIENTS
1 tablespoon olive oil
$1/2$ teaspoon cumin seeds
1 medium onion, diced
2 cloves garlic, passed through press
1 teaspoon grated fresh ginger root
$1/8$ teaspoon cayenne pepper
$1/2$ teaspoon paprika
$1/2$ teaspoon salt
1 ripe tomato, diced
24 to 30 ounces frozen lima beans, partially thawed
2 tablespoons shredded coconut
1 tablespoon chopped fresh dill

Heat oil in a skillet over medium heat. Add cumin seeds.
Cook until sizzling. Add onion, garlic, and ginger. Sauté
until onion is slightly golden, 8 to 10 minutes. Add cayenne,
paprika, and salt. Stir to blend. Sauté 1 minute to release
flavors. Add tomato. Sauté a few minutes to evaporate
liquid. Stir in lima beans and coconut. Heat thoroughly, 3 to
5 minutes. Put into serving dish. Sprinkle with chopped dill
and serve warm.

❧ Serves 6 to 8

Gorgonzola Stuffed Onions

INGREDIENTS
Vegetable oil
6 medium onions
4 ounces Gorgonzola cheese
2 tablespoons olive oil, divided
2 teaspoons chopped fresh rosemary
2 teaspoons chopped fresh thyme
Salt and freshly ground black pepper
³/4 cup water
Sprigs of fresh rosemary

Heat oven to 400°F. Lightly oil a baking dish large enough to hold the onions and suitable for presenting at table. Trim ends of onions and remove papery covering. With a melon baller, scoop out a large depression about 1 ¹/2 inches wide and 2 inches deep in each onion top. Arrange onions in prepared baking pan. Divide Gorgonzola evenly between onions, packing firmly into depressions. Drizzle 1 teaspoon olive oil over each onion. Sprinkle with rosemary and thyme. Season with salt and pepper to taste. Pour water into bottom of dish, cover tightly with foil. Bake for 55 to 60 minutes, until onions are tender. Remove foil. Garnish with fresh rosemary and serve.

Note: To get golden brown tops on the onions, remove the foil after 45 minutes of baking.

 Serves 6

Roasted Peppers with Feta

INGREDIENTS
¹/2 cup chopped walnuts
8 red or yellow bell peppers
4 ounces of Feta, crumbled
1 to 2 tablespoons of
   extra-virgin olive oil
1 tablespoon balsamic vinegar
2 tablespoons minced parsley
1 baguette, thinly sliced

Heat broiler unit. Place walnuts in a small baking pan and set aside. Set whole peppers on rack below heating element. As pepper skins turn black and blistery, turn using long handled tongs to char on every side. When peppers are blackened, remove and place in a large bowl and cover immediately or place in self sealing bag and close. Leave for 15 to 20 minutes. Place walnuts under broiler, turn off heat and let toast lightly, being careful not to burn.

Uncover peppers. Remove charred peel. It is okay if some skin remains. Cut peppers in half, remove seeds and stem. Cut each half into eighths and arrange on a large plate. Sprinkle with Feta and drizzle with oil and vinegar. Scatter walnuts and parsley over all. Serve at room temperature with bread slices.

 Serves 8

Fontina Baked Potatoes and Tomatoes

INGREDIENTS
Olive oil
3 large tomatoes
6 russet potatoes
6 ounces Fontina cheese, shredded
Salt and black pepper

Heat oven to 375°F. Brush a shallow 2-quart baking dish with oil. Wash and thinly slice tomatoes. Scrub, peel and thinly slice potatoes. Using one-third of potato slices, arrange in a slightly overlapping layer in prepared dish. Top with one-third of tomato slices. Sprinkle with salt and pepper and one-third of cheese. Repeat, making two more layers, ending with cheese. Cover with foil and bake 1 hour. Remove foil and continue to bake until top is golden brown, about 15 minutes more, and serve.

❧ *Serves 4 to 6*

Roasted Potatoes with Hazelnuts

INGREDIENTS
2 pounds sweet potatoes
2 pounds Yukon gold potatoes
12 cloves garlic, peeled
3 tablespoons olive oil
4 tablespoons butter, cut into small pieces
Salt and black pepper
3/4 cup chopped hazelnuts
Paprika

Heat oven to 400°F. Scrub, peel, and cut potatoes into 1-inch chunks. Place potatoes in a 12 x 17-inch roasting pan. Scatter in garlic. Drizzle with oil, dot with butter, and season with salt and pepper. Cover with aluminum foil. Bake for 30 minutes.

Uncover and bake for another 30 minutes, turning potatoes every 10 minutes. Sprinkle with hazelnuts and continue to bake another 5 to 10 minutes, turning occasionally, until very tender and well browned. Sprinkle with paprika and serve.

❧ *Serves 8*

Walnut Sage Potatoes

INGREDIENTS

2 pounds potatoes

3 tablespoons walnut oil

$1/2$ cup chopped onion

2 cloves garlic, minced

3 tablespoons minced fresh sage

3 tablespoons all-purpose flour

$1/2$ teaspoon salt

$1/4$ teaspoon black pepper

2 $1/2$ cups milk

4 ounces Gruyere cheese, shredded, divided

$1/2$ cup broken walnut pieces

Fresh sage leaves

Heat oven to 350°F. Grease a 2-quart round casserole. Scrub, peel, and thinly slice potatoes. Place slices in colander, rinse well with cold water, and let sit to drain. In a medium saucepan, heat oil over medium heat. Add onion, garlic, and sage. Sauté until tender but not browned. Using whisk, stir in flour, salt, and pepper. Stir in milk all at once, blending well. Continue to cook stirring occasionally until thickened and bubbling. Remove from heat.

Layer half the potatoes in casserole. Cover with half the sauce. Sprinkle with half the cheese. Repeat layers of potato and sauce. Cover with baking lid or foil. Chill remaining cheese. Bake potatoes for 45 minutes, then uncover and bake 20 to 25 minutes more until just tender. Sprinkle with remaining cheese and nuts. Bake uncovered 5 more minutes to melt cheese and lightly toast nuts. Remove from oven and let stand a few minutes. Garnish with sage leaves and serve.

 Serves 4

Wasabi Mashed Potatoes

INGREDIENTS

3 pounds white potatoes
3 tablespoons butter, cubed
3 cloves garlic, passed through press
$1/2$ cup chicken broth
1 cup half-and-half
2 tablespoons wasabi paste
$1/2$ cup chopped parsley
Sea salt

Scrub, peel, and cut potatoes into chunks. Place in a 4-quart pan, cover with water and bring to a boil over high heat. Reduce heat to medium and cook until tender, about 20 minutes. Drain well. Add butter and garlic, stir to mix, and let sit a minute or two to melt butter. Coarsely mash by hand. Add broth and half-and-half a little at a time, mashing between additions until smooth. Stir in wasabi and parsley. Scrape into warm serving bowl and sprinkle lightly with salt. Serve warm.

Note: Wasabi or Japanese horseradish is a root-like rhizome with a pungent flavor and bright green color. Fresh wasabi is becoming scarce and mixtures with western horseradish are being substituted. It can be found in both powdered and prepared forms. As a condiment, it is traditionally served with sushi, seafood, and noodle dishes.

❀ *Serves 4 to 6*

Gingered Sweet Potatoes

INGREDIENTS
4 tablespoons butter, divided
5 cloves garlic, thinly sliced
1 tablespoon minced fresh ginger root
1 1/2 cups half-and-half
4 medium sweet potatoes
Salt and black pepper

Melt 1 tablespoon butter in a small saucepan over medium-low heat and swirl to coat the bottom of the pan. Add garlic and ginger. Sauté, stirring occasionally, until garlic is golden, about 5 minutes. Add half-and-half and heat to reduce to about one cup, about 10 minutes. Keep warm.

Peel and cut sweet potatoes into eighths. Place in a large saucepan and cover with water. Bring to a boil over high heat and cook until tender, 20 to 25 minutes. Drain well. Coarsely mash by hand. Add reduced half-and-half and continue to mash until well blended. Add remaining butter, season with salt and pepper, and stir until smooth. Adjust seasonings to taste. Place in a warm serving bowl and serve.

Note: Using a variety of light and dark colored sweet potatoes adds a bit of interest.

❀ *Serves 4*

Sweet Potato and Currant Latkes

INGREDIENTS
1 cup boiling water
1/4 cup dried currants
3 medium sweet potatoes
2 eggs
1/3 cup finely chopped hazelnuts
1/4 teaspoon ground cinnamon
1/4 teaspoon ground cloves
1/8 teaspoon salt
1/4 cup all-purpose flour
2 to 3 tablespoons olive oil, divided
Applesauce

In a small mixing bowl pour boiling water over currants. Let stand 5 minutes. Drain well. Scrub potatoes, peel and shred. Place in a clean tea towel and squeeze out the excess liquid. In a large bowl, beat eggs until smooth. Add currants, hazelnuts, cinnamon, cloves, and salt. Stir in potatoes and flour, mixing well. Using 1/3 cup mixture for each latke, press into patties about 1/2-inch thick and set aside.

In a large skillet, heat 1 tablespoon oil over medium heat. Add several latkes and cook 3 to 4 minutes, until golden brown. Turn and cook other side. Remove from pan and set on paper towel to drain. Cook remaining latkes, adding additional oil as needed to prevent sticking. Arrange on warmed serving platter. Serve with applesauce.

Note: The secret to great latkes is to remove as much liquid from the potatoes as possible.

❋ *Makes about 10*

Kabocha Pumpkin with Caramelized Onions

INGREDIENTS
2 pounds Kabocha pumpkin
1/2 cup water
1/2 cup golden raisins
1/2 cup warm water
1/4 cup olive oil
2 large Maui onions, thinly sliced
1/4 cup sliced almonds
1/4 cup granulated sugar
1 teaspoon ground cinnamon
Salt and black pepper
Sliced almonds

Heat oven to 375°F. Slice pumpkin into 1-inch wedges and peel. Place in an ovenproof baking dish. Add 1/2 cup water and cover tightly. Bake until tender about 45 to 50 minutes. Place raisins in small bowl. Cover with warm water and let plump. In a large skillet over medium-low, heat oil and cook onions, stirring occasionally, 20 to 25 minutes until caramelized. Drain raisins and add to skillet with almonds, sugar, and cinnamon. Cook, stirring, for 5 more minutes. Drain off any excess water from cooked pumpkin. Season with salt and pepper. Spread onion mixture evenly over pumpkin. Sprinkle with additional almonds and serve.

Note: Sugar pumpkins or acorn squash may be substituted for Kabocha.

❋ *Serves 6*

Spinach and Garbanzo Beans

INGREDIENTS

2 tablespoons pine nuts
1 tablespoon olive oil
1 large onion, diced
2 cloves garlic, minced
1/2 teaspoon ground nutmeg
2 pounds fresh spinach, thinly sliced
15 ounces canned garbanzo beans,
    drained
1/2 cup dark or golden raisins
Salt and black pepper
1/4 cup plain yogurt

Heat a large skillet over medium heat. Add pine nuts and toast until golden. Remove and set aside. Heat oil in skillet. Add onion and garlic, sauté until soft, stirring occasionally, about 8 minutes. Add nutmeg and heat 1 minute. Add spinach, cover, and let steam just a few minutes until wilted. Add garbanzo beans, raisins, and pine nuts, stirring well. Season with salt and pepper to taste. Heat thoroughly, about 5 minutes.

Place in warmed serving bowl. Serve with dollop of plain yogurt. Also try serving with crusty bread and tomato salad or polenta and tomato sauce.

 Serves 4

Butternut Squash with Adzuki Bean

INGREDIENTS

1 small butternut squash
1 cup vegetable broth
1 tablespoon grated fresh ginger root
1 tablespoon tamari or soy sauce
1 tablespoon sesame oil
3 cups cooked adzuki beans
1 tablespoon miso
Salt and black pepper

Peel squash, remove seeds, and cut into 1-inch cubes. Set aside. In a large saucepan, bring broth, ginger, tamari, and oil to a boil over medium heat. Add squash, cover, and cook until tender, about 10 minutes. Stir in adzuki beans and miso, reduce heat and simmer 5 minutes. Season lightly with salt and pepper, add additional broth or water if too dry, and serve.

Note: Miso is a concentrated savory paste and good source of protein and carbohydrates, but high in sodium. It is made from fermenting soybeans with yeast and grain such as rice, barley, or wheat, and is then combined with salt and water. The mixture is aged from one month to three years.

 Serves 4

Curried Summer Squash

INGREDIENTS
¹/4 cup shredded coconut
2 tablespoons grape seed or other oil
5 medium summer squash, thinly sliced
1 sweet onion, thinly sliced
3 cloves garlic, minced
1 teaspoon grated fresh ginger root
1 ¹/2 teaspoons curry powder
¹/2 teaspoon ground cumin
Salt

Place a skillet over medium-high heat. Add coconut and heat in dry skillet just until lightly toasted, being careful not to burn. Remove from pan and set aside. Reduce heat to medium. Add oil to pan and heat. Add squash, onion, garlic, and ginger. Sauté until limp, about 8 to 10 minutes. Stir in curry powder and cumin. Season with salt to taste. Place in a warmed serving dish. Garnish with toasted coconut and serve.

❁ *Serves 6*

Stir-Fried Ung Choi with Miso

INGREDIENTS
2 pounds fresh ung choi
2 tablespoons soy sauce
1 tablespoon miso
2 teaspoons rice vinegar
2 tablespoons sliced almonds
1 tablespoon peanut oil
1 teaspoon sesame oil
1 teaspoon grated fresh ginger root

Wash ung choi, trim ends, and cut into 2-inch pieces. Set aside. Combine soy sauce, miso, and vinegar until smooth. Set aside. Heat a wok over high heat. Add almonds and stir-fry quickly until fragrant and toasted, about 45 seconds. Remove almonds and set aside.

Add peanut and sesame oils to wok and heat. Add ung choi and ginger and stir-fry until greens are tender, 2 to 3 minutes. Sprinkle with soy sauce mixture and heat through allowing sauce to reduce and thicken. Place in a serving bowl. Sprinkle with toasted sliced almonds and serve.

❁ *Serves 6*

Zucchini with Roasted Mushrooms

INGREDIENTS
4 tablespoons olive oil
1 tablespoon fresh thyme
3/4 teaspoon salt
1/2 teaspoon black pepper
5 small zucchini
1 1/2 pounds mixed fresh mushrooms

Heat oven to 400°F. Whisk together oil, thyme, salt, and pepper. Let sit a few minutes. Wash and halve squash lengthwise. Remove seeds and cut crosswise into 1/2-inch slices. Toss squash with 2 tablespoons thyme oil in a shallow baking pan, arranging in single layer. Wash mushrooms, remove stems and halve. Toss mushrooms with remaining 2 tablespoons thyme oil in another shallow baking pan spreading into single layer. Place in hot oven. Roast squash and mushrooms, stirring occasionally, and switching position of pans halfway through roasting, until vegetables are tender and liquid from mushrooms is evaporated, 40 to 45 minutes. Remove from oven. Combine zucchini and mushrooms in serving dish, toss to mix, and serve.

Note: Try with a combination of yellow zucchini or summer squash.

❦ *Serves 6*

Nightfall

Desserts

❧ by Yvonne Cheng

Desserts

Apricot Bars

INGREDIENTS
$1/2$ cup butter, softened
1 cup packed light brown sugar, divided
1 cup all-purpose flour
3 cups whole dried apricots
1 cup water
2 eggs
1 teaspoon vanilla extract
$1/2$ teaspoon ground cinnamon
$1/2$ teaspoon baking powder
$1/4$ teaspoon salt
$3/4$ cup chopped cashews

Heat oven to 350°F. If using glass pan, reduce heat to 325°F. Lightly butter a 9 x 9-inch baking pan and set aside. In a bowl, beat together butter and $1/2$ cup sugar. Blend in flour. Press evenly onto bottom of prepared pan. Bake until slightly golden, 20 to 25 minutes. Remove to wire rack.

In a saucepan, bring apricots and water to a boil over medium heat. Reduce heat to low and simmer uncovered until very soft, 10 to 15 minutes. Drain and set aside to cool. It is important that the apricots not be hot when the eggs are added or the eggs will curdle. In bowl, beat eggs with fork until light and fluffy. Beat in remaining $1/2$ cup sugar. Stir in vanilla, cinnamon, baking powder, and salt. Gently press apricots to rid of excess moisture. Chop into small pieces and stir into egg mixture. Beat until well blended. Pour over baked crust. Sprinkle with cashews.

Bake 25 to 30 minutes until set, puffy, and golden. Remove from oven and cool in pan on wire rack. Cut into sixteen squares.

❋ Makes 16

CRUST

1 1/4 cups rolled oats
1 1/4 cups all-purpose flour
3/4 cup shredded coconut
1/4 cup granulated sugar
1/2 teaspoon salt
3/4 cup butter, softened

FILLING

3/4 cup raspberry jam

TOPPING

3 egg whites
1/4 teaspoon cream of tartar
2/3 cup granulated sugar

Mauna Kea Bars

Heat oven to 325°F. In a large bowl, stir together oats, flour, coconut, sugar, and salt. Stir in butter, blending well. Press crust into bottom of a 9 x 13-inch baking pan. Bake 15 minutes until edges begin to brown. Let cool 5 minutes, spread evenly with jam, and set aside.

In a large bowl, whip egg whites and cream of tartar with an electric mixer on high speed until thick and foamy. Gradually add sugar and continue to whip until shiny and holds soft peaks. Gently spread meringue evenly over jam using spatula. Bake about 20 minutes until meringue is lightly browned. Remove from oven and cool 5 minutes on wire rack. Cut into 24 bars and let cool completely before removing from pan with spatula.

❀ Makes 2 dozen

PUMPKIN SQUARES

1 cup all-purpose flour
$^1/2$ teaspoon baking soda
$^3/4$ teaspoon ground cinnamon
$^3/4$ teaspoon ground ginger
$^1/4$ teaspoon ground nutmeg
$^1/4$ teaspoon ground allspice
$^1/8$ teaspoon ground cloves
$^1/2$ teaspoon salt
$^1/2$ cup unsalted butter
1 $^1/3$ cups packed dark brown sugar
1 egg, at room temperature
1 $^1/4$ teaspoon vanilla extract
1 cup cooked pumpkin
$^1/2$ cup coarsely chopped walnuts
$^1/2$ cup raisins

FROSTING

6 ounces white chocolate, chopped
6 ounces cream cheese, softened
$^1/4$ teaspoon vanilla extract
3 tablespons unsalted butter, divided

Frosted Pumpkin Squares

Position oven rack in center of oven. Heat oven to 350°F. Butter a 9 x 13-inch pan and dust with a little flour, tapping out the excess. Set aside.

In a medium bowl, whisk together flour, baking soda, cinnamon, ginger, nutmeg, allspice, cloves, and salt. In a large bowl, cream together butter and brown sugar until light and fluffy. Beat in egg until well blended. Beat in vanilla. Beat in half the flour mixture. Beat in half the pumpkin. Scrape down the side of the bowl. Beat in remaining pumpkin until smooth. Stir in remaining flour mixture just until combined. Fold in walnuts and raisins. Scrape batter into prepared pan and smooth the top with a rubber spatula. Bake for 25 to 30 minutes, or until a cake tester or toothpick inserted in center comes out clean. Cool completely in pan on wire rack before frosting.

Place white chocolate in top of a double boiler and melt, stirring, over boiling water. Set aside to cool.

In a medium bowl, beat cream cheese until light and fluffy. Beat in vanilla and butter. Gradually beat in the cooled white chocolate until smooth and shiny. If frosting starts to curdle at any time, continue to beat until smooth. Spread evenly over top of cooled pumpkin base. Refrigerate for 30 minutes, until slightly set. Using a large sharp knife, cut lengthwise into four strips, wiping the knife blade clean after each cut. Cut each strip into six pieces, again wiping the knife clean after each cut to make 24 squares. Keep any leftovers covered and refrigerated.

❧ *Makes 2 dozen*

Butter or Blueberry Mochi

INGREDIENTS
1/2 cup butter
1 pound mochiko
2 1/2 cups granulated sugar
1 teaspoon baking powder
3 cups milk
5 eggs, beaten
1 teaspoon vanilla extract
1/2 cup shredded coconut or
    12 ounces fresh or frozen blueberries

Heat oven to 350°F. Grease a 9 x 9-inch baking pan and set aside. Melt butter in a small saucepan over medium heat. Set aside to cool. In a large bowl, combine mochiko, sugar, and baking powder. Add milk, eggs, vanilla, and melted butter. Stir to mix well. Gently fold in coconut or blueberries. Pour into prepared pan. Place in center of oven and bake about 1 hour until set. Cool in pan on wire rack. Cut into 24 pieces.

Note: Mochiko is rice flour made from mochi; a sweet, short-grained, very glutinous rice with a high starch content.

❧ *Makes 2 dozen*

Brown Sugar Brownies

INGREDIENTS
1/2 cup butter, softened
1 cup packed dark brown sugar
2 eggs
3/4 cup raisins or other dried fruit
1 cup chopped walnuts
1/2 cup all-purpose flour

Heat oven to 350°F. Grease an 8 x 8-inch baking pan and set aside. In a large bowl, cream together butter and sugar until fluffy. Beat in eggs, one at a time, until well blended. Stir in raisins and nuts. Stir in flour. Pour into prepared pan and bake 22 to 25 minutes until a tester comes out clean. Cool in pan on wire rack. Cut into sixteen squares.

❧ *Makes 16*

Orange Cake Bars

INGREDIENTS
1 1/2 cups all-purpose flour
2 cups granulated sugar
1 teaspoon salt
1 cup butter, softened
4 eggs
2 teaspoons pure orange extract
2 teaspoons grated orange zest, divided
1 cup confectioners' sugar
2 tablespoons orange juice

Heat oven to 350°F. Grease a 9 x 12 x 2-inch pan and set aside. In a bowl, stir together flour, sugar, and salt. Add butter, eggs, orange extract, and 1 teaspoon orange zest and beat with a handheld electric mixer until well blended. Pour batter into prepared pan and bake for 30 minutes, or until light golden brown and set. Remove to wire rack. Stir together confectioners' sugar, orange juice, and remaining zest until smooth to make glaze. Pierce top of orange bars with a fork. Drizzle with glaze. Cool and cut into squares.

❋ Makes one 9 x 12-inch pan

At right, Hawaiian Style Scottish Shortbread, Mauna Kea Bars and Orange Cake Bars.

Rosemary and Pine Nut Bars

INGREDIENTS
^{1}/4 cup pine nuts
8 tablespoons unsalted butter, melted
^{1}/2 cup confectioners' sugar
1 tablespoon minced fresh rosemary
    or 2 teaspoons dried
1 cup all-purpose flour

Heat oven to 350°F. Spread pine nuts on a baking sheet and place in oven. Toast, shaking occasionally until slightly brown and fragrant, about 5 minutes. Watch carefully as pine nuts burn easily. Remove from baking sheet and set aside.

In a medium bowl, stir together butter, sugar, rosemary, and pine nuts. Add flour and stir to make a stiff dough. Spread evenly into an ungreased 8 x 8-inch baking pan and pat down. Bake about 20 minutes until golden and firm at the edges. Remove from oven to wire rack and cool in pan about 2 minutes, then cut into sixteen squares using a sharp knife. Let the bars cool in the pan for at least 10 minutes before removing with a small spatula.

Note: Good accompanied with a plate of grapes or pears and wedges of dessert cheese.

❧ *Makes 16*

Apricot-Sage Cookies

INGREDIENTS
1 $^3/_4$ cups all-purpose flour
$^1/_3$ cup granulated sugar
$^1/_4$ cup yellow cornmeal
10 tablespoons butter
2 tablespoons snipped fresh sage or
   2 teaspoons dried
3 tablespoons milk
4 tablespoons apricot preserves, melted
24 fresh sage leaves

Heat oven to 375°F. In a medium bowl, stir together flour, sugar, and cornmeal. Mix in butter until mixture resembles coarse sand and starts to cling together. Stir in snipped sage. Add milk and stir to combine. Form mixture into a ball and knead until smooth. Divide dough in half. On a lightly floured surface with lightly floured rolling pin, roll out each half to $^1/_4$-inch thickness. Cut out cookies with 2 $^1/_2$-inch round cutter or rim of glass. Gather together scraps and continue to use all of dough.

Place on an ungreased baking sheet. Bake about 10 minutes until edges are firm and bottoms are very lightly browned. Remove from baking sheet and cool on wire rack.

Cut any large pieces of fruit in preserves into smaller pieces. Spread preserves over cooled cookies. Top each cookie with a sage leaf.

Note: Lemon thyme is a nice substitute for the sage.

❀ *Makes 2 dozen*

Cappuccino Cookies

INGREDIENTS
12 tablespoons unsalted butter
4 ounces white chocolate
3 tablespoons instant espresso granules
2 1/2 cups all-purpose flour
1/2 teaspoon salt
1/2 teaspoon baking soda
1/4 teaspoon ground nutmeg
2 eggs
1 cup lightly packed light brown sugar
1/2 cup granulated sugar
2 teaspoons vanilla extract

Line two large baking sheets with parchment paper. Heat oven to 325°F. Adjust oven racks to upper and middle positions. In a saucepan, melt butter and white chocolate over low heat, stirring frequently. Add espresso granules and stir until dissolved. Set aside to cool.

In a bowl, stir together flour, salt, baking soda, and nutmeg. Set aside.

In another bowl, beat eggs until light. Add brown and granulated sugars and continue to beat until smooth. Beat in cooled butter mixture. Add vanilla. Stir in dry ingredients, mixing until just combined. Drop scant 1/4 cupfuls of dough onto prepared baking sheets, about 9 per sheet. Smaller baking sheets can be used, but baking time will need to be adjusted. If the kitchen is warm, place the unused cookie dough in the refrigerator while between batches.

Bake 13 to 18 minutes, switching baking sheet positions halfway through baking, until cookies are light golden brown and outer edges start to harden. Cool cookies on baking sheets before removing.

❈ Makes about 2 dozen

Caraway Cookies

INGREDIENTS
2 cups all-purpose flour
1 tablespoon caraway seed
1 teaspoon baking powder
$1/4$ teaspoon baking soda
$1/4$ teaspoon salt
$1/2$ cup butter, softened
1 cup granulated sugar
2 eggs

In a bowl, stir together flour, caraway seed, baking powder, baking soda, and salt. Set aside.

In a large bowl, beat butter and sugar together until light and fluffy. Beat in eggs, one at a time, until well blended. Stir in flour mixture. Form into a ball. Divide in half and roll each half into a 2-inch thick log. Wrap log in plastic wrap and chill about 3 hours until firm and easy to handle.

Heat oven to 375°F. Lightly grease baking sheets. Unwrap dough logs one at a time and cut into $1/8$ to $1/4$-inch thick rounds. Place rounds 2 inches apart on prepared baking sheets. Bake 7 to 9 minutes, depending on thickness, until edges are lightly browned. Remove from baking sheet and cool on wire rack.

❋ *Makes about 4 dozen*

Coconut Macaroons

INGREDIENTS
4 egg whites
3/4 cup granulated sugar
1/2 teaspoon salt
1 1/2 teaspoons vanilla extract
3 cups shredded coconut
6 tablespoons all-purpose flour
8 ounces bittersweet chocolate

In a heavy saucepan stir together egg whites, sugar, salt, vanilla, and coconut. Sift in flour and stir until well combined. Place over medium heat for 5 minutes, stirring constantly. Increase heat to medium-high and cook, stirring constantly, for 3 to 5 minutes until mixture has thickened and pulls away from side of the pan. Scrape mixture into a bowl and let cool slightly. Cover and chill just until cold.

Heat oven to 300°F. Lightly grease baking sheets. Using a small ice cream scoop, place dough 2 inches apart onto prepared baking sheets. Bake the macaroons in batches in the middle of oven for 20 to 25 minutes until pale golden. Remove from baking sheet and cool on wire rack.

Line a baking sheet or tray with foil. Finely chop chocolate. Place in a small metal bowl set over a pan of barely simmering water. Heat water to melt chocolate, stirring until smooth. Remove from heat and dip macaroon bottoms, one at a time, into chocolate, coating 1/4-inch up the sides. Let any excess chocolate drip back into pan. Transfer coated macaroons to prepared tray and chill for 30 to 60 minutes until set. Store chilled and separated by layers of wax paper, in an airtight container.

❀ *Makes about 1 1/2 dozen*

Cranberry Oatmeal Cookies

INGREDIENTS
1 cup butter
1 1/2 cups granulated sugar
2 eggs
1 teaspoon vanilla extract
2 cups all-purpose flour
1 teaspoon baking powder
1/2 teaspoon salt
1/4 teaspoon baking soda
2 cups rolled oats
1 cup raisins
1 cup chopped fresh or dried cranberries
1 tablespoon grated orange zest
12 ounces white chocolate chips

Grease two baking sheets and set aside. Heat oven to 375°F. Cream together butter and sugar in a bowl. Add eggs, one at a time, beating well after each addition. Beat in vanilla. Combine flour, baking powder, salt, and baking soda. Add to creamed mixture. Stir in oats, raisins, cranberries, and orange zest, mixing well. Stir in chips.

Drop by tablespoonfuls 2 inches apart onto prepared baking sheets. Bake 10 to 12 minutes until edges are lightly browned, switching baking sheet positions half way through for even baking. Remove from baking sheet and cool on wire rack.

❋ *Makes about 4 dozen*

Hawaiian Style Scottish Shortbread

INGREDIENTS
1 cup butter
1/2 cup granulated sugar
1 1/2 teaspoons vanilla extract
1/2 teaspoon almond extract
1 1/2 cups all-purpose flour
1/2 cup ground almonds
1/3 cup minced candied pineapple

Heat oven to 350°F. In a medium bowl, cream together butter and sugar until light and fluffy. Add vanilla and almond extracts. Mix in flour, almonds, and pineapple. Pat into a 9-inch springform or cake pan with removable bottom. Bake for 25 to 30 minutes until light golden brown around the edges. Remove from oven and using tines of fork, pierce shortbread, creating twelve wedges that will separate easily upon cooling. This must be done while still very warm. Let cool.

Note: For best results, be sure to use real butter and not substitutes.

❋ *Makes 1 dozen*

Lavender Lemon Cookies

INGREDIENTS

$3/4$ cup unsalted butter, softened
$3/4$ cup granulated sugar
$1/2$ tablespoon dried lavender buds
1 tablespoon grated lemon zest
1 egg
$1/2$ tablespoon vanilla extract
$1/4$ teaspoon salt
2 $1/4$ cups all-purpose flour

In a bowl, cream together butter and sugar until light and fluffy. Add lavender and lemon zest, blending gently. Add egg, vanilla, and salt, mixing briefly to combine. Gradually add the flour, mixing just until combined. Gather the dough together and pat it into a disk. Wrap with plastic wrap and refrigerate for at least 1 hour.

Heat oven to 350°F. Work quickly to keep dough from becoming too warm and soft. Roll out chilled dough on lightly floured surface to a $1/4$-inch thickness. Cut out shapes with a biscuit or cookie cutter. Place on baking sheets. Bake until cookies begin to color around the edges, about 10 to 12 minutes. Let sit on baking sheet a few minutes to firm up before transferring to wire rack, then cool completely. May be stored in an airtight container for up to one week.

Note: This is a very soft dough. Chilling it helps keep the dough firm enough to roll out easily. Place dough in refrigerator between batches.

❦ *Makes 2 dozen*

Lemon Sugar Cookies

INGREDIENTS
1 1/2 cups granulated sugar, divided
2 teaspoons lemon oil or
    3 teaspoons lemon extract, divided
2 1/2 cups sifted all-purpose flour
1/2 teaspoon baking soda
1/4 teaspoon salt
1 cup unsalted butter, softened
1/3 cup grated lemon zest
1 egg
2 tablespoons fresh lemon juice

In a small bowl, stir together 1/2 cup sugar and 1 teaspoon lemon oil or extract and set aside. In another bowl, sift together flour, baking soda, and salt. Set aside. In a large bowl, beat butter, remaining sugar, remaining lemon oil or extract, and lemon zest with an electric mixer on medium-high until light and fluffy. Add egg and lemon juice, beating well. Reduce speed to low and add flour mixture, mixing just until blended. Cover the dough with plastic wrap and place in freezer for 10 minutes or refrigerator for 30 minutes.

Position rack in middle of oven. Heat oven to 400°F. Lightly grease two large baking sheets and set aside. Form balls from tablespoonfuls of dough, roll in the lemon sugar, coating well, and place about 3 inches apart on the prepared baking sheets. Flatten each ball with the bottom of a glass until about 2 inches round and 3/8-inch thick. Sprinkle each cookie with a pinch of the lemon sugar mixture. Keep remaining dough in freezer to keep firm between batches.

Bake, one sheet at a time, for 8 to 10 minutes, until the edges are lightly browned. Wait 30 seconds before removing the cookies from the baking sheet to cool on wire rack but don't wait too long or cookies will stick to baking sheet.

❧ Makes 4 dozen

Lime Coconut Triangles

1 cup all-purpose flour
*1/3 cup sifted confectioners' sugar,
    plus extra*
1/4 cup chopped macadamia nuts
3/4 cup shredded coconut, divided
1/3 cup butter, melted
2 eggs
1 cup granulated sugar
1 tablespoon shredded lime zest
1/4 cup lime juice
1/4 teaspoon baking powder

Heat oven to 350°F. Grease an 8 x 8 x 2-inch baking pan and set aside. In a medium bowl, stir together flour, 1/3 cup confectioners' sugar, nuts, and 1/4 cup coconut. Mix in butter. Press mixture into prepared pan. Bake for 20 minutes. Remove from oven and set on wire rack.

In a medium bowl, beat eggs slightly. Beat in granulated sugar, lime zest, lime juice, and baking powder. Stir in remaining coconut, mixing to combine well. Pour over baked crust. Return to oven for 20 minutes until edges are lightly browned and center is set. Remove from oven and cool in pan on wire rack. Cut into four equal parallel sections. Cut each section into triangles. Place on serving plate and dust with confectioners' sugar.

❋ *Makes 1 1/2 dozen*

Lime Ginger Cookies

1 cup butter, softened
1/2 cup granulated sugar
1/2 cup packed light brown sugar
1 egg
1 tablespoon grated lime zest
2 1/4 cups all-purpose flour
1 teaspoon ground ginger
Pinch ground nutmeg
3/4 teaspoon baking soda
1/2 teaspoon salt
12 ounces white chocolate chips

Heat oven to 350°F. In a bowl, cream together butter, granulated and brown sugars. Beat in egg and lime zest. Combine flour, ginger, nutmeg, baking soda, and salt and add to butter mixture. Stir in chips. Drop by rounded tablespoonfuls onto ungreased baking sheets. Bake for 12 to 14 minutes until lightly browned. Remove from baking sheet and cool on wire racks.

Note: These can be made with orange peel, cinnamon, and clove instead of lime, ginger, and nutmeg.

❋ *Makes about 3 dozen*

Macadamia Mea'ono

INGREDIENTS

1 cup butter, softened
1/2 cup plus 2 tablespoons
   confectioners' sugar, divided
2 teaspoons water
2 teaspoons vanilla extract
2 cups all-purpose flour
1 cup macadamia nut bits

In a large bowl, cream butter and 1/2 cup sugar together until light and fluffy. Beat in water and vanilla until combined. Stir in flour just until blended. Fold in nuts. Form into a mound, cover with plastic wrap, and refrigerate for 2 to 3 hours.

Heat oven to 350°F. Roll tablespoonfuls of dough into 1-inch balls. Place on ungreased baking sheets about 1-inch apart. Bake 18 to 20 minutes until lightly golden. Remove from baking sheet to wire rack to cool. Dust with remaining confectioners' sugar.

❀ *Makes about 3 dozen*

Pistachio White Chocolate Chunk Cookies

INGREDIENTS

1 1/4 cups unsalted butter, softened
1 cup granulated sugar
1 cup packed dark brown sugar
2 eggs
2 tablespoons milk
2 tablespoons vanilla extract
2 1/2 cups all-purpose flour
1 teaspoon baking soda
1 teaspoon baking powder
1 teaspoon salt
1 cup rolled oats
1 1/2 cups chopped pistachios, divided
10 ounces white chocolate chunks

Heat oven to 350°F. Lightly grease two baking sheets. Cream together butter, granulated and brown sugars. Beat in eggs, milk, and vanilla. Combine flour, baking soda, baking powder, and salt. Process oats in blender or food processor until smaller in size but still coarse. Mix into flour. Gradually add flour mixture to butter mixture, mixing well. Stir in 1 cup pistachios and white chocolate chips. Drop mixture by heaping teaspoons onto prepared baking sheets, an inch or two apart. Press remaining pistachios on top of cookies. Bake 8 to 10 minutes until golden brown. Let cool slightly on baking sheet before removing to wire rack, then cool completely.

❈ *Makes 3 to 4 dozen*

Baked Apples

FILLING
1 1/2 cups chopped pecans
1/2 cup diced dried papaya
4 tablespoons honey
2 tablespoons butter, softened
1 teaspoon ground cinnamon
1/4 teaspoon ground nutmeg

APPLES
8 Granny Smith apples
2 tablespoons lemon juice

SAUCE
3 tablespoons butter
1 teaspoon ground cinnamon
4 tablespoons honey
1 cup good white wine
Fresh mint leaves

Place pecans in a bowl with papaya, honey, butter, cinnamon, and nutmeg. Stir to combine and set aside. Heat oven to 350°F. Grease a baking dish large enough to hold all the apples and set aside. Remove core from apples making a 1-inch diameter hole but keeping bottom intact. With a sharp knife, form a decorative design on each apple by scoring and removing part of the peel exposing the flesh. Brush with lemon juice to prevent discoloring. Fill apples with nut mixture, dividing evenly. Arrange in prepared baking dish and bake 40 minutes until tender. Remove from oven and set on wire rack.

Melt butter in a small saucepan over medium heat. Add cinnamon and cook, stirring for 1 minute. Add honey and cook, stirring for 1 minute. Stir in wine. Reduce heat and simmer 8 to 10 minutes to form a syrup. Remove from heat and set aside. Carefully scoop apples into individual serving bowls. Drizzle with syrup. Garnish with fresh mint and serve.

 Serves 8

Mango Raspberry Cobbler

INGREDIENTS
3 cups fresh diced mango
$1/4$ cup fresh or frozen raspberries
2 tablespoons packed light brown sugar
$1/4$ cup granulated sugar, divided
2 teaspoons cornstarch
$1/8$ teaspoon ground cinnamon
$3/4$ cup all-purpose flour
$1/2$ teaspoon baking powder
$1/4$ teaspoon baking soda
Pinch salt
2 tablespoons unsalted butter, cut into small pieces
$2 1/2$ tablespoons plain yogurt
2 teaspoons milk
$1/4$ teaspoon vanilla extract

Heat oven to 400°F. In a 9-inch round casserole or baking dish, stir together mango, raspberries, brown sugar, 1 tablespoon granulated sugar, cornstarch, and cinnamon. Set aside.

In a bowl, sift together flour, 2 tablespoons granulated sugar, baking powder, baking soda, and salt. Blend in butter using fork or pastry blender. In another bowl, whisk together yogurt, milk, and vanilla. Add to flour mixture, stirring until just combined. Knead dough lightly. Divide into five or six parts. Shape into rounds about $3/4$-inch thick and place around the fruit mixture. Sprinkle remaining tablespoon sugar on dough.

Bake for 23 to 28 minutes until biscuits are golden, cooked through, and sauce is slightly thickened. Remove from oven and set on wire rack to cool slightly. Can be served with scoops of ice cream.

❦ Serves 4 to 6

Mango with Sticky Rice

INGREDIENTS
10 ounces sticky rice
1 cup thick coconut milk
2 tablespoons granulated sugar
1/2 teaspoon salt
3 large ripe mangoes
2 tablespoons coconut cream

Put rice in a bowl. Cover with cold water and soak for at least 3 hours, or overnight if possible. Drain and rinse thoroughly. Line steamer basket with a double thickness of muslin or cheesecloth. Add rice. Fill bottom pot of steamer with water. Put on stove over medium heat and bring to a boil. Cover with top basket and steam rice about 30 minutes until tender, adding water as needed.

In a large bowl, mix together coconut milk, sugar, and salt, stirring until sugar is dissolved. Add warm cooked rice. Stir to mix well. Cover and set aside for 30 minutes. Peel mangoes. Working over a bowl to catch juice, slice the two outside cheeks of each fruit as close to the pit as possible. Cut any remaining fruit off. Discard the pit. Slice mango into pieces lengthwise and place in bowl. Mound rice in the center of a serving dish. Arrange mango slices around. Drizzle coconut cream over rice and serve.

Note: Coconut milk is not the liquid inside a coconut. It is made by soaking grated coconut meat in hot water or scalded milk and straining off the liquid. Coconut milk is classified as thick, thin, and cream. Thick is the result of the first soaking and pressing. If not shaken, it separates into two layers. The upper layer is the coconut cream and bottom layer is the thin milk. For thick coconut milk, shake the layers back together before using. Thin milk can also be produced from a second steeping and pressing of the coconut meat.

 Serves 4 to 6

Oranges in Wine Syrup

INGREDIENTS
$^1/_2$ cup fresh orange juice
$^3/_4$ cup water
$^1/_2$ cup white wine
$^1/_4$ cup granulated sugar
1 teaspoon anise seed
3 oranges

Combine orange juice, water, and wine in a heavy saucepan and bring to a boil over medium-high heat. Cook 5 minutes to reduce. Stir in sugar, heating until dissolved. Reduce heat, add anise seed, and simmer gently for a few minutes. Remove from heat, cover, and let cool for 1 hour. Strain wine syrup through fine sieve to remove seeds. This can be made ahead.

Peel oranges, removing all of the white pith. Slice thinly crosswise. Place in a glass bowl and pour in wine syrup. Cover and refrigerate for at least 1 hour to infuse flavors before serving.

❋ Serves 4

Basil Grilled Pineapple

INGREDIENTS
1 large pineapple
36 basil leaves
$^1/_4$ cup granulated sugar
$^1/_4$ cup lemon juice
Basil flowers

Twist off top and peel pineapple. Cut crosswise into slices about $^1/_4$-inch thick, allowing two slices per serving. Heat a grill pan over medium high heat. Place pineapple slices in hot pan a few at a time and sear until lightly browned. Press three basil leaves on each pineapple slice. Turn pineapple using tongs and sear other side until lightly browned. Carefully remove slices with basil, using tongs, and set on serving platter. Repeat with remaining pineapple slices and basil leaves. The pineapple can be seared ahead of time and reheated just before serving.

Combine sugar and lemon juice in small saucepan. Cook over medium heat for a few minutes to blend. Drizzle over grilled pineapple. Garnish with basil flowers and serve.

❋ Serves 6 to 8

Papaya Risotto with Rum Cream

PAPAYA RISOTTO
5 cups whole milk
1 tablespoon light olive oil
1 cup Arborio rice
1/2 cup diced dried papaya
3/4 cup granulated sugar
Fresh mint

RUM CREAM
3 egg yolks
3 tablespoons granulated sugar
1 1/2 cups heavy cream
1 heaping tablespoon sour cream
1/2 Hawaiian-grown vanilla bean
3 tablespoons light rum

In a medium saucepan, heat milk over medium heat until hot. Set aside but keep warm. Heat oil in a large saucepan over medium heat. Add rice and stir until all grains are coated. Add papaya and continue to stir for an additional 2 minutes. Add 1 cup warm milk and cook, stirring constantly until liquid is absorbed. Add 3 cups warm milk, one cup at a time, stirring frequently until liquid is absorbed after each addition. Add remaining cup milk and sugar. Cook, stirring, until tender. Let rice cool to almost room temperature. Use ice cream scoop to mound rice on individual dessert plates. Drizzle with Rum Cream, garnish with mint, and serve.

Note: Preparing Arborio rice differs from most other rice preparations. The liquid is added a little at a time, rather than all at once, and Arborio rice must be stirred as it cooks. This helps to release the starch and promote creaminess.

Rum Cream: In a medium bowl, whisk together egg yolks and sugar until pale yellow and smooth. In a medium saucepan, combine heavy cream and sour cream. Split vanilla bean lengthwise to expose the seeds, scrape out and add to pan with pod. Bring to a boil over medium heat. Whisk half the cream mixture into the egg yolks until well combined, then pour all back into the saucepan. Stir mixture constantly with a wooden spoon until it coats the back of the spoon. Remove vanilla bean, scrape off any remaining seeds using back of knife and return to cream. Discard pod. Pour into clean metal bowl set over iced cold water. Leave until chilled, stirring occasionally. Cover and refrigerate.

 Serves 6

Pineapple with Lilikoi Cream

INGREDIENTS

1 fresh pineapple
12 ounces cream cheese, softened
6 ounces lilikoi juice concentrate
3/4 cup finely diced ripe mango
4 ounces strawberries, diced
2 tablespoons granulated sugar

Twist off top and peel pineapple. Cut in half crosswise. Stand one half of pineapple upright. Position a large sharp knife at top of pineapple, and cut downward to slice pineapple into eight pieces. Set aside two center pieces containing core. Repeat with the other half of pineapple. Remove flesh from core sections and save for another use. Discard core. Beat together cream cheese and lilikoi juice concentrate in a food processor or electric mixer until very smooth. Scrape into a bowl. Fold mango into cream cheese mixture and refrigerate for at least 2 hours until firm. Place strawberries and sugar in a food processor or blender and puree until smooth. Cover and refrigerate.

Heat broiler. Grease a baking sheet. Lay pineapple slices on baking sheet. Broil until lightly browned, 5 to 10 minutes.

Lay one slice of broiled pineapple on each of four plates. Spread with lilikoi cream, top with another slice of pineapple and more lilikoi cream. Finish with a third slice of pineapple. Drizzle with strawberry sauce. Serve.

Note: Guanabana, also called soursop, is a white-fleshed fruit popular in Latino cooking. The purée is sold frozen and can be used in place of the lilikoi.

❧ *Serves 4*

Rhubarb Foolery

INGREDIENTS
5 cups diced fresh rhubarb
$^3/_4$ cup water
$^1/_2$ cup plus 1 tablespoon
   granulated sugar, divided
3 tablespoons quick cooking tapioca
$^1/_4$ teaspoon ground cinnamon
Dash ground ginger or $^1/_2$-inch piece
   fresh ginger root, grated
1 cup whipping cream
Dash vanilla extract

Place diced rhubarb in a large saucepan. Add water, $^1/_2$ cup sugar, tapioca, cinnamon, and ginger. Heat over medium, stirring frequently, about 10 minutes until mixture is slightly thickened and tapioca is clear. Remove from heat and cool. Pour into a serving bowl. Cover and refrigerate at least 2 hours.

Whip cream. Blend in remaining sugar and vanilla. Spoon rhubarb mixture into bowls, top with a dollop of whipped cream, and serve.

 Serves 4 to 6

Sautéed Pears

INGREDIENTS
4 firm, ripe pears
$^1/_2$ cup pistachios
2 tablespoons granulated sugar
Pinch ground cloves
1 tablespoon butter
2 teaspoons grated fresh ginger root
$^1/_4$ teaspoon ground cinnamon
$^1/_4$ cup apple juice
$^1/_4$ cup packed dark brown sugar
1 quart vanilla ice cream

Peel, core and slice pears. Set aside. Lightly toast pistachio nuts over medium-low heat in a heavy skillet. Add sugar and cloves, stirring until sugar melts. Scrape into a dish and set aside. Clean skillet. Add butter and melt over medium heat. Add ginger and cinnamon, and cook 1 minute, stirring. Add apple juice and brown sugar, stirring to dissolve sugar. Add pear slices and sauté until tender. Scoop ice cream into individual serving bowls, top with pears, sprinkle with toasted nuts, and serve.

 Serves 4

Kula Style Strawberries

INGREDIENTS
1/3 cup pine nuts
1 quart fresh Kula strawberries
4 teaspoons granulated sugar
Pinch of ground cloves
3 tablespoons balsamic vinegar
Fresh mint leaves

Lightly toast pine nuts in a skillet over medium-low heat just until golden. Remove and cool. Wash, hull, and slice strawberries. Place in a glass serving bowl. Combine sugar and cloves and sprinkle over berries. Drizzle with vinegar. Cover and chill, or let sit at room temperature, at least 30 minutes, stirring occasionally.

Uncover and sprinkle with toasted nuts. Garnish with mint and serve. This can be served with vanilla frozen yogurt or ice cream.

❋ *Serves 4 to 6*

Strawberry Shortcake

INGREDIENTS
1 pound Kula strawberries
2 tablespoons Cointreau
2 1/4 cups all-purpose flour
1/3 cup granulated sugar
2 1/2 teaspoons baking powder
1/2 teaspoon baking soda
1/4 teaspoon salt
6 tablespoons unsalted butter,
  cut into small pieces
2 tablespoons minced crystallized ginger
3/4 cup buttermilk
Whipping cream
Sprigs of fresh mint

Place strawberries in a glass bowl. Sprinkle with Cointreau, cover, and refrigerate. Heat oven to 425°F. Grease or line baking sheet with parchment paper and set aside. In a large bowl, sift together flour, sugar, baking powder, baking soda, and salt. Blend in butter with fork or pastry blender until mixture resembles coarse sand. Stir in ginger, blending well. Gently stir in buttermilk to form a soft dough. Transfer to a lightly floured surface and pat out to 3/4-inch thick. Cut out 3-inch rounds with a cookie or biscuit cutter or rim of glass. Place rounds on prepared baking sheet. Bake 10 to 12 minutes until golden. Transfer to rack to cool.

Whip cream. Split shortcakes and place in shallow individual serving bowls. Spoon in strawberries and replace top. Add dollop of whipped cream, garnish with mint, and serve.

❋ *Serves 6*

INGREDIENTS
2 cups whole milk
3 tablespoons fresh basil, thinly sliced
3/4 cup granulated sugar, divided
Pinch salt
4 egg yolks
1 cup heavy or whipping cream

Basil Ice Cream

Bring milk, basil, $1/4$ cup sugar, and salt to a boil in a 2-quart heavy saucepan. Stir, remove from heat, and let steep 30 minutes. Transfer to a blender and blend until basil is finely ground. Beat together yolks and remaining $1/2$ cup sugar in a medium bowl with an electric mixer or whisk until thick and pale, about 1 minute. Add cream, blending well. Add milk mixture in a stream, beating until well combined. Pour mixture back into saucepan and cook over medium heat, stirring constantly with a wooden spoon, until mixture coats back of spoon, about 10 minutes. Do not allow to boil. Immediately remove from heat and pour through a fine-mesh sieve into a metal bowl. Set bowl in a larger bowl of ice water and stir until cold, 10 to 15 minutes. Freeze in an ice cream maker according to manufacturer's instructions.

❦ *Makes about 1 quart*

Ginger Ice Cream

INGREDIENTS
2 cups whole milk
4 egg yolks
1 cup granulated sugar
1/8 teaspoon salt
2 cups well-chilled heavy or
  whipping cream
1 teaspoon vanilla extract
3/4 cup minced crystallized ginger
Crystallized ginger, cut into thin strips

Heat water in bottom of double boiler to a simmer. Bring milk to a simmer in a saucepan over medium heat. Remove from heat and set aside. In the top of a double boiler off the heat, whisk egg yolks with sugar and salt until pale yellow, 3 to 4 minutes. Gradually add the hot milk, whisking constantly until fully incorporated. Set the top pan over but not touching the simmering water of bottom pan and cook, stirring slowly and continuously with a wooden spoon, until the custard thickens, 8 to 10 minutes. A finger drawn across the back of the spoon should leave a path. Do not allow the custard to boil. Remove from heat and stir in cream and vanilla. Pour the custard through a fine-mesh sieve into a clean bowl and refrigerate for 20 minutes.

Transfer the custard to an ice cream maker and freeze according to the manufacturer's instructions. When the ice cream is halfway into the freezing process, add the crystallized ginger. Complete the freezing process. Transfer the ice cream to a chilled container, cover and freeze until firm, at least 3 hours or up to 2 days, before serving. Scoop the ice cream into chilled ice cream dishes or bowls. Garnish with strips of crystallized ginger and serve.

❋ *Makes about 1 quart*

Green Tea Ice Cream

INGREDIENTS
3 cups half-and-half
1/4 cup whole green tea leaves
1 cup well-chilled heavy or
  whipping cream
3/4 cup granulated sugar
Grated zest of 1 lime
1/8 teaspoon vanilla extract

In a heavy saucepan, bring half-and-half and tea to a boil over medium heat, stirring occasionally to prevent bottom from scorching. Remove from heat and set aside for 5 minutes to infuse. Pour liquid through a fine-meshed sieve into a bowl, pressing firmly on the tea leaves to extract as much liquid as possible. Discard leaves. Add heavy cream, sugar, and lime zest. Stir to dissolve sugar completely. Stir in vanilla and set aside to cool. Cover and refrigerate until cold. Freeze in an ice cream maker according to manufacturer's instructions.

❋ *Makes about 1 quart*

Honey Lavender Ice Cream

INGREDIENTS
2 cups whole milk
2 cups half-and-half
Scant 1/4 cup dried lavender flower buds
3/4 cup honey
1 teaspoon vanilla extract

In a medium saucepan, combine milk, half-and-half, lavender, and honey. Bring to a gentle boil, cover, and remove from heat. Let steep 5 minutes. Pour through fine-meshed sieve into a bowl. Press lavender to extract liquid. Discard lavender. Stir in vanilla. Pour into a bowl, set in an ice-water bath and let stand until chilled, stirring occasionally. Freeze in an ice cream maker according to manufacturer's instructions.

❀ *Makes about 1 quart*

Lychee Coconut Sorbet

INGREDIENTS
15 to 20 ounces canned lychee, drained
*1 cup thick coconut milk or coconut
   cream, not Coco Lopez*
3 1/2 tablespoons fresh lime juice, divided
1 large ripe mango
1 teaspoon grated lime zest

Drain lychees and place in a blender with coconut milk and 2 1/2 tablespoons lime juice. Puree until smooth. Freeze in ice cream maker according to manufacturer's directions. Or, place in freezer-proof dish and set in freezer for several hours, stirring every 30 minutes until smooth and frozen. Peel mango and slice into mixing bowl. Combine with lime zest and remaining lime juice. Arrange mango slices in serving dishes. Scoop sorbet over fruit slices. Serve.

❀ *Makes about 1 pint*

Basic Granita Recipe

INGREDIENTS
1/2 cup granulated sugar
1 cup water
3 cups fruit juice
2 teaspoons freshly squeezed lemon juice

Place a 13 x 9-inch freezer-proof pan in freezer. Combine sugar and water in a medium saucepan and bring to a boil, stirring until the sugar dissolves. Remove from heat and let cool. Stir in the fruit juice and lemon juice. Pour into chilled baking pan. Place in freezer, stirring every 30 minutes to evenly distribute the ice crystals, until the mixture is firm.

❋ *Makes 1 quart*

Raspberry Pineapple Granita

INGREDIENTS
1 fresh pineapple
1/3 cup granulated sugar
2 tablespoons fresh lemon juice
2 cups fresh or frozen raspberries
1 teaspoon grated lemon zest

Chill a 9 x 9-inch non-reactive metal baking pan in freezer at least 30 minutes. Twist off pineapple top. Peel, core and dice pineapple. Measure out 2 cups diced pineapple, saving the rest for another use, and combine with sugar and lemon juice in a blender or food processor. Puree. Add raspberries and puree to combine. Scrape into chilled baking pan. Freeze until ice crystals form around the edges, 30 to 60 minutes. Stir with fork to evenly incorporate ice crystals into mixture. Return to freezer. Mash and stir mixture every 30 minutes until uniformly frozen, about 3 hours.

Note: Granita should be slightly soft for easier serving. If it is too firm, place in refrigerator for a few minutes and mash. Serve scoops in chilled bowls and garnish with grated lemon zest.

❋ *Makes 1 1/2 pints*

Zesty Lemon Granita

GRANITA
2 $^1/2$ cups water
$^1/2$ cup fresh lemon juice
$^1/2$ teaspoon lemon zest
$^1/2$ cup granulated sugar

CANDIED LEMON STRIPS
1 large lemon
1 cup sugar
$^1/3$ cup corn syrup
$^1/3$ cup water

Bring water to a boil in a medium non-reactive saucepan. Add lemon juice, zest, and sugar. Reduce heat to low and simmer to blend flavors, stirring occasionally, about 30 minutes.

Transfer syrup to a non-reactive freezer proof bowl and cool to room temperature. Place in freezer and freeze, stirring every 30 minutes evenly distribute ice crystals. Repeat until mixture is just solid, 3 to 4 hours. Scoop granita into chilled serving glasses. Garnish with candied lemon strips and serve immediately.

Candied Lemon Strips: Cut the zest of a large lemon into fine julienne strips. Bring sugar, corn syrup and water to a boil. Add zest strips and cook 1 to 2 minutes. Remove from heat and let stand for 30 minutes. Store in an airtight container for up to one week.

❋ *Makes 1 $^1/2$ pints*

Apple Macadamia Nut Tart

INGREDIENTS
3/4 cup macadamia nut pieces
1 1/4 cups all-purpose flour
3/4 cup plus 1 tablespoon
    granulated sugar, divided
3/4 cup butter, cut into small pieces,
    divided
1 egg yolk
3 eggs
2 to 3 Granny Smith apples
1/4 cup lilikoi or apricot jam
2 tablespoons Cointreau

Heat oven to 325°F. Spread nuts in bottom of a small baking pan and bake until golden, about 5 to 8 minutes, watching carefully so nuts do not burn, shaking pan often. Pour from pan to a dish and let cool. Keep oven on.

In a bowl, mix flour and 1 tablespoon sugar. Add 1/2 cup butter. Blend together with fork to form texture of fine sand. Add egg yolk, mixing until dough holds together. Gather and pat into a smooth ball. Place in a 9-inch tart pan with removable bottom. Working from center out, firmly press dough over bottom and up sides of pan. Set aside.

Put toasted macadamia nuts and remaining sugar in food processor. Pulse until nuts are finely ground. Add remaining butter and whole eggs and whirl until smooth. Set aside.

Peel, core, and slice apples 1/8-inch thick. Arrange apple slices, overlapping, neatly in tart pan. Drizzle with nut mixture. Bake 50 to 60 minutes until crust is browned and apples are tender. Remove to wire rack and cool. Filling will be puffy then settle upon cooling.

In a small bowl, stir together jam and liqueur. Drizzle over cooling tart. Let sit at least 30 minutes before removing rim. Serve warm or cooled, cut into wedges.

❧ *Serves 8 to 10*

Frangipane Tart

INGREDIENTS
1 sheet puff pastry, thawed
1 cup blanched almonds
$1/2$ cup granulated sugar
$1/4$ teaspoon salt
1 teaspoon vanilla extract
$1/4$ teaspoon almond extract
1 egg
4 tablespoons butter, softened
2 ripe mangoes
Almond slices

Heat oven to 400°F. Line a baking sheet with parchment paper. Lay puff pastry on prepared baking sheet. In a food processor, pulse almonds and sugar until nuts are finely ground. Add salt, vanilla and almond extracts, and egg. Pulse until blended. Add butter and process until smoothly blended. With a rubber spatula, spread frangipane evenly over puff pastry, keeping an inch or so away from all edges. Peel mango and cut flesh from seed in slices. Arrange slices decoratively on top of frangipane. Roll in or fold over edges to create a slight rim.

Bake about 30 minutes until frangipane is golden and set when the pan is gently shaken. Remove to wire rack and cool. Garnish with almonds. Serve at room temperature or chilled.

Note: Fresh pears or peaches may be used instead of mango.

Frangipane is a rich almond-flavored pastry cream and another name for the fragrant plumeria flower.

❋ *Serves 8 to 10*

Ginger Macadamia Tart

INGREDIENTS
1 1/3 cup all-purpose flour
1/4 cup granulated sugar
4 tablespoons cold butter,
   cut into small pieces
1 egg yolk
3 eggs
1 cup packed light brown sugar
1/2 cup minced crystallized ginger
1 tablespoon grated fresh ginger root
1 teaspoon vanilla extract
3 cups salted, roasted macadamia nuts

Heat oven to 300°F. In a food processor or by hand, combine flour and sugar. Cut in butter until mixture is the texture of fine sand and crumbly. Add egg yolk and mix until dough holds together. Press evenly over bottom and up sides of an 11-inch tart pan with removable bottom. Bake 12 to 15 minutes just until golden. Set aside. Increase oven to 350°F.

In a medium bowl, beat eggs until foamy. Add brown sugar, crystallized ginger, fresh ginger, and vanilla, mixing well. Stir in nuts. Pour into baked pastry shell. Bake on lowest rack in oven about 35 to 40 minutes, until top is golden and filling is set. Remove to wire rack and cool. Remove pan rim. Serve in wedges. Can be accompanied by vanilla ice cream and warm chocolate sauce.

❀ Serves 10

Mango Lime Cream Pie

INGREDIENTS

1 1/2 cups graham cracker crumbs
4 tablespoons unsalted butter, softened
1/4 cup fresh lime juice
1 1/2 teaspoons unflavored
   powdered gelatin
12 ounces cream cheese, softened
1/2 cup confectioners' sugar
2 1/4 teaspoons grated lime zest
1 cup mango puree
2 cups well chilled heavy or
   whipping cream
2 firm ripe mangoes

Heat oven to 350°F. Line bottom of a 10-inch springform pan with parchment paper and set aside. In a bowl, combine graham crackers with butter and mix well. Press firmly into bottom of the prepared pan and bake until firm, 10 to 15 minutes. Remove from oven and cool completely on a wire rack.

In a small saucepan, heat lime juice and gelatin over low heat until the gelatin dissolves, about 3 minutes. Remove from heat and let cool slightly. In a large bowl, beat cream cheese until light and fluffy with electric mixer or by hand. Add sugar and lime zest and beat until well blended. Add the softened gelatin and mango puree and mix to combine. In a bowl, whip the cream until soft peaks form. Using a rubber spatula, fold into the mango puree mixture and pour over crust, smoothing the top. Cover with plastic wrap and refrigerate at least 4 hours until firm. Peel mangoes, remove seed, and dice flesh. Cover and chill. Serve garnished with diced mango.

❧ Serves 10 to 12

Pear Crostata

RICH PASTRY
2 cups all-purpose flour
1 tablespoon granulated sugar
1 teaspoon salt
3/4 cup cold unsalted butter,
   cut into small pieces
2 egg yolks
3 tablespoons milk

ALMOND CREAM
1/2 cup butter, softened
1/2 cup granulated sugar
2 eggs
1/2 teaspoon vanilla extract
1 1/4 cups ground almonds
1 tablespoon all-purpose flour
Pinch salt

CROSTATA
6 Bosc pears
1-inch piece fresh ginger root, grated
1 cup granulated sugar
1/2 cup dried cranberries
4 ounces crumbled blue cheese

In a bowl or electric mixer, combine flour, sugar, and salt, mixing well. Add butter and work in until mixture resembles coarse sand. Whisk together egg yolks and milk in a small bowl. Add to flour mixture and mix to form a soft dough. Transfer to a sheet of plastic wrap, wrap well, and store in the refrigerator for several hours. The dough will keep for several days.

In a bowl, cream together butter with sugar until light and fluffy. Add eggs and vanilla, beating well. Stir in ground almonds, flour, and salt, mixing just until combined. Cover almond cream and chill.

Heat oven to 350°F. Lightly grease a baking sheet and set aside. Peel, halve, core, and slice pears. Set aside. Mix ginger with sugar and set aside. Roll out pastry on a lightly floured work surface into a circle about 12 to 14 inches in diameter and 1/8-inch thick. Transfer the dough to prepared baking sheet. Using a spatula, spread a circle of Almond Cream about 8 inches in diameter in the center of the dough. Arrange the pears in concentric circles in two layers on top. Sprinkle with gingered sugar. Scatter with cranberries. Fold the edges of the dough in, slightly covering the pears, to create a free-form tart. Bake 30 minutes. Sprinkle with blue cheese and continue baking another 20 to 30 minutes until pastry is golden brown. Remove to wire rack and cool before serving.

 Serves 8

Persimmon Pie

INGREDIENTS

2 1/2 pounds firm ripe persimmons
1/3 cup granulated sugar
1/3 cup packed brown sugar
2 1/2 tablespoons quick cooking tapioca
1 teaspoon ground cinnamon
1/2 teaspoon grated orange peel
1/2 teaspoon grated lemon peel
3 tablespoons lemon juice
Double crust pastry for 9-inch pie
1 tablespoon butter, cut into small pieces

Rinse persimmons and trim off tops. For a softer texture, persimmons can be blanched and peeled before slicing. Slice crosswise into thin rounds and place in a large bowl. Add granulated and brown sugars, tapioca, cinnamon, orange and lemon peels, and lemon juice. Stir gently to blend. Let stand 15 minutes.

Set oven rack to lowest position. Heat oven to 375°F. Pour fruit mixture into pastry shell, layering persimmon slices. Dot with butter, cover with remaining pastry, and crimp edges together to seal. Cut decorative slits into top crust. Bake about 1 hour until juices bubble in center of pie and crust is nicely browned. Remove to wire rack and cool.

❧ Serves 8

COCONUT CUSTARD
1 egg, beaten
4 egg yolks
$^1/_2$ teaspoon ground mace or nutmeg
$^1/_2$ cup granulated sugar
2 $^1/_2$ cups shredded coconut
3 cups half-and-half
1 teaspoon vanilla extract

LIME MERINGUE
$^1/_4$ teaspoon salt
4 egg whites
6 tablespoons sugar
$^1/_2$ teaspoon vanilla extract
1 $^1/_2$ tablespoons fresh lime juice

BRANDY CREAM SAUCE
$^1/_2$ cup heavy or whipping cream
$^1/_4$ cup brandy

Baked Coconut Custard with Lime Meringue

Butter eight 2 $^1/_2$-inch deep individual baking dishes or ramekins. Arrange in large roasting pan and set aside. Heat oven to 350°F.

In a large mixing bowl, beat together egg and egg yolks. Add mace and sugar, beating until light and fluffy. Stir in coconut, half-and-half, and vanilla. Fill prepared baking dishes $^3/_4$ full. Add enough boiling water to pan to fill 1-inch deep. Bake 35 to 40 minutes until firm.

Remove from oven and water bath. Reduce oven to 325°F. Top each dish with Lime Meringue, return to oven and bake 12 to 15 minutes until meringue is lightly golden. Remove to wire rack and cool. Serve at room temperature or chilled with a bit of Brandy Cream Sauce.

Lime Meringue: In a large bowl, add salt to egg whites. Beat with electric mixer until soft peaks form, about 5 minutes. Beat in sugar 1 tablespoon at a time. Continue beating to form stiff peaks. Beat in vanilla and lime juice. Cover and chill.

Brandy Cream Sauce: In a small bowl, whip cream until stiff. Fold in brandy. Cover and chill.

❧ *Serves 8*

Blueberry Bread Pudding

INGREDIENTS
4 eggs
2 cups heavy or whipping cream
2 cups milk
1 cup packed light brown sugar
1 teaspoon vanilla extract
1/2 teaspoon ground cinnamon
6 cups cubed day-old bread
6 ounces white chocolate chips
2 cups fresh or 1 cup dried blueberries
3 tablespoons butter, melted

AMARETTO CREAM
1/4 cup Amaretto
1 tablespoon cornstarch
1 1/2 cups heavy cream
1/4 cup granulated sugar

In a large bowl, beat eggs with a whisk until light and fluffy. Beat in cream, milk, brown sugar, vanilla, and cinnamon. Add bread, chocolate chips, and blueberries, stirring gently with spoon. Drizzle with melted butter and stir to mix. Let stand for 30 minutes for bread to absorb the egg mixture.

Heat oven to 350°F. Butter a 10 x 14-inch baking dish. Scrape in bread mixture, distributing evenly. Bake about 1 hour until firm when pressed in the center. Remove to wire rack and cool about 20 minutes until just warm.

In a small bowl, combine Amaretto and cornstarch with a whisk until smooth. In a medium saucepan, bring cream to a boil over medium heat. Add sugar and beat with a whisk until dissolved. Add Amaretto, stirring constantly with whisk and return to a boil. Reduce heat to low and cook, stirring until thickened. Remove from heat and let cool to room temperature.

Top individual servings of bread pudding with Amaretto Cream.

 Serves 8

Chai Tea Pudding

INGREDIENTS
3 1/2 cups water
1 teaspoon whole cloves
1 teaspoon whole cardamom seeds
1 whole star anise
1/2 teaspoon ground ginger
8 bags black India tea
14 ounces sweetened condensed milk
1/4 cup cornstarch
3 egg yolks
Toasted sliced almonds

In a large saucepan, combine water, cloves, cardamom, star anise, and ginger. Bring to a boil over high heat. Add tea bags, remove from heat, cover, and let steep 10 minutes. Remove tea bags but do not squeeze. In a large bowl, whisk together sweetened condensed milk with cornstarch until blended. Pour tea through fine meshed strainer into condensed milk mixture. Discard spices. Stir to mix then return to saucepan. Cook a few minutes over medium heat, stirring, until mixture comes to a boil and thickens slightly. Remove from heat. Beat egg yolks in a medium bowl. Slowly whisk hot pudding into yolks then return to saucepan. Bring to a simmering boil and heat about 1 minute, stirring gently to cook eggs.

Spoon into eight to ten demitasse cups. Cover and refrigerate at least 2 hours. Garnish with a few toasted almond slices and serve chilled.

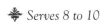 Serves 8 to 10

Coconut Pearl Tapioca Pudding

INGREDIENTS
5 cups milk
1/2 cup granulated sugar
3/4 cup small pearl tapioca
12 to 14 ounces canned coconut milk
1 cup frozen passion fruit juice
    concentrate, thawed
1 to 2 teaspoons fresh lemon juice

In a large saucepan, combine milk and sugar and cook over medium heat until simmering, stirring frequently. Add tapioca, reduce heat to low, and simmer, stirring frequently for 45 to 60 minutes until tapioca pearls are soft. Stir in coconut milk and cook 15 minutes more, stirring frequently.

Pour into individual serving bowls. Let cool, cover, and chill overnight. In a small bowl or pitcher with spout, stir together passion fruit concentrate and lemon juice. Cover and chill. Serve puddings topped with passion fruit syrup.

 Serves 6

Jasmine Rice Pudding

INGREDIENTS
1/2 cup Jasmine rice
2 cups milk
Pinch salt
1 Hawaiian-grown vanilla bean
1/3 cup granulated sugar
1/2 teaspoon gelatin
1 tablespoon water
1 cup well chilled whipping cream
Fresh raspberries

Combine rice, milk, and salt in a medium saucepan. Split vanilla bean lengthwise and add to pan. Place over medium-high heat and bring to a boil, stirring frequently to prevent scorching. Reduce heat to very low, cover, and simmer until milk is absorbed, about 20 minutes, stirring occasionally. Remove from heat. Remove vanilla bean, scrape out seeds, return seeds to cooked rice, and discard pod. Stir in sugar, mixing well. Dissolve gelatin in water, stirring until smooth. Add to rice, stirring to mix. Whip cream until peaks form and fold into rice. Spoon into molds or ramekins. Chill. Unmold. Serve garnished with berries.

Note: Madagascar, Mexico, and Tahiti have long been famous as sources for vanilla beans, the green bean-like seed pod of the *Vanilla Planifolia* orchid. Recently Hawai'i has joined this prestigious group and begun to grow these orchids due to the appropriate soil, temperature, humidity, and climate necessary to produce this exotic delicacy.

 Serves 8

INGREDIENTS

2 cups heavy cream
6 star anise
3 cups milk
1/2 cup medium-grained rice
1 cup granulated sugar, divided
Dash salt
5 egg yolks
1/2 teaspoon vanilla extract
8 teaspoons loose brown sugar, optional

Star Anise Rice Pudding

In a medium saucepan, bring cream and star anise to a simmering boil over medium heat. Remove from heat, cover and let steep for 30 minutes. In another pan, bring milk to a boil over medium-high heat, stirring occasionally to prevent scorching. Add rice, 1/2 cup sugar, and salt. Reduce heat to low, cover, and cook slowly 35 to 40 minutes until all the milk is absorbed and rice is tender. Remove from heat, place in a large bowl, and set aside.

Heat oven to 325°F. Remove star anise from cream. Return saucepan to stove and heat over medium. In a bowl, whisk egg yolks until light. Beat in remaining sugar and vanilla. Slowly add half the hot cream to eggs while whisking vigorously to blend. Whisk in remaining cream. Stir into cooked rice. Ladle into eight 4-inch ramekins being sure to distribute rice evenly. Place into one or two large baking pans. Add 1/2-inch boiling water. Bake 30 minutes until set. Remove from water bath and let cool. Serve warm, at room temperature, or chilled.

For crème brulee-style pudding, sprinkle each ramekin with 1 teaspoon brown sugar. Use a kitchen torch or place under broiler a few seconds to caramelize sugar.

❧ *Serves 8*

Coconut Cheesecake

CRUST
1 cup graham cracker crumbs
$1/4$ cup granulated sugar
3 tablespoons butter, melted
$1 1/2$ cups shredded coconut

FILLING
2 pounds cream cheese, softened
1 cup granulated sugar
5 eggs
14 to 16 ounces canned cream of
    coconut, such as Coco Lopez
1 cup thick coconut milk
$1/4$ teaspoon salt
$1/8$ teaspoon grated lemon zest
1 teaspoon vanilla extract

TOPPING
3 tablespoons butter
$1/4$ cup packed brown sugar
$1/2$ cup chopped macadamia nuts,
    toasted

Heat oven to 375°F. In a small bowl, mix together graham cracker crumbs, sugar, and melted butter. Press onto bottom of a 10-inch springform pan. Bake 10 minutes. Remove from oven, sprinkle with coconut and cool. Reduce oven to 350°F.

In a large bowl, beat cream cheese until light. Add sugar and beat until blended. Add eggs, one at a time, beating just until combined. Stir in cream of coconut, coconut milk, salt, lemon zest, and vanilla. Blend well. Pour onto coconut sprinkled crust. Bake about 1 hour to 1 hour and 15 minutes, until cheesecake is set but moves just slightly when shaken. Top may crack. Run a knife between side of pan and cheesecake to loosen edge. Remove to wire rack and let cool. Cover and chill several hours or overnight.

Release pan sides. Using a long spatula, loosen bottom and slide cheesecake onto serving plate. Melt butter and brown sugar over medium heat in a medium saucepan. Remove from heat and stir in macadamia nuts. Spread over cheesecake. Cut into wedges and serve.

Note: Cream of Coconut is a homogenized cream made from the meat of the coconut and blended with cane sugar to result in a smooth sweet coconut cream.

✤ *Serves 10 to 12*

Molasses Cheesecake

CRUST
1 1/4 cups gingersnap cookie crumbs
3 tablespoons granulated sugar
3 tablespoons butter, melted

FILLING
24 ounces cream cheese, softened
1/3 cup packed dark brown sugar
1/4 cup molasses
1 1/2 tablespoons cornstarch
1/2 teaspoon baking soda
3 eggs, at room temperature
1 egg yolk
2 teaspoons vanilla extract
1/4 cup gingersnap cookie crumbs

Grease bottom of a 9-inch springform pan and set aside. In a small bowl stir together cookie crumbs and sugar. Add melted butter and stir until well combined. Press crumb mixture evenly onto the bottom of prepared pan. Place in freezer while preparing filling.

Heat oven to 350°F. In large bowl, combine cream cheese, brown sugar, molasses, cornstarch, and baking soda. Beat with an electric mixer until smooth. Add eggs and egg yolk one at a time, beating well after each addition. Beat in vanilla. Pour over chilled crust, spreading evenly with rubber spatula. Sprinkle with cookie crumbs. Bake 15 minutes. Lower temperature to 300°F and bake 1 hour and 15 minutes until the center no longer looks wet or shiny. Turn off oven.

Remove cake from oven and run a knife around inside edge of pan. Return cake to sit in warm oven for an additional hour. Remove to wire rack and let cool completely. Cover and chill several hours or overnight. Run a knife between side of pan and cheesecake to loosen edge. Release pan sides. Using long spatula, loosen bottom and slide onto serving plate. Cut into wedges and serve.

Note: Lightly oil or spray the inside of the measuring cup before measuring the molasses and it will slip easily out of the cup.

❈ *Serves 10 to 12*

White Chocolate Mango Cheesecake

CRUST

2 cups graham cracker crumbs
1 cup slivered blanched almonds or
    macadamia nuts
4 tablespoons butter
8 ounces fine quality white chocolate

FILLING

2 pounds cream cheese, softened
1/2 cup plus 2 tablespoons
    granulated sugar
4 eggs
1 teaspoon vanilla extract
2 cups finely diced mango
1/2 cup fresh red raspberries

Set aside a few nuts and berries for garnish.

In a food processor, blend together graham cracker crumbs and nuts until finely ground. Add butter and combine well. Press mixture onto the bottom and part way up the side of 10-inch a springform pan. Grate white chocolate into a bowl. Sprinkle over crust. Chill.

Heat oven to 325°F. In a large bowl, beat cream cheese until light and fluffy by hand or with electric mixer. Add sugar and beat well. Add eggs, one at a time, beating after each addition. Beat in vanilla. Scatter mango and raspberries over crust. Carefully pour in the filling. Bake in middle of oven for 1 hour until top is firm to the touch.

Remove to wire rack and run knife around inside edge of pan. Let cool in pan. Cover loosely with plastic wrap and chill several hours or overnight. Run a knife between side of pan and cheesecake to loosen edge, then release pan sides. Using long spatula, loosen bottom and slide onto serving plate. Garnish with reserved nuts and berries. Cut into wedges and serve.

❀ *Serves 10 to 12*

Okinawan Sweet Potato-Haupia Cheesecake

CRUST
1 1/2 cups graham cracker crumbs
1/4 cup granulated sugar
3 tablespoons butter, melted

FILLING
2 pounds cream cheese, softened
3/4 cup granulated sugar
4 eggs
1 teaspoon vanilla extract
1/4 teaspoon salt
3 cups cooked mashed Okinawan
    sweet potato

HAUPIA TOPPING
12 to 14 ounces canned thick
    coconut milk
3/4 cup granulated sugar
3 tablespoons cornstarch
3 tablespoons water
1 tablespoon vanilla extract

Heat oven to 350°F. In a small bowl, mix together graham cracker crumbs, sugar, and melted butter. Press onto bottom of a 10-inch springform pan. Bake 10 minutes. Remove to wire rack and let cool.

In a large bowl, beat cream cheese until light. Add sugar and beat until blended. Add eggs one at a time, beating just until combined. Stir in vanilla, salt, and mashed sweet potato until blended. Pour onto baked crust. Bake about 1 hour 15 minutes, until cheesecake is set but moves just slightly when shaken. Top may crack. Remove to wire rack. Run a knife around inside edge of pan.

In saucepan, bring coconut milk and sugar to a boil, stirring frequently, over medium heat. Mix together cornstarch and water. Add to hot coconut milk, stirring until thickened. Remove from heat and stir in vanilla. Let stand 5 minutes, stirring occasionally before pouring onto cheesecake. Cover and refrigerate several hours or overnight to set. Run a knife between side of pan and cheesecake to loosen edge. Release pan sides. Using long spatula, loosen bottom and slide onto serving plate. Cut into wedges and serve.

❀ Serves 10 to 12

INGREDIENTS
1 cup butter, softened
1 1/2 cups granulated sugar
6 eggs
1 tablespoon lemon zest
3 cups all-purpose flour
1/2 teaspoon baking powder
1 cup buttermilk
Confectioners' sugar

Lemon Cake

Heat oven to 350°F. Grease two 9-inch cake pans and set aside.

Place butter in the bowl of an electric mixer. Beat until light and creamy. Add sugar slowly and beat until well blended. Add eggs one at a time, beating after each addition. Stir in lemon zest. Sift flour with baking powder. Alternately add the flour and buttermilk to the butter mixture, combining well. Scrape into prepared pans and spread evenly using a rubber spatula.

Bake for 30 to 35 minutes until a cake tester inserted into center comes out clean. Remove to wire rack and let cool. Place each cake on a cake pedestal or serving platter. Cut each cake into ten to twelve wedges and sprinkle with confectioners' sugar.

❋ Serves 20

Pear Cake

CAKE

3 firm ripe Bosc pears
1 $^1/_3$ cups all-purpose flour
$^1/_2$ teaspoon ground cinnamon
1 teaspoon baking powder
$^1/_2$ cup butter, softened
1 $^1/_4$ cups plus 1 tablespoon
    granulated sugar, divided
3 eggs
1 teaspoon vanilla extract
$^1/_3$ cup milk
$^1/_2$ cup chopped pitted prunes or raisins
$^1/_2$ cup lightly toasted pine nuts

SAUCE

2 eggs
1 cup half-and-half
$^1/_2$ cup sugar
4 tablespoons butter
1 teaspoon vanilla extract
1 tablespoon rum or brandy
1 teaspoon ground cinnamon

Heat oven to 350°F. Lightly butter and flour a 9-inch springform pan. Set aside. Peel, core, and dice pears into $^1/_2$-inch cubes. Set aside. In a bowl, whisk together flour, cinnamon, and baking powder. Set aside.

In another bowl, cream together butter and 1 $^1/_4$ cups sugar until light and fluffy. Add eggs, one at a time, beating well after each addition. Beat in vanilla. Beat in half of flour mixture, then milk, and rest of flour just until combined. Fold in pears, prunes, and nuts. Scrape into prepared pan and spread evenly using rubber spatula. Sprinkle with remaining tablespoon sugar. Bake in middle of oven 45 to 50 minutes until a tester inserted in center comes out clean. Remove to wire rack and let cool in pan.

In a small bowl, beat eggs with a whisk until light and smooth. Heat half-and-half and sugar in saucepan over medium-low heat until hot. Add butter and stir until melted. Whisk in vanilla, rum, and cinnamon. Slowly pour a little of the warm milk into the beaten eggs, while beating well. Slowly, so as not to scramble the eggs, pour egg mixture back into saucepan, beating with a whisk. Heat until sauce is slightly thickened and thoroughly cooked. Remove from heat. Serve slices of cake with warm sauce.

❧ *Serves 10 to 12*

Volcano Cakes

INGREDIENTS

4 ounces semisweet chocolate, chopped
$^1/_2$ cup butter, cut into small pieces
$^3/_4$ cup whipping cream, divided
$^1/_2$ teaspoon vanilla extract
$^1/_4$ cup all-purpose flour
$^1/_4$ cup plus 2 tablespoons
   granulated sugar, divided
2 eggs
2 egg yolks
Confectioners' sugar

Heat oven to 400°F. Butter six 4-ounce custard cups. Dust with a little sugar. Set aside.

Combine chopped chocolate, butter, and $^1/_4$ cup cream in a small heavy saucepan. Cook over low heat, stirring occasionally, until butter and chocolate have melted and mixture is blended well. Remove from heat. Stir in vanilla. Using a wire whisk, stir in flour just until mixture is smooth. Set aside. In medium bowl, beat $^1/_4$ cup sugar, eggs, and egg yolks with a whisk until thick and light in color, about 5 minutes. Gently fold egg mixture into chocolate mixture, one-third at a time, until blended.

Divide batter evenly among prepared custard cups. Place cups in shallow baking pan for easier handling. Place in center of hot oven and bake 8 to 10 minutes until edges of cakes are set but centers still jiggle when gently shaken. Cool in pan on wire rack 3 minutes. Whip remaining $^1/_2$ cup cream with 2 tablespoons sugar. Add a few drops of vanilla extract if desired. Run a thin knife around edge of each cake to loosen from custard cup. Invert onto individual plates and gently remove cups. Dust with confectioners' sugar. Top with a dollop of whipped cream. Serve immediately.

❋ *Makes 6*

Chocolate Truffles

INGREDIENTS

3/4 cup heavy cream

4 tablespoons unsalted butter,
  cut into small pieces

10 ounces bittersweet chocolate,
  chopped

1 tablespoon brandy

2 teaspoons grated lime zest

2 teaspoons minced crystallized ginger

Unsweetened cocoa powder or
  finely shredded coconut

Place cream and butter in a saucepan. Bring to a full boil over medium heat, stirring frequently. Turn off heat. Add chocolate bits. Gently stir to melt chocolate. Let stand 5 minutes. Add brandy, lime zest, and ginger, whisking slowly to combine. Scrape mixture into a bowl using a rubber spatula. Cover and refrigerate until firm, about 4 hours or overnight.

Line a baking sheet with waxed or parchment paper. Using a melon baller or very small ice cream scoop, portion chocolate and roll between palms of hands to form mixture into 1-inch balls. If mixture is too hard, let stand at room temperature 5 to 10 minutes before shaping. Place on prepared pan. Chill 10 to 15 minutes to firm.

Place a small amount of cocoa in a small deep dish. Remove chocolate balls from refrigerator. Roll each ball between the palms of hands to warm up slightly. Drop in cocoa and swirl to coat. Return truffles to baking sheet. Chill at least 1 hour until firm. Store in airtight container in refrigerator.

❋ *Makes about 2 dozen*

INGREDIENTS
2 cups packed brown sugar
²/3 cup milk
²/3 cup sesame tahini
1 teaspoon vanilla extract

Halvah

Butter an 8 x 8-inch pan and set aside.

In a saucepan, heat sugar and milk over medium, stirring to just under the soft-ball stage (230°F). Remove from heat. Add tahini and vanilla but do not mix in immediately. Let cool about 2 minutes then beat with wooden spoon for 10 to 15 seconds and quickly pour into prepared pan. Let stand until firm. Cut into pieces and serve.

Note: To test for soft ball stage, fill a small bowl with cold water. Drop a bit of sugar syrup into water. Mixture should form into a soft flexible ball that can be flattened.

Tahini is a paste made from raw or toasted sesame seeds and can be found in Middle Eastern food stores, specialty sections of grocery stores, or natural food stores.

❀ *Makes one 8 x 8-inch pan*

Toffee Fudge Bites

INGREDIENTS
7 ounces unsweetened chocolate,
   chopped
3 ounces bittersweet chocolate, chopped
1 cup plus 1 tablespoon unsalted butter
1 1/2 cups cake flour
3 tablespoons unsweetened
   cocoa powder
1/2 teaspoon salt
2 1/4 cups toffee bits
5 eggs
2 cups granulated sugar
1/3 cup packed dark brown sugar
2 teaspoons vanilla extract

Heat oven to 350°F. Grease a 9 x 13 x 2-inch baking pan and set aside.

In a medium saucepan, melt unsweetened and bittersweet chocolate with butter over medium-low heat, stirring frequently. Remove from heat and set aside to cool slightly.

Whisk together cake flour, cocoa powder, and salt. Add toffee bits and stir to mix. Scrape chocolate-butter mixture into a medium bowl with a rubber spatula. Whisk to blend. Add eggs, one at a time, beating well after each addition. Beat in granulated sugar, brown sugar, and vanilla. Stir in dry ingredients and mix until combined. Scrape batter into prepared pan. Bake for 25 to 30 minutes just until set. The center will be soft and edges will shrink slightly from sides of baking pan.

Remove to wire rack. Cover and refrigerate for 2 hours until firm enough to cut into pieces. Cut into 1 x 1-inch pieces. Return to refrigerator. Bring to room temperature before serving. Store leftovers in refrigerator.

Note: One cup sifted cake flour can be substituted with 3/4 cup sifted bleached all-purpose flour mixed with 2 tablespoons cornstarch.

❦ Makes 2 1/2 dozen

Acknowledgements

This book would not have been possible without the research, planning, implementation, and talents of the individuals involved.

Mahalo to the following:

JLH Commercial Products Cookbook Committees
2003-04 Vanessa Applbaum, Lurlyn Brown, Tracy Jones, Coral Rasmussen, Wendy Shewalter. Carole Berg, Chair.

2004-05 Heather Ardoin, Monique Canonico, Tracy Jones, Melinda Kohr, Suzanne Lee, Kristi Nicholson, Coral Rasmussen, Wendy Shewalter, Barbara Sniezek, Susan Worley. Carole Berg, Chair.

2005-06 Dianne Bosworth, Lurlyn Brown, Jodie Ching, Marisa Gumpfer, Heather Henken, Tracy Jones, Melinda Kohr, Nancy Page, Coral Rasmussen, Nina Pfaffenbach, Oleana Sagapolutele, Wendy Shewalter, Susan Worley. Tanya Hertel, Austen Cook, Carole Berg, Co-Chairs.

2006-07 Dianne Bosworth, Sue Chouljian, Marisa Gumpfer, Tracy Jones, Melinda Kohr, Lauren Lewis, Lisa Matsuda, Heather McDermott, Nancy Page, Rose Smith, Kimi Takazawa. Carrie Allport, Lee Ann Del Carpio, Anna Grisi, Co-Chairs. Carole Berg, Advisor.

For their generosity, time, and talents
Buzz Belknap, John De Mello, Robert C. Godbey, Lorry Kennedy, Dick Lyday, and Nina Pfaffenbach.

For their generosity and artistic talents
Pegge Hopper for the cover, "Under a Magnolia Moon"
Susanne Ball, "Breakfast Delight," pages 9 and 10
Yvonne Cheng, "Untitled," pages 327 and 328
Patrice Federspiel, "Growing From the Inside Out," pages 69 and 70
Roberta Goodman, "Tropical Fruit," pages 197 and 198
Susan Szabo, "Lanikai Afternoon," pages 141 and 142

For contributing, testing, and tasting recipes over the last three years the volunteers of The Junior League of Honolulu, Inc., their families, relatives, and friends.